The ... st date

Social Services

Education Policy Perspectives

General Editor: Professor Ivor Goodson, Faculty of Education, University of Western Ontario, London, Canada N6G 1G7

Education policy analysis has long been a neglected area in the UK and, to an extent, in the USA and Australia. The result has been a profound gap between the study of education and the formulation of education policy. For practitioners, such a lack of analysis of new policy initiatives has worrying implications, particularly at a time of such policy flux and change. Education policy has, in recent years, been a matter for intense political debate – the political and public interest in the working of the system has come at the same time as the breaking of the consensus on education policy by the New Right. As never before, political parties and pressure groups differ in their articulated policies and prescriptions for the education sector. Critical thinking about these developments is clearly imperative.

All those working within the system also need information on policy-making, policy implementation and effective day-to-day operation. Pressure on schools from government, education authorities and parents has generated an enormous need for knowledge amongst those on the receiving end of educational policies.

This Falmer Press series aims to fill the academic gap, to reflect the politicalization of education, and to provide the practitioners with the analysis for informed implementation of policies that they will need. It offers studies in broad areas of policy studies, with a particular focus on the following areas: school organization and improvement; critical social analysis; policy studies and evaluation; and education and training.

The Politics of Linking Schools and Social Services

The 1993 Yearbook of the Politics of Education Association

Edited by

Louise Adler

and

Sid Gardner

Center for Collaboration for Children, California State University, Fullerton

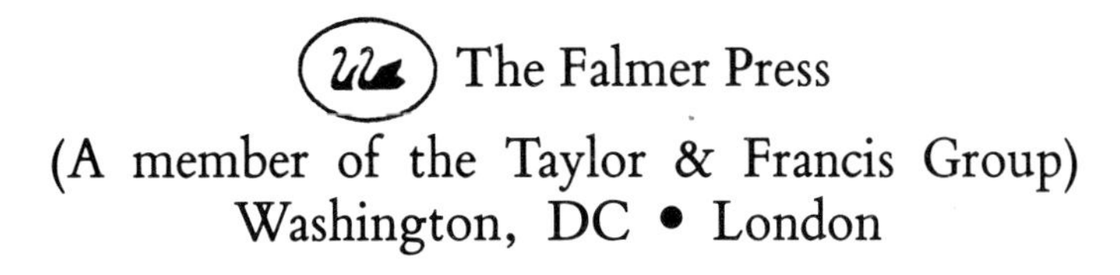

The Falmer Press
(A member of the Taylor & Francis Group)
Washington, DC • London

USA Falmer Press (North America) 1900 Frost Road, 101, Bristol, PA 19007
UK Falmer Press Ltd, 4 John Street, London WC1N 2ET

First published 1994

Library of Congress Cataloging-in-Publication data are available on request

A catalogue record for this book is available from the British Library

ISBN 0 7507 0222 2 cased
ISBN 0 7507 0223 0 paper

Typeset by RGM Associates, Lord Street, Southport, England
Cover Design by Caroline Archer

Printed in Great Britain by Burgess Science Press, Basingstoke on paper which has a specified pH value on final paper manufacture of not less than 7.5 and is therefore 'acid free'.

Contents

Politics of Education Association

Yearbook Sponsor

The **Politics of Education Association (PEA)** promotes the development and dissemination of research and debate on educational policy and politics. PEA brings together scholars, practitioners, and policy makers interested in educational governance and politics; is affiliated as a Special Interest Group with the American Educational Research Association (AERA); and meets each spring in conjunction with AERA's annual meeting. The annual membership dues for PEA are $US25.00 (subject to change). Members receive a copy of the annual *Yearbook* and the *Politics of Education Bulletin*, which includes news on member activities and occasional short scholarly pieces. Membership dues should be sent to Robert Wimpelberg, PEA, College of Education, University of New Orleans, New Orleans, LA 70148, USA.

The Politics of Excellence and Choice in Education
William Boyd and Charles Kerchner (1987)

The Politics of Reforming School Administration
Jane Hannaway and Robert Crowson (1988)

Education Politics for the New Century
Douglas Mitchell and Margaret Goertz (1989)

Politics of Curriculum and Testing
Susan Fuhrman and Betty Malen (1990)

The Politics of Urban Education in the United States
James G. Cibulka, Rodney J. Reed, and Kenneth K. Wong (1991)

The New Politics of Race and Gender
Catherine Marshall (1992)

POLITICS OF EDUCATION ASSOCIATION YEARBOOK, 1993, ix–xi

About the Editors and Contributors

Louise Adler is an Associate Professor of Educational Administration at California State University, Fullerton and a Fellow at the Center for Collaboration for Children. Her primary research interest is the impact of politics on decision making by school districts.

Sid Gardner is the Director of the Center for Collaboration for Children at California State University – Fullerton. He has extensive experience in improving services for children and families, particularly through collaborative efforts across agencies and disciplines.

R. Michael Casto is President of the Interprofessional Commission of Ohio. Formerly, he was Acting Director of the Commission on Interprofessional Education and Practice at Ohio State University.

Joan L. Curcio is an Associate Professor at Virginia Tech University, Northern VA Graduate Center, where she specializes in education law and governance, particularly the superintendency.

Patricia F. First is a Professor and Chair of the Department of Educational Leadership at Western Michigan University. She is a member of the Board of Directors of the National Organization on Legal Problems of Education and co-editor of NOLPE's *School Law Reporter*.

James R. Garvin is the Director of the Project for Urban Education and Community Development housed in the College of Urban and Public Affairs at the University of New Orleans. His research interests center on urban education systems, public housing environments, and the effect of social isolation on children and their families.

Gloria Guba is a high school principal and a doctoral candidate in the Department of Education Leadership and Policy Studies at Temple University. Her research interests focus on school restructuring and the links between schools and service providers.

Unni S. Hagen is a Research Fellow at the Institute for Educational Research, University of Oslo, where she is working on a comparative project on educational policy and school leadership. She worked as a primary school teacher for thirteen years in three Norwegian municipalities, including the period of the 1980 reforms.

Katharine Hooper-Briar is Director of the Institute on Children and Families at Risk at Florida International University (Miami). She was Assistant Secretary for the Children, Youth & Families unit of the Washington State Department of Social and Health Services.

Stephanie Kadel is pursuing a PhD at Syracuse University. Her research interests include school restructuring and educational policy. As a writer for SERVE, the regional educational laboratory for the southeast, she has published guidebooks for practitioners on implementing collaborative services, reducing violence in schools, and creating innovative educational programs.

Michael S. Knapp is an Associate Professor of Educational Leadership and Policy Studies at the University of Washington, specializing in research on the education of 'disadvantaged' groups, professional development, and the policymaking process. He co-authored the chapter in this volume collaboratively with five other professors at University of Washington: **Kathryn Barnard** (School of Nursing), **Richard Brandon** (School of Public Affairs), **Nathalie Gehrke** (College of Education), **Albert Smith** (College of Education), and **Ted Teather** (School of Social Work).

Julia E. Koppich is Deputy Director of Policy Analysis for California Education (PACE) at the University of California – Berkeley. She previously worked on the staff of the California legislature, taught high school government, and served on the staff of the American Federation of Teachers. Her research interests include the policies of education, public sector labor relations, integrated services for children and the reform of educational systems.

Hal A. Lawson is a Professor in the School of Education and Allied Professions at Miami University, Ohio; an Associate in the Institute for Educational Inquiry; participant in the Danforth Foundation's School Leader's Program; and member of the Association of Teacher Educators' National Commission on Interprofessional Education.

Jane Clark Lindle of the Department of Administration & Supervision, University of Kentucky, teaches courses in Educational Administration. Her research interests include micropolitics, methods of instruction in Educational Administration, and knowledge application in administrative practice.

Hanne B. Mawhinney is an Assistant Professor in the Faculty of Education at University of Ottawa. Her research interests focus on education politics and policy. Her research for this chapter was supported by a Canadian Social Sciences and Humanities Research Council Doctoral Fellowship.

Douglas E. Mitchell is a Professor of Education and Director of the California Educational Research Cooperative (CERC) at the University of California, Riverside which is one of the nation's largest research and development centers. His own research and scholarly interests are focused on school politics and policy.

Dorothy K. Routh is Deputy Director of SERVE, the regional educational laboratory for the southeast US. Her work focuses on facilitating change and the shifting roles of teachers and administrators. She was a Program for Educational Leadership Fellow at Columbia University Teacher's College.

Charles J. Russo of the University of Kentucky, Department of Educational Administration & Supervision, teaches education law. His research focuses on the legal dimensions of school reform, the relationship between religion and public education, and the role of unionization and collective bargaining in the schools.

Jo-Anne Schick is an instructor in Second Language Education in the Department of Curriculum and Instruction at the University of Houston. Her research interests include the use of computer-assisted instruction and linguistic-minority students.

Linda D. Scott is Assistant Research Educationist with the California Education Research Cooperative (CERC) at University of California, Riverside. She specializes in curriculum development and English Language Arts, K–12 and is active in curriculum and staff development for Native American Education.

Jacqueline A. Stefkovich is Assistant Professor, Department of Educational Leadership and Policy Studies, Temple University where she teaches courses in qualitative research and school law. Her major research interests focus on school restructuring, school discipline, and the impact of court decisions on school policies and practices.

Kip Tellez is Assistant Professor of Education in the Department of Curriculum and Instruction at the University of Houston. His research interests include teacher education, ESL instruction, urban professional development schools, and the philosophy of education

Felisa L. Tibbitts is a Senior Consultant with IMTEC (Norwegian consulting organization) where she works as an educational evaluation specialist on various international projects. In the US, she has worked primarily as a teacher trainer and qualitative researcher in the areas of education and social services.

William A. White is a Consultant for Healthy Start in the California Department of Education. He formerly coordinated the statewide drug, alcohol, tobacco, and HIV/AIDS programs for the Department. He is also a former manager of Medi-Cal policy and budget with the California Department of Health Services.

William C. Wilson is Dean of the School of Education at California State University, Dominguez Hill. His co-authors are: **Patricia Karasoff**, Director, Integrated Services Partnership Training Project, San Francisco State University; and **Barbara Nolan**, Project Assistant and Doctoral Student in Educational Administration, University of California, Berkeley.

Alma H. Young is Professor of Urban and Public Affairs and director of the doctoral program in Urban Studies at the University of New Orleans. Her current research interests focus on welfare reform and its impact on children, women and the urban environment and the political economy of urban development.

Dalton L. Young is a doctoral student at University of Oklahoma in the Department of Educational Leadership and Policy Studies. He is also a public school teacher with a special interest in programs for teenage mothers.

POLITICS OF EDUCATION ASSOCIATION YEARBOOK, 1993, 1–16

Introduction and overview

Louise Adler

Linking schools and social services has become a nationwide and, as the authors of these chapters show, an international movement. There are a variety of definitions of what constitutes linking schools and social services. Almost all of the definitions include the following:

- families and children ought to be able to access all necessary services at a center located at a local school or some other facility in their neighborhood;
- a wide variety of services should be available such as health, mental health, recreation, job development, child development and care, education, and housing;
- the service providers should work collaboratively to meet all of the needs of children and families in a holistic way;
- the services should stress community development and family support that prevents problems rather than being crisis-driven;
- planning to meet the needs of the community should empower both families and the line workers who provide direct services;
- organizations that provide community and family services will have to develop new ways of working together;
- more flexibility must be created in how categorical funding can be used; or, ideally, new blended funding streams should be created to support collaborative services on an ongoing basis;
- professionals who work in community and family services will need training to develop new skills, and the preparation of professionals also needs to be changed; and
- to achieve these goals systemwide changes will be necessary.

The statistics and political processes that have propelled these issues toward center stage in the policy arena are well documented in this volume. In an attempt to provide a framework for this discussion, organizational, economic, and political issues will be outlined. This will be followed by a discussion of two important themes which are raised by many of the authors – the necessity of explicitly defining the ethos that supports linking schools and social services, and the central role of interpersonal ties in the collaboration process.

Organizational issues

The pervasiveness of organizations is a critical feature of modern life even for children. Most children are born in a hospital which is part of a network of health care organizations which continue to serve them throughout their lives. Not very long after

0268–0939/93 $10·00 © 1993 Taylor & Francis Ltd.

the birth of a child, parents begin to read or hear about the advice of child development experts, and to buy developmental toys which are the child's initial contact with a wide network of educational organizations. Unless the child's family is exceptionally lucky or wealthy, the child will probably come in contact with some of the various public and private organizations which minister to the social and psychological well-being of children.

One of the recurring debates in western culture is between: (1) those who view organizations as instruments of de-humanization that put the interests of the organization ahead of the interest of the individuals who depend on the organizations for employment, services or goods; and (2) those who view organizations as the social institutions that allow people to work together to achieve collective aims that may transcend individual self-interest.

As you will find reading this volume, the arguments for linking schools and social services depend in large measure on arguments drawn from both sides of this debate about organizations. Those in the forefront of the movement to link schools and social services argue that services are fragmented in various discrete organizations which may be efficient for the organizations, but not for children – failure by fragmentation. This basic argument finds the current system of serving children 'organizationally' deficient.

At the same time, the argument for linking schools and social services is based on an optimistic view of organizations – that they can solve problems impacting on children's lives if they act collaboratively. Thus, the argument is that the prescription to improve children's lives is 'organizational.' This argument is based on the assumption that one cannot isolate a child's biological, psychological, and social needs and assign different organizations to meet each category of need. Further, the needs of the child cannot be met fully by organizations that attempt to deal with the child in isolation from families and communities. Thus, the movement to link schools and social services can be viewed as a logical extension of the reform movement which began in the progressive era with concerns about public health and universal access to education and has continued more recently with movements to protect children from child abuse and to require inoculations against childhood diseases. All of these reforms have been based on a belief that organizations can help to improve the lives of children. The new argument for linking schools and social services posits that integrating services once provided by separate organizations will result in substantially better services for children than the services provided by separate organizations which do not collaborate.

Bridging institutional networks

To understand the politics of linking schools and social services we must recognize that schools and social services have been parts of different institutionalized networks of organizations (Perrow 1986, Meyer and Rowan 1983, Meyer *et al.* 1983). These networks have different norms, dialects, and missions. Bringing together professionals from these various networks is bound to create a fertile ground for conflict, negotiations, and coalition building – the *sine qua non* of politics. These political processes are played out at the various levels within society (see figure 1). At the direct service site, professionals must negotiate new roles, struggle to understand each other's terminology, and search for ways to coordinate their efforts (see Mitchell and Scott: Ch. 5, Kadel and Routh: Ch. 8). Leaders of organizations such as school districts, county human service agencies, and voluntary associations such as United Way must deal with the tension that exists between the need to work cooperatively, to deal with an ever-increasing demand and reduced resources, and the need to maintain organizational identity and professional integrity.

At the universities similar problems are addressed (see Knapp: Ch. 9) when various schools and departments explore the curriculum and resource implications of training professionals in various fields so that they are capable of effective cross-disciplinary collaboration to meet the needs of children and families. Universities are common elements in almost every institutional network of organizations that focus on a human service. Thus, they may have an important role to play beyond the preparation of professionals – that of provocateur of collaboration between organizations in the community. Teitel (1993) points to the important role of 'third parties' in promoting such partnerships (see Garvin and Young: Ch. 6).

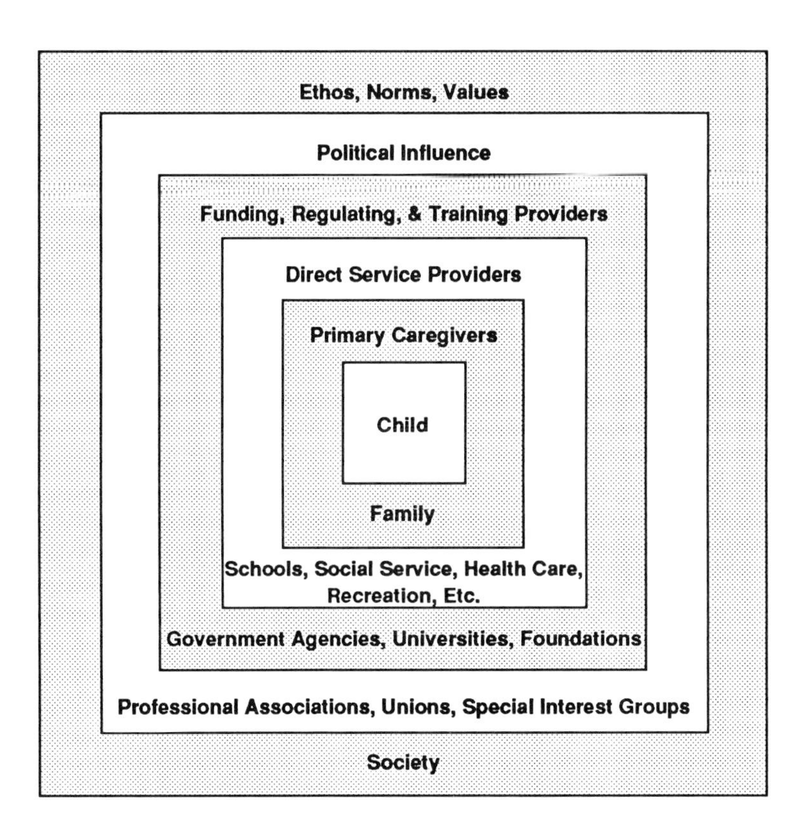

Figure 1

The concept of interorganizational networks provides a way to describe and study connections between different types of organizations all of which focus on a particular service or product. Perrow (1986) used citywide health services as an example. The network contained hospitals (public and private), universities that train doctors and nurses, the city government, labor unions and professional associations, and the dominant political party organization. Similar networks can be described for education and other social services. These visual representations of interorganizational exchanges are useful tools for understanding what we are about when we attempt to construct school-linked social services. Each of the various services (for example: social, health, education, recreation, child care, juvenile justice, employment development) exists within its own institutional network of organizations. Each network consists of similar types of organizations: direct service providers, professional training and certification organizations, public and private funding organizations, professional and union organizations, regulatory government agencies, special interest groups, and research organizations. An illustration of the education network for a typical city shows the complexity of each of these networks (see figure 2). When an organization begins a collaborative effort, it is constrained by its institutional network. For example, norms for practice may make collaboration more difficult. Funding may require focused attention on only one type of problem or need. Training needed to get a license or certificate may not have sufficient flexibility to allow additional or revised activities to learn about collaboration.

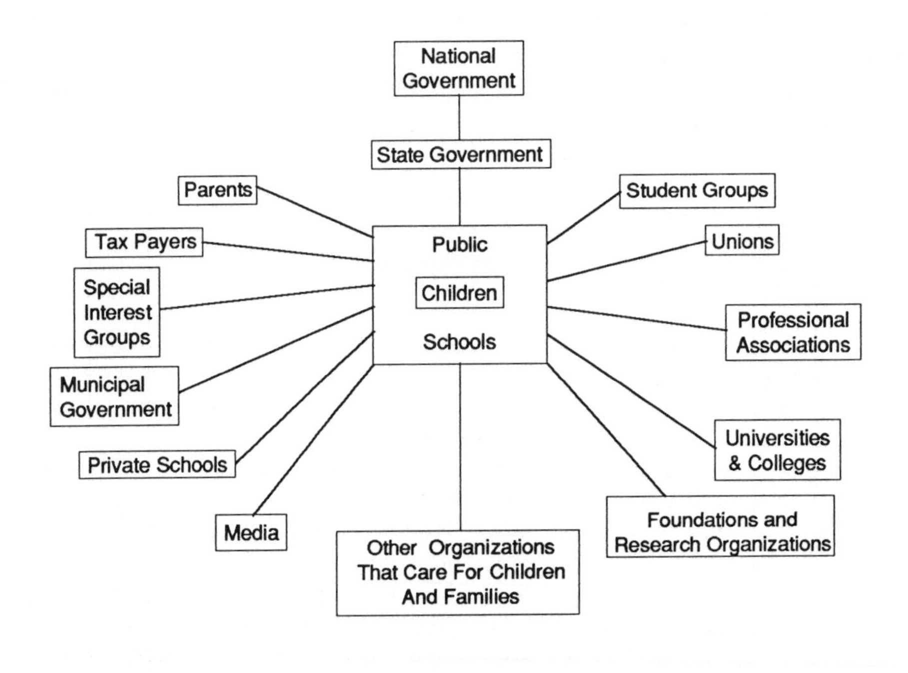

Figure 2

Berman and McLaughlin's (1978) landmark study of the implementation of federal programs supporting educational change (a) raised cautions about the ability of legislative programs to change the operations of organizations that are loosely coupled to higher governmental structures, and (b) pointed out the important role that the 'street-level' service provider or 'line worker' has in shaping the outcome of policies. The federal programs they studied involved only educators. Implementation problems increase geometrically when professions from various types of agencies situated in different institutional networks must collaborate. Any innovation requires the investment of resources and time in planning. The necessary investment grows with the number of players in the game. The willingness of state and local governments to fund such efforts systemwide in the face of resource deficiencies is not at all clear at this time, although a number of pilot programs have been funded. At the most basic level it is also not yet clear how well these collaborations will be able to agree on common definitions of the problems, models of service delivery, and outcome measures.

When we discuss links between various services and the public schools, the inter-organizational connections become complex and difficult to negotiate. Hall (1991) suggests that, as the environments of organizations become more turbulent, inter-organizational relationships increase. Increasing turbulence in the health, social service, and education organizational networks that serve children has been caused by the economic downturn which has resulted in reduced funding for services. At the same time, the need for such services has increased due to stress on families caused, in part, by the weak economy. Also, the USA has been experiencing higher levels of immigration in the last decade, a pattern that has been repeated in other western countries as they respond to the need to shelter refugees.

The organizational theory literature provides an important warning for those who advocated linking schools and social services. Perrow (1986) pointed out that, 'coordination has costs associated with it, as well as presumed benefits; and there may be substantial gains with redundant, uncoordinated activity and substantial costs with coordination that eliminates backup facilities' (p. 207).

Political issues

Public policy development

Political scientists and scholars of the politics of education have frequently pointed out that the process of public policy development in the USA is unique because of the fragmentation caused by our federal system of government which requires the various levels of government to work cooperatively to move a policy issue forward, often resulting in policy stagnation (see Koppich: Ch. 3 and First, Curcio and Dalton: Ch. 4) (Robertson and Judd 1989). The term 'children's policy' was largely unnoticed in public policy discussions before the 1980s, though it was preceded by a discussion of 'family policy' in academic circles and foundations during the 1970s (Grubb and Lazerson, 1982). The emergence of 'children's policy' signifies an effort to unify the various levels of government and agencies which provide services for children. If school-linked social services are widely adopted, it will reverse the policy trend toward fragmentation and categorical programs.

Children's issues became part of the public policy agenda in large part because of the publication of very alarming statistics about the conditions of children. Various interest groups, such as the Children's Defense Fund and the Child Welfare League of America, advocated for children being an important policy issue. Policy Analysis for California Education (PACE) published *Conditions of Children in California* which become a model of the 'report card' presentation of data about children's slide from their protected status in our society. The demographic statistics were so dramatic and widely reported that they captured center stage for 'children's issues.' Private foundations and nonprofits such as the Stuart Foundation, the William T. Grant Foundation, the Annie E. Casey Foundation, and California Tomorrow provided funding and/or technical assistance for demonstration projects that used school-linked collaborative service delivery models. New Beginnings in San Diego, California; New Futures in Little Rock, Arkansas and Savannah, Georgia; and the K-SIX Program in Fresno, California are examples of these efforts. Thus demographic shifts, advocacy groups, policy centers and foundations all played an interdependent role in moving school-linked social services onto the policy agenda.

Redistributive v. allocational politics

Peterson (1981) described three policy arenas: redistributive, allocational, and developmental. 'Developmental policies enhance the economic position of the city. Redistributive policies benefit low-income residents . . . . Allocational policies are more or less neutral in their economic effects' (p. 14). Education and social services have been treated quite differently in terms of public support and funding. While public education is seen as a service that is provided to every child and is, thus, allocational in nature, social services which have means tests and are designed to serve those in special need are considered redistributive. As some commentators have pointed out, there is a broader public support for allocational programs that serve everyone (e.g., public schools and social security) than there is for programs that are redistributive (e.g., Aid for Families of Dependent Children and other 'welfare' programs).

> The public's discontent with the welfare system is captured by one remarkable statistic. The *New York Times*/CBS News [nationwide] Poll asked a question in May about the level of spending for 'assistance to the poor,' and two-thirds of the public said it was 'too little.'
>
> That question was immediately re-asked, with one small change: the word 'welfare' was substituted for 'assistance to the poor.' Only 23 percent said the nation was spending 'too little' on 'welfare.' (Tonner 1992: 13)

Political support for education is much stronger. A recent survey in one of the most conservative counties in the USA (Orange County, California) found that, 'for the most part, parents are already fairly satisfied with the quality of local public schools even though a majority also think the schools are underfunded' (Lesher and Wride 1993: A30).

Some commentators have begun to frame the linking of schools and social services as a developmental argument. Thus, well-educated children are an economic resource. Provision of collaborative services in this view serves to increase the economic base of a community by growing healthier, better-educated adults. In past generations, natural resources were seen as the key to economic prosperity. In the information age, people are seen as the key resource.

> Social scientists, corporate leaders, and government officials have all expressed concerns about the potential weakening of America's competitive position if we fail to confront the growing shortage of skilled workers. These concerns have led to a heightened awareness of the consequences of poverty, poor education, and joblessness. (Wilson 1990: 80)

It is not clear how public support for education and social services will shift as social services are linked to public education. In fact, as the resource base of government has constricted, these public services have often been in competition for public funds. One of the arguments advanced in support of school-linked social services is that it may bring improved efficiency in the use of tax dollars. Child advocates are quick to point out, however, that collaboration and coordination will not overcome inadequate funding and growing demands that are driven by demographic shifts and socioeconomic changes.

One way to deal with resource scarcity is to target services to those most in need. This has been the pattern in many of the collaborative efforts to date. Conversely, efforts which seek to provide collaborative services for all children seem more likely to gain widespread political support because they will be seen as a reform effort rather than as a new 'welfare' program. Additionally, targeting services to 'poor areas' means that children who may be in desperate need, but do not live in those areas, will not be served.

If collaborative school-linked social services are only made available in poor neighborhoods, the potential benefits of improved services will not be demonstrated in middle and upper class neighborhoods; and a chance to build a stronger constituency for linking services will be lost.

The politics of allocation or development are more likely to build a wide coalition of support for linking schools and social services. Wilson (1990) made a similar argument for policies that are seen as assisting a broad range of citizens rather than just minority groups.

> Full employment policies, jobs skills training, comprehensive health care legislation, educational reforms in public schools, child care legislation, and crime and drug abuse prevention programs – these are the race-neutral policies likely to begin making a difference for the poor, black and white.... These programs should be presented, however, not as ways to address the plight of poor minorities (though they would greatly benefit from them), but as strategies to help all groups, regardless of race or economic class. (Wilson 1990: 79).

Legislative action

The history of legislative action in both education and social services has been the development of categorical programs and projects targeted to deal with specific problems such as teen pregnancy, drug abuse, child abuse, students who do not speak English, and special education students. These categorical programs have isolated funding streams that require funds to be used to solve the targeted problem, rather than helping the individual recipient to solve a range of interrelated problems (see Koppich: Ch. 3).

Hearings were held in the summer of 1989 in the US House of Representatives on the establishment of a National Youth Policy. Prior to President Bush's Education Summit the National Association of Elementary School Principals issues a statement calling for coordination of services: 'it is not better teachers, textbooks or curricula our children need most; it is better childhoods. We will never see permanent school reform until we first see childhood reform' (NAESP 1989). During the 1990 California election, gubernatorial candidate Pete Wilson announced his Healthy Start Program (see White: Ch. 10). New Jersey and Kentucky (see First *et al.*: Ch. 4, Russo and Lindle: Ch. 11) have implemented statewide education programs that seek stronger links to family resource centers and other school-linked services.

Wang *et al.* (1993), commenting on the work of the Commission on Chapter 1, which is trying to craft reforms of the federal education program, noted that it will be difficult for schools to participate in integration of services for children if their own internal programs are not integrated. They urged that it is time to reform all education categorical programs such as Chapter 1. Others have argued that Congressional reauthorization of Chapter 1 provides a 'window of opportunity for collaboration' (Dunkle and Usdan 1993: 34). At the least, some have argued that schools should be able to use a portion of their Chapter 1 funding as 'matching funds' for non-educational programs that students need. In this sense the funds could be used as the 'glue' to bring together a wider array of services (Kirst 1992).

Community empowerment issues

All of the advocates for linking schools and social services have at least paid 'lip-service' to the notion that families who will be the recipients of such services should be part of the planning process (see Garvin and Young: Ch. 6 and Kadel and Routh: Ch. 8). Prior efforts at community involvement, such as those of the War on Poverty programs, raise a caution about the difficulties of these efforts. Who decides what is defined as a need: the community, the professionals, or the politicians? How is community participation structured? Critical theorists suggest that unless institutions change how they conceptualize the role of community members, government actions will result in replicating the current social structure which empowers some and disenfranchises others.

Tyack (1992) makes a similar point when discussing resistance by some immigrant parents to the provision of health services in public schools during the Progressive Era.

> It is important to consult and involve the clients, to discover what they want and need. The rational plans of outsiders often fail, for parents in the past have found ways to sabotage services they found intrusive. (p. 30)

Interest group opposition

All of the many categorical education programs have the support of special-interest groups which lobby to protect these programs. Koppich (Ch. 3) discusses the need to change this political paradigm if we are going to have systemic change. But there are other interest groups from outside the various social service and educational institutional networks that pose threats to the development of collaborative school-linked services.

The religious right has found much in the linking of schools and social services to oppose. They blend together political conservatism with patriarchal views of the family (Adler 1990, 1992). Their conservatism resists any change, particularly if it involves more government spending. They also oppose aspects of linking schools and social services because they value the traditional family structure with a 'stay-at-home mother' and oppose efforts to support families that do not fit this mold. A project funded by the New American Schools Development Corporation in Gaston County, North Carolina was opposed by 'conservative Christian activists' (Sommerfield 1993: 1). The project included plans for coordination of education, health, and social services along with other educational reforms.

Efforts that involve provision of health services have also been opposed by the religious right because of concerns that access to abortion or family planning services might be provided. In many cases, the individuals objecting to the provision of health services are not the parents of children in the public schools; and in some cases they are not even residents of the school district where the services would be provided. A California district's effort to provide health services for poor, elementary school students, using private foundation and Medi-Cal funding, was opposed by people from the religious right who maintained there was a 'chance' that a pregnant elementary school child's family might be given a referral to an agency that might discuss abortion. Health screenings at two of the schools showed that 88% of first- and fourth-grade students had untreated health problems. Eventually, the opposition was overcome; and the health services are being provided. But there was a protracted and very public debate about this issue (Smith 1991). This was also the case in several other Califonia districts that submitted proposals for Healthy Start funding. Reports of discussions with staff from other districts indicate that some districts decided not to apply for funding because of the controversies surrounding provision of health services. A similar 'echo effect' has been documented in school districts that respond to controversial curriculum challenges in nearby districts by limiting the range of textbooks they consider for adoption (Adler 1993).

In another California district, a dispute erupted over a drug abuse counseling program at a high school. The services were provided by a county agency to students, during the school day, at the high school campus. An anonymous phone call to the school district alleged that students were being provided free access to birth control and '$5·00 abortions' through the cooperative venture between the county and the district. Investigation by the district later revealed that the county counselor had invited the local Medi-Cal (state-funded health care for indigents) worker to the school to complete the paper work for hundreds of students to get services through a special program for children aged 12–20 requiring services related to family planning, drug abuse counseling, pregnancy, sexual assault, sexually transmitted diseases, and psychological treatment. This mechanism was used to cover the cost of the counseling program which could not be funded out of district or county funds due to budget reductions. The children did not need parental consent to access any of these services. The school district, unaware of the range of services being offered, actually had a long-standing policy which stated that students would not be excused from school to receive medical services without parent permission.

The resulting controversy was used in the campaigns of two candidates supported by the religious right who won seats on the local school board. The county agency removed the services when the district planned to notify parents generally of the services because this would, in the county's view, violate the students' rights to confidentiality. Subsequently, the district contracted with the county agency to provide only drug abuse counseling through the remainder of the school year. Thus, the interplay of pressure from the religious right and poorly maintained lines of communications between the organizations threatened the provision of much needed services for students.

In addition to concerns about linking the provision of health services and public schools, the religious right has also raised concerns about using databases to keep records on children and families; 'overzealous' child abuse reporting; using the term 'at risk;' programs designed to improve self-esteem; and what they generally describe as 'usurping parental responsibility or authority' and 'social engineering.'

Economic issues

Clearly, the continuing slow economic recovery exacerbates the difficulties of children and families. A child whose parents have been laid off from their jobs will have much greater difficulty obtaining health care and, ultimately, will have greater difficulty benefiting fully from education. The economic system is an important part of the ecological context for children. (See Mawhinney: Ch. 2 for a discussion of the importance of an ecological context.)

Many commentators have noted that poverty is a variable that is often found in describing the difficulties of children and families who face social or educational problems. Further, some commentators have begun to point to poverty as one of, or perhaps the root, cause of social problems. 'We must search for root causes (e.g., poverty and unemployment) for which other problems (e.g., substance abuse, school failure, child abuse) are the equivalent of symptoms' (Lawson and Hooper-Brier, Response 2, this volume). Wilson (1991) has also pointed to the critical role of the economic base of a community in impacting on social structures.

> Urban minorities have been highly vulnerable to structural changes in the economy, such as the shift from goods-producing to service-producing industries, the increasing polarization of the labor market into low-wage and high-wage sectors, innovations in technology, and the relocation of manufacturing industries out of the central city. These shifts have led to sharp increases in joblessness and related problems of highly concentrated poverty, welfare dependency, and family breakup .... (Wilson 1990: p. 78)

The importance of the economic system as a key component of the ecology of families must not be overlooked in developing collaborative services for families. Families that lack the potential for economic viability will always be at risk. Thus, if we are serious about prevention, we must focus on how to improve the economic viability of communities. Efforts to rebuild the job base of communities through economic development, providing job skills training, and providing access investment capital need to be addressed as a part of collaboration efforts. Unless we address issues of economic empowerment, we will never be able to build enough homeless shelters, provide enough compensatory education programs, or move more families off welfare roles than come onto them.

> As we approach the end of the twentieth century the problems of poverty, joblessness and social isolation in the inner-city ghetto remain among the most serious challenges facing municipal and national polity makers in the United States. A successful public policy initiative to address these problems requires a close look not only at the declining labor-market opportunities for the truly disadvantaged, but also at the declining social organization of inner-city neighborhoods that have continued to reinforce the economic marginality of their residents. (Wilson 1992: 21)

Thus, the economic problems of families must be addressed as part of the efforts to link together all of the support services that families may need. The argument made here is that we cannot get better childhoods for children unless we build better communities. That cannot be done without attending to all aspects of a community, both social and economic. Further, we cannot improve the community by simply training people for jobs, if the jobs are not accessible to people from the community.

Major themes

Several themes seem to support the concepts presented in all of the chapters, though to varying degrees. First, the fact that people, not organizations, collaborate means that time is a critical resource constraint. Second, because collaboration is a complex task it is very important that a common ethos drive the process.

Interpersonal ties and the value of time

Early on in our discussions at the Center for Collaboration for Children, Julia George, a Fellow at the Center and a nursing educator, pointed out that people from various organizations are the actual collaborators, not the organizations. Organizations can constrain or enable interorganizational efforts, but collaboration is a person-to-person activity. Thus, interpersonal ties are critical to the success of interorganizational relationships. Galaskiewicz and Shatin (1981) stressed that interpersonal ties become more important during periods of environmental turbulence. Smith (comments made at a meeting of the Center for Collaboration for Children on April 21, 1993 by Ralph Smith from the Philadelphia Children's Network) suggests an interesting paradox between the need for interpersonal ties and the resistance to change. He pointed to the importance of the 'B Team' in considering linking schools and social services. These are the people in organizations who tell reformers: 'I've *b*een here *b*efore you came and I'll *b*e here after you go!' A similar point is made by Stefkovich and Guba (Ch. 7) in their discussion of the need to empower line workers who are expected to carry out reform efforts.

In analyzing the salience of the 1978 change agent study which she co-authored McLaughlin (1990) pointed to the importance of professional connections between teachers in implementing new programs or policies. 'We did not look beyond the policy structure to consider that the embedded structure of greatest import to teachers might have nothing or little to do with policy – it might have to do with professional networks, school department, or other school-level associations, or colleagues however organized . . . ' (p. 15). Thus, policy makers may try to impose a reform but the 'B Team' has the power to resist or implement a reform.

Beck and Marshall's (1992) study of how sexuality educators use interpersonal ties to deal with a politically turbulent environment by forging informal ties that span various organizations which may not have formal relationships is an excellent example of the fact that people, not organizations, collaborate. In their example the 'B Team' forged inter-organizational ties that helped them proactively to shape and respond to their environment.

Time is a critical factor necessary to allow the development of these interpersonal ties as the Mitchell and Scott, Kadel and Roth and Garvin and Young chapters suggest. It takes time for professionals to learn the language and customs of their colleagues from other disciplines. Time is also required to forge the trusting, cross-institutional personal relationships that are crucial to overcoming organizational inertia and resistance.

> 'This is tough stuff – it's not going to be a quick fix,' said Kathleen J. Emery, executive director of the New Futures project in Dayton. . . . 'I don't think anybody thinks we are on the wrong track,' Mr. Van Vleck [Casey Foundation representative] said. 'What has changed . . . is our understanding and acceptance that this is not a 5- or even 10-year effort, but a 15- to 20-year process of retooling and reshaping the youth-service system.' (Cohen 1991: 12)

Kadel and Roth stress the importance of staff development efforts in providing the framework to support changes in attitudes and acquisition of new skills. Knapp discussed the importance of socializing new members to collaborative efforts at universities and that it is a time-consuming process. In fact, this volume would not exist in its present form except for the time provided to interested faculty Fellows (including the editors of this volume) over a three-year period by the Center for Collaboration for Children at California State University, Fullerton.

Common ethos

In the *1991 Yearbook*, King and McGuire contend that, 'it is imperative to seek reforms that elicit agreement in value positions among internal and external groups' (p. 124). The chapters that discuss the Norwegian and Canadian efforts both show the strong guiding ethos of program in those countries. The process of adopting 'white papers' and establishing study commissions assures that reforms in these countries reflect value positions that are developed over some time and once implemented do not change rapidly. The policy process in the USA is, conversely, notorious for the 'quick-fix' approach, after which, a policy issue moves out of public attention. Ours is a pragmatic and incremental system which often develops value characteristics as an 'afterthought' rather than by design. However, as Mawhinney suggests, the process of gaining consensus on the values to be advanced by a reform is critical to community building.

Lawson and Hooper-Briar (Response 2) pose the global question: what is our vision for a good and just society and how do our efforts to link schools and social services advance that vision? Newmann (1993), in discussing education restructuring, argued that, 'a technically collaborative organization is particularly effective when guided by the ethos of [a] caring community' (Newmann 1993: 9). No single way of expressing an undergirding ethos for linking schools and social services has yet emerged in the USA.

However, it is clear from the work of authors in this volume that the outlines of this ethos are clear. It values empowerment of both line workers and families. It recognizes the strong interrelationsips between children, families, and communities. Thus, it takes a stance that is both holistic and ecological. It places the child and the family at the center of the purposes of this reform effort. Rather than seeing families as patriarchal islands, it assumes that families are connected to the community and need community caring and support. And further, that families have a reciprocal responsibility to care for the whole community. It sees public and private agencies as both a source of problems – fragmentation and restricted resources – and as a potential source of solutions – collaborative approaches to caring for children and families.

Categorical programs which have been developed to deal with specific social problems seemed to be based on conceptions of 'rights.' Thus, every citizen was seen as having a right to be caught in a safety net of services if they 'fell off the norm.' This system of fragmented services has been driven by notions of individualism and rights-based entitlements. Services were only provided to the individuals in greatest need because their need gave greater 'rights' to the services. In this way we developed a system that was crisis driven and deficit based (assumes that there is something wrong with the person needing assistance).

The notion of 'caring' which Newmann uses can provide a key concept in defining the ethos for linking schools and social services. This ethos stresses the notion of responsibility for others and interconnectedness. Gilligan (1982) describes morality as based on caring:

> This conception of morality as concerned with the activity of care centers moral development around the understanding of responsibilities and relationships, just as the conception of morality as fairness ties moral development to the understanding of rights and rules. (p. 19)

Noddings (1984) makes a similar point:

> Human caring and the memory of caring and being cared for, which I shall argue form the foundation of ethical response, have not received attention except as outcomes of ethical behavior. (p. 1)

> Our efforts must, then, be directed to the maintenance of conditions that will permit caring to flourish . . . . Since caring and the commitment to sustain it form the universal heart of the ethic, we must establish a convincing and comprehensive picture of caring at the outset. (pp. 5–6)

It is interesting to note that (a) the work of both Gilligan and Noddings, which calls our attention to 'caring,' focuses on the study of women's moral and psychological development, and (b) that many of the line workers who will be implementing collaborative school-linked social services are women. The ethos of caring can provide language to harmonize American individualism and our desperate need to act collectively to address social problems and to address those problems in a way that empowers those in need of our care. Etzioni (1993) seems to be making a similar point in a discussion of the communitarian movement's efforts to establish a sense of collective responsibility.

Overview of the *Yearbook*

This volume explores what can best be described as an emerging area of study. It is one which can surely be enriched by applying lessons learned from past efforts to reform policies and services provision. It brings together a wide array of research and public policy issues to focus on a new configuration of service provision – linking schools and social services. It is thus a conceptually complex enterprise. In addition, this volume attempts to capture the scope of the enterprise at a rather early stage – the first stages of implementation in some states. Thus, this volume lacks the benefit of 'hindsight.'

We have attempted to 'walk the thin line' between providing a work that is purely theoretical and one that is a handbook for practitioners by situating this proposed policy direction in a theoretical framework and, at the same time, by being 'close to the ground' in describing what is actually happening as the policy is implemented. 'True believers' in the value of school-linked social services may be concerned about the way that we have attempted to balance the possibilities with the problems that are suggested by the theoretical literature.

Those familiar with past *Yearbooks* will perhaps note that there are more chapters written by groups of co-authors in this volume. It would seem that the authors have reflected in their scholarly work the practices recommended to service providers – collaboration and interdisciplinary approaches. We note, however, that in some academic settings co-authors receive less credit for tenure than single authors – a powerful disincentive for collaboration. The contributors also reflect a wide array of experience. There are some authors who have written about other issues in politics of education. There are also authors with backgrounds in law, urban studies, and children's issues. Additionally, there are authors who are 'practitioners.'

In selecting the topics to be included in this *Yearbook* we were faced with a common dilemma – whether to stress the broad scope of the issues or to focus on in-depth analysis. We attempted a compromise but were unable to cover every issue. Evaluation is an important issue in any innovation, which is only touched on in these chapters. Gardner discusses the importance of outcome measures in the Afterword. We are indebted to the previous work done by King and McGuire in the 1991 *Yearbook*, and the work of colleagues that was published by the Packard Foundation, *The Future of Children* (Behrman 1992).

Part 1 – Cross-national Perspectives identifies the policy processes that impact on children's issues in Norway and Canada. These chapters also suggest that Norwegian and Canadian approaches to policy development are different from the process found in the USA. More importantly, they illustrate the importance of a clear ethos that drives the policy process.

Hagen and Tibbitts (Ch. 1) present a descriptive analysis of the Norwegian government's practices related to *barns oppvekstkår*, a policy orientation that is 'child-centered' and dependent on close cooperation between the family, schools and municipal authorities. They also discuss the tension between local autonomy and the pressure for increased accountability. Teachers are suppose to play a vital role as 'human links' with municipal service delivery. Hagen and Tibbitts discuss the limited research available and suggest that widespread professionalization of teachers for these new roles has not yet occurred.

Mawhinney (Ch. 2) makes the case that ecological perspectives from the child development literature; family service interventions; and research on the relationship between families, schools and communities supports an ecological approach to meeting the needs of children and families. She argues that this philosophy undergirds a holistic approach which is beginning to take hold in Ontario, Canada. She urges that we engage the public in rethinking the delivery of services for young people because only this will facilitate the kind of large-scale social and structural changes that are necessary.

Part 2 – State and Local Perspectives has six chapters that focus on the implications of linking local schools and social service in the USA. Koppich (Ch. 3) first traces the development of the many categorical programs that currently shape service delivery. The chapter then 'unpacks' the political dynamics that tend to maintain the categorical nature of services. California's Healthy Start program is seen as a shift in the paradigm, but on a modest scale. Koppich argues that to expand such efforts the rules of the political game must be altered.

First, Curcio and Young (Ch. 4) argue that the 'full-service school' movement is not following traditional policy models. They argue that innovations pioneered at the local level seem to be influencing state policy. They trace examples of policy development across a number of states and describe an instrument for assessing the strength of the state role in shaping policy.

Mitchell and Scott (Ch. 5) argue that success of collaboration between schools and social service agencies is contingent upon the development of appropriate institutional and professional cultures. They argue that interagency collaboration can supplement competent individual-level professionalism but cannot replace it. Further, the failures in the current system are systemic in character. Thus, the system is doing what it was designed to do but is not meeting the needs of children and families.

Garvin and Young (Ch. 6) discuss efforts in New Orleans to reconnect schools and cities. Resource issues such as use of grant funding, time as a critical resource, outcome assessments, and blending reource streams are explored. They discuss the concepts of proximal benefits and proximal concerns to explain the value various stakeholders place on collaborative efforts.

Stefkovich and Guba (Ch. 7) focus on the restructuring movement in education and its relationship to school-linked social services. They characterize schools as 'open systems' which must elicit the support of other providers and the community. Three nationally recognized initiatives (The Yale Child Study Center's School Development Program, Philadelphia Children's Network, and New Beginnings in San Diego) are used as examples of restructuring that include school-linked social services.

Kadel and Routh (Ch. 8) discuss the implementation process for linking schools and social services and give examples from the field of how the various stages have been addressed in actual collaborative efforts. They also discuss the limitations of using implementation literature based on changes within organizations to predict the success of cross-organization and systemwide changes.

Part 3 – The Role of the Universities consists of a chapter by Knapp (Ch. 9) and his colleagues at the University of Washington and four responses from colleagues at five other universities. Knapp argues that since the university is a central player in the preparation of professionals it is challenged to adjust curriculum to support interprofessional collaboration. The chapter explores credentialing and licensing issues, disciplinary and interdisciplinary issues, curriculum development, and practicum sites. Casto (Response 1) raises very salient issues about funding for interprofessional education. Lawson and Hooper-Briar (Response 2) focus on the need to define a vision which is based on conceptions of a just society. Wilson (Response 3) and his colleagues argue that universities should create change within the existing system by enhancing the skills of current professionals and then, in the long term, change discipline specific programs. Tellez and Schick (Response 4) raise critical questions about the ability of teacher education as it is currently configured in many locations to infuse collaborative training into preparation programs. They also pose critical multicultural issues.

Part 4 – Lessons from the Field focuses on two states – California and Kentucky. White (Ch. 10) discusses the Healthy Start reforms in California and the important role of private foundations in developing and carrying out the initiative. Russo and Lindle (Ch. 11) discuss implementation of the Kentucky Education Reform Act which resulted from a court decision declaring the state's education finance system unconstitutional. Important issues about how to maintain local flexibility and centralized accountability are illustrated.

References

ADLER, L. (1990, April) 'Decisions fired with emotion', *Urban Education*, 25(1), pp. 3–13.

ADLER, L. (1992, July) 'Curriculum challenge from the Religious Right', *Urban Education*, 27(2), pp. 152–173.

ADLER, L. (1993, spring/summer) 'Curriculum challenges in California', *Record in Educational Administration and Supervision*, pp. 10–20.

BECK, L. G. and MARSHALL, C. (1992, September) 'Policy into practice: a qualitative inquiry into the work of sexuality educators', *Educational Policy*, 6(3), pp. 319–334.

BEHRMAN, R. (ed.) (1992) *The Future of Children* (Los Altos, CA: David and Lucile Packard Foundation).

BERMAN, P. and MCLAUGHLIN, M. (1978) *Federal Programs Supporting Educational Change*, Vol. VIII: *Implementing and Sustaining Innovations* (Santa Monica, CA: Rand).

COHEN, D. (1991, September 25) 'Reality tempers "New Futures" leaders' optimism', *Education Week*, pp. 1, 12–13, 15.

DUNKLE, M. and USDAN, M. (1993, March 3) 'Putting people first means connecting education to other services', *Education Week*, pp. 34, 44.

ETZIONI, A. (1993) *The Spirit of Community* (New York: Crown).

GALASKIEWICZ, J. and SHATIN, D. (1981) 'Leadership and networking among neighborhood human service organizations', *Administrative Science Quarterly*, 26(September), pp. 454–479.

GILLIGAN, C. (1982) *In a Different Voice* (Cambridge, MA: Harvard University Press).

GRUBB, W. N. and LAZERSON, M. (1982) *Broken Promises: How Americans Fail Their Children* (New York: Basic Books).

HALL, R. H. (1991) *Organizations: Structures, Processes and Outcomes* (New Jersey: Prentice Hall).

KING, R. and MCGUIRE, C. (1992) 'Political and financial support for school-based and child-centered reforms', in J. Cibulka, R. Reed and K. Wong (eds) *The Politics of Urban Education in the United States, 1991 Yearbook of PEA* (London: Falmer Press), pp. 123–135.

KIRST, M. (1992) 'Supporting school-linked children's services', in A. Odden (ed.) *Rethinking School Finance: An Agenda for the 1990s* (San Francisco: Josey-Bass), pp. 298–321.

LESHER, D. and WRIDE, N. (1993, June 13) 'Voucher plan gets high marks', *OC Los Angeles Times*, pp. 1, 26, 28–30.

MCLAUGHLIN, M. W. (1990) 'The Rand Change Agent Study revisited: macro perspectives and micro realities', *Educational Researcher*, 19(9), pp. 11–16.

MEYER, J. and ROWAN, B. (1983) 'Institutionalized organizations: formal structure as myth and ceremony', in J. Meyer and W. R. Scott (eds) *Organizational Environments* (Beverly Hills: Sage), pp. 21–43.

MEYER, J., SCOTT, W. R. and DEAL, T. (1983) 'Institutional and technical sources of organizational structure: explaining the structure of educational organizations', in J. Meyer and W. R. Scott (eds) *Organizational Environments* (Beverly Hills: Sage), pp. 45–67.

'NAESP: childhood reform essential to education reform' (1989, October 2) EDCAL (Sacramento, CA: Association of California School Administrators).

NEWMANN, F. (1984) *Caring: A Feminine Approach to Ethics and Moral Education* (Berkeley, CA: University of California Press).

PACE (1989) *Conditions of Children in California* (Berkeley, CA: Policy Analysis for California Education).

PERROW, C. (1986) *Complex Organizations: A Critical Essay* (New York: Random House).

PETERSON, P. (1981) *City Limits* (Chicago: University of Chicago Press).

PORTNEY, K. (1986) *Approaching Public Policy Analysis* (New Jersey: Prentice Hall).

ROBERTSON, D. and JUDD, D. (1989) *The Development of American Public Policy: The Structure of Policy Restraint* (Boston: Scott, Foresman).

SOMMERFELD, M. (1993, March 10) 'Christian activists seek to torpedo NASDC project', *Education Week*, pp. 1, 18–19.

SMITH, S. (1991) '*School-based health clinics*', unpublished master's project (Fullerton, CA: California State University, Fullerton).

TEITEL, L. (1993, March) 'The state role in jump-starting school/university collaboration: a case study', *Educational Policy*, 7(1), pp. 74–95.

TONER, R. (1992, July 5) 'Politics of welfare: focusing on the problems', *The New York Times*, pp. 1, 13.

TYACK, D. (1992) 'Health and social services in public schools: historical perspectives', in Behrmann, R. (ed.) *The Future of Children* (Los Altos, CA: David and Lucile Packard Foundation), pp. 19–31.

WANG, M., REYNOLDS, M. and WALBERG, H. (1993, March 24) 'Reform all categorical programs', *Education Week*, p. 64.

WILSON, W. (1990, Spring), 'Race-neutral programs and the Democratic coalition', *The American Prospect*, pp. 74–81.

WILSON, W. (1992) 'Race, class, and poverty in urban neighborhoods: a comparative perspective', keynote speech, conference on Building Strong Communities: Strategies for Urban Change, Cleveland, Ohio, May 13–15, 1992.

PART 1
Cross-national perspectives

POLITICS OF EDUCATION ASSOCIATION YEARBOOK, 1993, 19–32

The Norwegian case: child-centered policy in action?

Unni Hagen and Felisa Tibbitts

In this chapter we will present a descriptive analysis of the Norwegian government's practices related to *barns oppvekstkår*, the closely intertwined set of laws and value systems related to the conditions under which children grow up, including education, health and social well-being. Effective local practices involve close cooperation between the family, schools and municipal authorities. We will examine formal policy and the limited empirical evidence that is available in appraising Norway's success in carrying out 'child-centered policy.'

The Norwegian model is an instructive one for the USA, not only for the ways in which the institutionalization of the child ombudsman role has been attempted from the central level on down, but because of the struggles that continue today as Norwegians attempt to balance the sometimes contradictory impulses between local governmental autonomy, the integrity of the family unit and the pressure for increased accountability within the system as a whole. These impulses have been laid bare in particular since the mid-1980s, when new policies were enacted that decentralized to municipalities responsibility for developing their operating budgets (while maintaining financial support from the center in the form of block grants).

Although there is insufficient evidence to judge the delivery of local services, and particularly any changes since decentralization, the Norwegian case illustrates how a system can be set up so that parents, teachers, health care professionals, social care providers and government officials at all levels can cooperate in meeting the multiple needs of children. In the wake of substantive educational reforms, policies have steadfastly assured that the pedagogical and social needs of children ultimately will take priority over financial considerations and will drive the configurations of service delivery. With increased accountability and teacher professionalization related to recent reforms, Norway will be in an even better position to guarantee that meeting children's needs remains the highest priority.

Some background on Norway

Norway has a landmass of over 839,062 square miles, approximately the same area as New Mexico. With a population of only about 4·2 million, it is one of the most sparsely populated countries on the European continent, with most of the inhabitants living in small towns. Slightly over 20% of the population is under the age of 15.

Norway is a social democratic country with a history of social policies geared towards equalization among its populace – in terms of both equality of opportunity and equality of outcomes. There is also a strong tradition for recognizing the special needs of children and women. Norway's egalitarianism has been traced partly to its scattered population, which, in former times, precluded the development of a feudal class. A certain populism, engendered in rural roots and early experiences with mass democracy, has also contributed to the country's commitment to equality.

> Norway was the first of the five [Nordic] countries to come close to mass democracy: Stein Kuhnle has offered estimates indicating that around 45 percent of all men 25 years and older were formally enfranchised in 1814. The free peasantry were given political rights .... In fact, the decision of the elite of officials to extend political rights to such large numbers was to a considerable extent based on the conviction that the peasants would remain tied to their parochial affairs and interfere very little in the running of the new state. (Rokkan 1981: 62)

A late-comer to the industrialized world, Norway's drilling of North Sea oil, beginning in the 1970s, has enabled one of the highest levels of living in the world. 'Level-of-living' was a concept established by a Swedish study in 1971. The indicator incorporates measures for health, nutrition, housing, family origins and family relations, education, work and work milieu, economic resources, political resources, leisure and leisure-time pursuits (Castles 1978: 79).

A considerable amount is spent on education, both in absolute and per capita terms. In 1987, public expenditure on education was approximately 7·8% of the gross national product (Utdannings- og forskningsdepartementet 1990: 5). This figure represents a real growth in total educational spending since 1980, attributable mostly to salary increases, although with concurrent reductions in equipment and materials acquisitions. During this period, there were renewed efforts to support teachers in the classroom. The 29 hour/week teaching load for primary school teachers was reduced to 27 hours as of the 1984–85 school year, teachers were given release time to develop local curricular plans (1987–88) and the maximum number of students from primary school classrooms was to be reduced from 30 to 28 by 1990 (Kirke-, utdannings- og forskningsdepartementet 1992: 8, 10–11).

Egalitarianism and welfare policies

Since the post-Second World War period, Norway and the other Scandinavian countries have gained international recognition for their centrally driven efforts in meeting the social and educational needs of citizens. The Social Democrats in Norway, who dominated the political scene following the Second World War and into the 1980s, have been most closely associated with these efforts. The policies themselves have been characterized by explicit guidelines and financial support earmarked from the center.

> [I]n terms of social structures, forms of government, and predominant attitudes towards society, the five Nordic countries have many common features. [T]he similarities stem from political thinking and actions, which in the latter part of our century have been characterized as an attempt to create 'welfare societies.' This catch-word has had a broader meaning and wider political consequences than in most other countries, where more often it has been seen solely as a matter of income redistribution, or adopted just as convenient political rhetoric. (Eide 1992: 9)

At the same time, a strong tradition of elective local government remains.

> Norway should be seen as a case of 'reluctant centralism'. From 1837, when local self-government was legally recognized, the rights of local people to influence schools have been strongly defended .... Local autonomy derives from Norway's political traditions and geographical circumstances; historically, Norway's rural and seafaring population constituted a 'free' peasantry only weakly incorporated into the state. (Rust and Blakemore 1990: 505)

Policies within Norway's educational, health, social service and even labor spheres have been characterized by a strong commitment to equalization. Within the economic domain, for example, this is reflected in a progressive tax system. Within the educational system, policies have evolved to increase the participation of traditionally underserved populations within Norway.

The equalization, both of opportunity and outcome, explicitly undergirds Norwegian policies concerning '*barns oppvekstkår*'. Education is almost exclusively in the hands of public institutions; although the number of students enrolled in private institutions increased by over 60% during the 1980s, that figure represents no more than two or three percent of all students (Rust and Blakemore 1990: 515).

Norwegian educational traditions

Education as community

For over 100 years, schools have been seen as a key support to families in the education and bringing up of children. The roots go back to a brand of populism, which upholds 'the importance of altruistic cultural values rooted in family life with a bias towards rural communities' (Lauglo 1992: 8).

The Norwegian model for 'child upbringing' has several basic features: parental control; multiple services organized by the schools; municipal-level responsibilities for all services to children and youth; substantial block grants from central government to the municipalities; and coordination and oversight at the national level.

Teachers, principals and schools have had formal responsibility for promoting the welfare of children, not only in terms of providing an education, but also in terms of the general well-being of the child. What distinguishes Norway from many other systems is not its commitment to this goal, but the ways in which it has tried to carry this out in practice within the welfare state.

As one example, in the area of health, municipal staff have an office on primary school grounds, where immunization, regular check-ups and non-emergency health care problems can be directly handled. If the office is not located on school grounds, students are taken to the local health center, not merely for routine medical services but in order to become familiar with the center's location. Formal policy promotes cooperation between schools and health centers, even as a common concern for the children forges a natural partnership. Once a child enters school, it is the teacher who is relied upon to work most closely with the parents to promote the child's welfare. In this manner, educators ideally serve as a human link between families and other services available on the municipal level. This role has been further formalized in recent educational reforms, bringing new challenges, which will be addressed later in the chapter.

Features of the school reflect the earlier traditions of Norway, when villages were scattered and travel to school was quite some distance. Family ties tend to be strong, community membership is meaningful, and schools are, theoretically, extensions of these personal relationships. The upbringing of children is recognized as a family affair, with schools there more to assist families in this task than to serve as a substitute.

> The political thinking behind this is partly based on the belief that a good school should have close contacts with parents and with the local community, which would not be possible for large school factories. Furthermore, schools are seen as essential to the life of the local community, and moving them to large centers will tap the life-blood of the local community. (Eide 1992: 10)

Even as Norway has become industrialized and cities have emerged (bringing urban problems), educational policy and practice have remained true to their original roots. Schools are relatively small. The average size of a school for grades 1–6 is about 150 pupils, and, for middle school (grades 7–9), the average is 250 pupils. A parliamentary decision placed a ceiling on the enrollment level of new lower secondary schools at 450 pupils. It is important to note that in Norway, educational policy makers have resisted the temptation to develop 'supermarket' schools that can sometimes be inspired by large student populations. Instead, Norway has kept the 'rural school' reference point, a contrast to many of the developments in other western nations.

> Small communities, small schools and small classes are greatly valued in their own right in this country, without much pause to think of the possibility that the choice and variety which large size allow can be an advantage. (Lauglo 1992: 2)

The philosophy and practice of Norway's services to the child are reminiscent of the themes of the community education movement that became popularized in the USA in the 1970s. Although community education has sometimes been defined as providing school programs for adults, a broader understanding of the concept implies 'the utilization of all resources in the community for the benefits of its members' (Seay *et al.* 1974: 11). Concern with 'restoring community' has a long history in thought on education and society in urban industrial societies, but Norwegians have a strong attachment to it at the level of ideology (Lauglo 1993: i).

> Community leaders began to think in terms of community-wide, institutionalized forces which were performing – and could be expected to perform better – the functions society entrusted to education. They saw that the time had come for the school-centered concept to grow into a community education concept. (Seay *et al.* 1974: 28)

The Norwegian philosophy resembles the so-called family support and education approach in the USA, which 'take an "ecological" approach to child development, recognising the importance of the immediate family, the extended family, and the community to the growth and development of the young child' (Seppanen and Heifitz 1988: 1).

In some community education programs, a new professional 'home–school counselor' was introduced, who would provide a link between the school and family and help to coordinate the efforts of educational and social service agencies (Tolbert 1978: 270). This sounds much like the role formally assigned to teachers in the Norwegian system.

The Norwegian system in practice

Beginning in the 1930s, educational coordination and oversight at a national level came into practice. The policies of the Norwegian model are now characterized by explicit guidelines and financial support from the center. The 454 municipalities are responsible for administering the nine-year 'basic school'. In every municipality there is an elected council, assisted by a chief education officer. Compulsory schools are run by the local authorities, even as the central government – through financial support and curriculum guidelines – aims to secure equality of education across the country. Per pupil expenditures in poorer municipalities are equal to the national average. Although there is minimal evidence, compulsory schools are generally considered to be of equal quality.

All Norwegian schools are organized similarly for the first nine years (6 + 3), with a great deal of attention to the primary school years. Pupils of differing abilities are kept together in the same classes, and cooperative group learning is strongly encouraged. No examinations or grades are assigned, just as there is no streaming according to ability. During the primary school years, it is not unusual to have the same teacher for at least a few years (e.g., 1–3, 4–6, even 1–6); this policy is maintained in some form in the lower secondary schools, where students keep the same homeroom teacher for three years. This practice allows for continuity in the contact between teacher and students, an inter-disciplinary curricular approach, and overall greater contact between parents, teachers and students. One conscious trade-off is the lack of subject-area specialization; a potential downside is prolonged contact between students and teachers who are not compatible.

Student-centered policies, with such sensitivity to equality, cooperation, and teacher autonomy, are reminiscent of the 'open school' phenomenon that took place in the USA in the 1970s. This progressive movement was characterized by team teaching, an interdisciplinary curricular approach, and pedagogical variety (such as lectures, small cooperative group work, individualized instruction and flexible scheduling). While this movement has waxed and waned in the USA, it appears to have reinforced and further developed child-centered pedagogy in Norway.

In Norway, there is a particular concern for vulnerable populations, which is exemplified in the treatment of handicapped and special needs students. Full mainstreaming is expected under the most extraordinary circumstances. Their protection is incorporated into every existing law affecting education. Beginning in 1975, a revision of the 1969 Education Act stated that, as far as possible, disabled children should be integrated into regular school services (Grunnskoleloven 1991). Disabled students were given explicit priority in their right to upper secondary-level education in an act of the same name (revised in 1987), and, in 1975, legislation relating both to primary- and secondary-level education reaffirmed the importance of education for disabled students.

Processes of educational reform

Educational policy making in Norway is coordinated with cultural policy, social policy, manpower policy and also regional policy – all within the rubric of welfare policies. The advent of educational law in Norway is normally the culmination of a long process of discussion and consensus-building, and often follows, rather than precedes, changes in practice. The consensus-building model can be explained in part by the origins of Norwegian democracy, which can be understood only by analyzing the processes of mobilization, bargaining and decision making within and among trade unions, other voluntary bodies, and the organization of issue movements. After the Second World War, 'the Nordic political systems were crisscrossed by networks of interest organizations, and the parties in the parliaments were increasingly forced to legislate within the frameworks set by these bargaining circuits' (Rokkan 1981: 75, 77).

A first step towards large-scale reform is the establishment of study commissions. These multi-partisan commissions collect the relevant research, consider various perspectives on an issue and ultimately make concrete recommendations for action. The study commissions are known for the thoroughness of their investigations, which have taken several years to complete. Once their recommendations have been released, input is encouraged from stakeholders in the educational community – organizations, institutions and individuals alike. Ultimately, educational law may be enacted in the *Storting* (Parliament). In this manner, commission reports are part of a consensual democratic process (Rust 1989: 286–288).

Educational initiatives may also come directly from the Ministry of Education, associated with the ruling political party. When the Ministry intends to promote a new policy, a position paper known as a Parliamentary, or White, Paper is developed. Like the commission reports, the Parliamentary Papers are also developed in consultation with pedagogical experts and become broadly available for comment. At this stage, it is still considered to be a partisan document of the Minister's ruling party.

However, the *Storting*, through a specially designated, multi-party committee, can develop 'interpretive guidelines' in response to a Paper. These guidelines include a summary of the Paper, majority and minority interpretations, and some concluding recommendations. In this form, a Parliamentary Paper can also be developed into a bill that is ultimately legislated by the *Storting* although, by this point, widespread consensus has already been reached on the policy. Again, this entire process of discussion and consensus-building can take years.

Educational reforms of the 1980s

In the 1980s, shifts in Norwegian economic and social environments influenced the educational sector. New realities included the rapid economic integration of Europe, concern for international competitiveness, and relatively higher levels of unemployment. In many respects, educational reform in Norway during the 1980s followed a pattern recently proposed by Ginsberg *et al.* as being 'likely [to] occur during periods of economic crisis and restructuring in the world system and relate to other economic, cultural, and political crisis in nation-states' (Ginsberg *et al.* 1990: 497).

The temptation to adopt a more market-oriented approach to policies culminated politically in an unusual break from Social Democratic (Labor Party) rule. Between 1983 and 1990, party dominance vacillated between the Labor Party and a coalition of conservative parties. One of the trademarks of those times was an increased demand for decentralization, which tipped the scale towards the tradition of local autonomy and away from the center-directed approach that had predominantly characterized the Norwegian government following the Second World War.

In 1980, this trend became evident in education with the publication of a report by the *Hovedkomite for reformer i lokalforvaltningen* (Blue Ribbon Commission), which called for increased administrative decentralization (Kommunaldepartementet 1991). Several important pieces of legislation and ensuing regulations were enacted.

In the sphere of curriculum, schools and local authorities were given more freedom to determine their programs. The 1987 revised *Mønsterplan* (national curricular guidelines) included an outline of the basic principles and objectives of compulsory education and the framework of the content of the various subjects and allocation of teaching periods. 'On the basis of the given guidelines, the individual schools are expected to work out plans indicating the further tasks of the school. It is specified that the individual school or local education authority is responsible for curriculum planning and further definition of syllabus content' (Utdannings- og forskningsdepartementet 1990: 14–15).

Following the 1987 reform, schools and teachers, having always been required to work cooperatively with parents, were now explicitly instructed to take the first initiative and, even before the child began to attend school, to inform parents about the possibilities for participation in school life (Kirke- og utdanningsdepartementet 1987: 66–67). Specifically, teachers were formally obliged: (1) to inform parents and other professionals in the social and educational networks of any special needs of students, and (2) to negotiate for adequate financial and physical support so that the student would thrive (Kirke- og utdanningsdepartementet 1989). The teacher had become the crucial intersection between local autonomy, decentralization efforts, and centralized guidelines.

In the area of budgets, municipalities no longer received direct grants with funds earmarked for educational, health, housing, cultural and other services. Instead, beginning in 1986, local authorities received lump-sum grants for all central government transfers. 'The intention was to give local and regional authorities more autonomy and to support local priorities in the use of resources in various sectors' (Granheim and Lundgren 1991: 482). These block grants required new budget-justifying practices on the part of schools and service providers, including more explicit goal setting for local programs.

> Previously, government allocations to primary and lower secondary schools were earmarked and calculated according to a differentiated scale designed to even out differences between the various regions and make it possible for each municipality to provide equally good schooling. In 1986 this system was revised and improved. Government allocations are no longer earmarked for specific purposes, which means that more of the responsibility is being transferred to the municipalities themselves. (Bjørndal 1992: 9)

We note that although municipalities can technically spend the money as they please, existing national guidelines combined with earmarked salaries and previous practice probably mean that less than 10% of the educational budget can be considered discretionary. Municipalities are also bound by agreements made between the association of municipalities and the Ministry, on the one hand, and the teachers' unions on the other.

In a system characterized in the past by considerable resource commitments to children, thoughtful policy development and widespread implementation, educational changes cannot be taken lightly. Under the recent decentralization, an obvious question arises: how can one ensure that the financial support and guidance from the center are sufficient to deliver the necessary services to children? The Norwegian system, known for its consistency in educational policy practice, is faced with new administrative and accountability challenges.

Coordination at the national level

At the central level, the *Barneombud* ('Child Ombudsman' office) – which had been established in 1981 – was incorporated in 1991 into a new *Barne- og familiedepartement* (Ministry of Children and Families). This new Ministry was given a formal role in assisting municipalities in their increased responsibilities. *Barne og familiedepartementet* was expected to serve as an 'institutional child ombudsman' in coordinating the existing policies of eight other agencies whose policies affect children, such as *Kirke-, utdannings- og forskningsdepartementet* (Ministry of Church, Education and Research), *Kulturdepartementet* (Ministry of Culture) and *Sosialdepartementet* (Ministry of Social Welfare).

In practice this means that the Ministry of Children and Families is responsible for providing citizens with information on governmental policies, administrative contacts, and funds that are available for earmarked purposes. A 1993 publication, entitled *Tiltak for barn og ungdom* (Programs for Children and Youth), overviews the array of services available for children through the system:

- Family support (including automatic stipends for children and housing subsidies);
- Children and preschool;
- Foster care;
- Local traffic safety;
- Education and training;
- The labor market;
- Stipends and loans to individuals;
- Loans to communities and non-profits for building construction;
- Leisure time and culture;
- Children and youth organizations;

- International youth exchanges;
- Research and development programs;
- Health and social policies and programs.

The nuances of reorganization: the case of handicapped children

The Norwegian government is still searching for ways to apply the new decentralization law that both respect local autonomy and ensure the best possible service to pupils. The reorganization of special needs centers has been a lightning rod for the discussion about administrative decentralization efforts and is, therefore, suggestive of the ways that administrative issues in other educational areas may be handled in Norway.

By law, municipalities and counties are responsible for the education of the disabled; nonetheless, until recently, services were provided to many children in centrally run special needs centers. In 1990, Parliamentary Paper No. 54 (St.meld.nr 54 1989–90) called for radical decentralization. The 40 special needs service centers operated by central government would be reduced to only ten within two years, with all resources, ensuing responsibilities and personnel (to the extent that specialists would be willing to associate with local educational authorities) transferred to the municipalities and counties. The objective was to further the mainstreaming of handicapped pupils by requiring schools to provide on-site services to students. Consistent with the educational reform trends of the 1980s, the guidelines for municipalities would be quite explicit without being overly directive, local teams would be developed in the schools, and handicapped students would be treated as part of their community.

A new educational minister was appointed in 1990 and a subsequent Parliamentary Paper proposed a slowing of the elimination of 40 centers to 20 instead of 10. A review of both Parliamentary Papers by a *Storting* committee reaffirmed the policy that education should be provided as close to the family residence as possible; however, Innar.S.nr.160 (1990–91) emphasized that it was effective service of the child, rather than the institutional preferences for a purely decentralized or centralized model, that should ultimately govern how services are organized. Handicapped children should first look to their municipalities for services; however, if these could not be met there, parents could choose either to send their child to one of the centers, or to require that the services be provided locally.

The report included other details as well, but the key points reveal the stability of the Norwegian educational model in reaffirming that:

- the pedagogical and social needs of the child take priority over both financial considerations and preferences for organizational 'models';
- teacher training should reflect the real demands of schooling;
- whenever possible, services should be provided locally and on-site;
- the central government has an ongoing oversight function to ensure that children receive the services they require;
- all human beings are entitled to the same quality of life, including full membership in the community; and
- parents have the final say.

Reaffirming the rights of the individual child is certainly laudable. The ensuing question is how teachers and local authorities manage to translate such policies into classroom practice.

Early reflections on decentralization policies

Vacuum in accountability

The new decentralized policies imply that new measures must be developed to ensure the delivery of educational services, to track the use of resources, and possibly to capture educational outcomes as well. In a 1988 report, the Organization for Economic Co-operation and Development (OECD) also recognized the need for increased accountability, recommended the use of school-evaluations and asserted a strong need to develop a model of evaluation that reflects the redistribution of responsibilities at various governmental levels (OECD 1990). Currently there is no systematic way of knowing whether and how services to children have been improved. Consequently, it is extremely difficult to assess the impact that various structural and content reforms have had in the Norwegian classroom and on Norwegian students.

> We know very little about Norwegian education. This was said clearly in the OECD review of Norwegian education more than two years ago. The OECD experts had difficulty evaluating the schools' use of material resources and the achieved results of teaching. It was the data which was not good enough, even the statistics on education were imperfect. The experts could not quite understand how one could direct school and education on such a fragile basis. (Sjøberg 1991: 67)

One direct indicator, however imperfect, is the number of complaints that have been lodged by parents against municipalities for failing to serve their children properly. The national *Barneombud* has unsuccessfully attempted to bring to court three municipalities on the basis of grievances filed on behalf of a child.

Decentralized budgetary decision making would seem to necessitate increased accountability at the municipal or national levels; however, movements in this direction have been slow and tentative. As one step in this direction, counties have appointed a director of education, who will be responsible for overseeing the coordination of services within the county and ensuring the pursuit of national education objectives (Bjørndal 1992: 14). With the increased emphasis on the role of the teacher as the 'human link' for municipal service delivery, a study into the delivery of these multiple services to children is essential.

New skills required at local level

Due to a lack of research, we cannot determine how well teachers understand and are able to practice their role as a 'human link' between municipal services and the child's family. Although the guidelines are fairly clear that the school is responsible for initiating and maintaining contact with families, and for ensuring that the needs of children are met (even if these require services outside the school), practices and methods for measuring these have not been spelled out. How do the teachers know what to do? How do teachers work 'as partners' with parents in ensuring the well-being of their students, particularly when parents are recognized as the formal upbringers and educators? How often are they the source of referrals to health centers or social services?

A case study of two municipalities in Norway's Finmark county – one of the few studies that have been conducted on the school–family relationship – suggested that parents felt closed off from the school and were consulted outside of the bi-yearly meetings only when their child was having some difficulty or if there were transportation problems. Without more information about the inner life of the school and greater opportunities for participation and influence, parents argued, communication could flow only from the school to the community, rather than in the reverse direction (Hovdenak 1992: 186).

Although teacher and schools have been criticized for failing to live up to their expanding responsibilities, widespread professionalization of teachers for these new roles has apparently not been forthcoming. In a system which offers insufficient training for such roles and only general guidelines, misunderstandings and variations in implementation are inevitable. Langerud, representing a parent organization, offered the following observation:

> The individual teacher and parent have to interpret the content of the [educational] policies themselves. Within the school, we as parents are often confronted with different interpretations, and this creates uncertainty and as a result, mistrust in each teacher's understanding of the content and the boundaries for the teaching profession. (Langerud 1991: 45)

While the reforms of the 1980s have pushed schools and teachers into an expanded role in their communities for guaranteeing the delivery of services to children, schools have also been placed in a head-to-head competition with health, social service and other municipal-level offices for block-grant funding. The first implication is that local service providers are learning how to maneuver in political waters that are deeper than ever before. In particular, principals and teachers are now obliged to work closely together and with members of their educational communities in defining their needs, developing associated budgets and promoting their case to local politicians. Many consider this a time-consuming task that is distracting from the 'real work' of schools. Educators and politicians alike are searching for suitable methods to appraise the effective delivery of services, methods that would, under ideal circumstances, actually contribute to the improvement of these services.

However, the unavoidable underbelly of increased accountability is a certain atmosphere of distrust. Educators now see themselves as having to 'defend' themselves to their local communities. Their general vulnerability is attenuated only by the fact that other local providers are in the same tenuous position. Clearly, increased accountability and improvement in services will hinge on schools having adequate skills to present their cases and continued public trust so that their proposals can be accepted at face value.

New roles for schools

Perhaps of greater import in the long run are shifting social and economic realities, which call into question the fundamental role that schools have played in the past. To a large degree, the 'human link' activities that teachers have performed have been premised on parents being actively responsible for the well-being of their children. Serving as a link between the child and local services, while respecting the authority of the parent, implies that the teacher must essentially be a parent educator. However, because the ultimate goal of the teacher is to help ensure that the basic needs of the child are met, there is a potential gray area within which the teacher must operate. In situations where parents are not taking responsibility for the full welfare of their child, who has the right or responsibility to intervene? Already overburdened, educators continue to question the limits of the roles they can play in helping to coordinate services for children.

> The teacher's tasks have been dramatically increased during the last 20 years. The teacher has taken over several tasks previously performed by the parents and the community. In addition, new subjects, themes and fields of work have been squeezed in – often without much reflection and with roots in different pressure groups. Soon there will be no limits to the responsibilities that teachers are given .... As a result, many in society are not

> satisfied with the school. The teachers are not satisfied because they are not able to do half of what they are expected to do. (Mæhle 1989: 39)

Complicating the picture is that, even in resource-rich Norway, financial struggles have become acute. The Norwegian economy has been seriously shaken by the closing of a number of banks and central government has had difficulty balancing the budget. This general atmosphere has been further clouded by the competition for resources at the local level.

Possible lessons for the USA

As presented in the previous discussion, Norwegian practice is a combination of a tradition of child-centered policy, administrative guidance from the center and respect for the autonomy not only of parents, but of the local community. These latter two are also strongly characteristic of the USA, with its decentralized educational and social service system, as well as its formal emphasis on community links. The areas of obvious difference between the US and Norwegian system are the organization of the services and the level of resource commitment. It is at the programmatic level that we see the Norwegian case influencing the US policy debate.

The organization of pupil personnel – that is, school health personnel, social workers, child psychologists and guidance counselors and placement workers – is, to a considerable degree in the USA, a matter of administrative practicality. Such staff may be attached to a centralized bureaucracy or decentralized within the region or to individual schools. Although demand for these services should dictate where and how personnel are assigned, departmental divisions, lack of coordination and resource struggles can undermine the delivery of effective services to children. As specialists have proliferated in the US school system, the concurrent need for articulation has increased. As a guidance manual from over 30 years ago asked: 'What problems should be referred to nurses, to visiting teachers, to child study workers, to guidance counselors? Is it advisable to group together structurally two or more departments which devote their major efforts to the same type of problems, but from differing points of view and with varying techniques?' (Rosecrance and Hayden 1960: 202). Others have pointed out that the social service delivery system has been fragmented in its efforts, often debilitated by poor timing as well as a lack of coordination (Barron 1981: i). Under such conditions, early intervention strategies are particularly difficult to implement.

The Norwegian system appears to have addressed this problem by creation of a comprehensive program that encompasses not only the school years, but those preceding and following schooling. During the educational years, it is the primary school teacher and, later, the homeroom teacher who remains primarily responsible for communication with the family regarding the welfare of the whole child, and for promoting solutions when problems arise. This is the model, at least. Even as Norway must learn how to clarify and support the role of schools and teachers in ensuring children's well-being, the government has established a clear expectation that the schools have a role to play. In the complex social web that the government has created for those responsible for the child – a quadrangle of relationships, including the child, the parents, the teacher, and other municipal agents – the government appears to have declared the teacher as its final representative in ensuring the well-being of the child. Although there is a continued risk of overlap with parental authority, the Norwegian child appears to be guaranteed an ombudsman. It is the side on which Norway has decided to err – that of overlapping oversight responsibilities between parents and so-called ombudsmen at all levels – that is most provocative for the USA.

One might argue that whereas, in Norway, the school system has consistently strived to remain in partnership with the families and communities they serve, in the USA schools began to supplant roles traditionally performed by families, churches and volunteer agencies. 'They provided school lunches, dental and medical inspections, nursing care, physical education, health classes, playgrounds and recreation, psychological counseling and mental health facilities, student government and extracurricular activities, and other programs aimed at the welfare of youth' (Tyack 1979: 45). Norway has not attempted to simplify organizationally the delivery of services to the child by making the school the 'primary service provider.' It has, in contrast, forged a delivery system which is theoretically coordinated along both vertical and horizontal structural dimensions, and which has institutionalized 'child ombudsmen' at all levels.

Perhaps the most similar model in the USA was a spin-off proposal of the community education movement: to develop community-wide guidance and pupil personnel programs, which would be overseen by community councils and implemented by local educational, housing, health, social, religious and recreational agencies (Rosecrance and Hayden 1960: 216). Characteristic of American culture, the proposal captured the idea of local, democratic and self-governing bodies that would both establish policy and guarantee delivery of services. In the Norwegian context, such decision making has typically been made through national politics, although the 1980s reforms opened the possibility for some local variations.

We do find within the US social service sector some models reflective of Norwegian practice. The search for effective solutions at the local level has resulted in a trend towards what might be called 'client-centered' policies. Multi-service agencies to serve the income maintenance, housing and employment needs of clients have become more popular. Some cities have established an Office for Children. Even if bureaucracies have not always been quick to respond, delivery models at the local level have become increasingly experimental in response to the increasing needs of local children. Intervention strategies tailored to the special needs of the community can be developed, and successful programs have the possibility of being replicated and expanded upon.

Given the US political system, it is probably only at the local level that we could realistically expect to find the possibility of consensus on a delivery system model. Although localized decision making brings with it the prospect of tailoring programs to community needs and infrastructure, a great deal of energy is required to establish and build on such conditions.

> Policy makers facing decisions about location or auspices have a number of questions to consider: whether to base the initiative within a single agency or to cast it as an inter-agency effort; whether to create a new organization to provide services, or expand the mission of an existing organization (e.g., public schools, child welfare agencies, or community development agencies) to include working directly with parents to strengthen and reinforce the role of the family; what kind of funding mechanism to create; which families to serve (all, or some particular 'at-risk' group); what service or configuration of services to provide (e.g., parent and child development education, mental health services, health and developmental screening, adult basic education, job training); and how the initiative will interact with existing services for children and families in the community. (Seppanen and Heifitz 1988: iii)

The special Norwegian case cannot address directly the issue of horizontal and vertical articulation between educational and social service organizations in the USA – except to say the obvious, that such articulation is crucial for both countries. However, there may be something to learn in the area of child ombudsmen. Perhaps in the USA those most frequently in contact with the children can be made more formally responsible, as partners with parents, for the welfare of children. This would mean enlarging the informal roles that health care workers and teachers currently play, and formally recognizing the need to treat the family as a unit of which the child is a part. Needless to say, such a move would require considerable training on the part of the teachers and a much closer alignment between schools, families and other local social service agencies.

Norway may serve to exemplify the possibility of child-centered policy – a policy that has developed out of the unique cultural, social and political history of that country, but whose ideals and practical approaches have been proposed in the USA over the last 30 years through the family support and community education movements. Much of what we are witnessing in the current educational reform movement in the USA, in fact, harks back to the themes of these earlier grass-roots movements: parent involvement, treatment of the whole child, integration of the child into community, and collaboration – all in the best interest of the child. That Norway has had both the resources and commitment to attempt to implement such a child-centered policy sets a rare example. Further developments there, however imperfect, will continue to be enlightening.

Solutions in the USA will obviously require a much greater dedication of resources, organizational experimentation and coordinaiton. In addition to programmatic changes, there must be a reorientation towards serving the whole child, rather than focusing on segmented needs. Under these circumstances, countries such as Norway, which continue to evolve in their own efforts to serve 'the whole child' can serve not only as an ideal of sorts, but as a country with lessons to impart to those eager to learn.

References

BARN-OG FAMILIEDEPARTEMENTET (Ministry for Children and Families) (1993) *Tiltak for barn og ungdom: Regjeringens forslag til statsbudsjett* (Programs for Children and Youth), Enclosure to St.prp.nr.1 (Parliamentary Bill No. 1) (1992–93) (Oslo: Falch Hurtigtrykk, Academica).

BARRON, M. (1981) 'Early intervention: a strategy to provide school based social services to adolescents', unpublished qualifying paper submitted to Harvard Graduate School of Education, Cambridge, MA.

BJØRNDAL, I. (1992) *The Norwegian Educational System* (Oslo: The Royal Ministry of Foreign Affairs, in cooperation with the Royal Ministry of Education).

CASTLES, F. G. (1978) *The Social Democratic Image of Society: A Study of the Achievements and Origins of Scandinavian Social Democracy in Comparative Perspective* (London: Routledge & Kegan Paul).

EIDE, K. (1992) 'The future of European education as seen from the north', *Comparative Education*, 28(1), pp. 9–17.

GINSBERG, M. B., COOPER, S., RAGHU, R. and ZEGARRA, H. (1990) 'National and world-system explanations of educational reform', *Comparative Education Review*, 34(4), pp. 474–499.

GRANHEIM, M. K. and LUNDGREN, U. P. (1991) 'Steering by goals and evaluation in the Norwegian education system: a report from the EMIL project', *Journal of Curriculum Studies*, 23(6), pp. 481–505.

Grunnskoleloven (1991) *av 13.juni 1969 nr.24 med endringer, sist ved lov av 20.juli 1991 nr.69* (Educational Act, 13 June 1969, No 24, including changes, Last Act of 20 July 1991) (Oslo: Grøndahl og Søn Forlag A.S., Lovdata).

HOVDENAK, S. S. (1992) 'Skolen – en stat i staten?' (The school – a state within the state?), *Norsk Pedagogisk Tidsskrift*, No. 4, pp. 184–192.

INNST.S.NR.160 (Recommendation Paper No. 160) (1990–91) *Instilling fra kirke- og undervisningskomiteen om opplæring av barn, unge og voksne med særskilte behov*.

KIRKE- OG UTDANNINGSDEPARTEMENTET (Ministry of Church and Education) (1989) *Forskrift for Grunnskolen* (Oslo: H. Aschehoug & Co., W. Nygaard).

KIRKE- OG UTDANNINGSDEPARTEMENTET (Ministry of Church and Education) (1987) *Mønsterplan for Grunnskolen* (Curricular Guidelines for the School) (Oslo: H. Aschehoug & Co., W. Nygaard).

KIRKE- UTDANNINGS- OG FORSKNINGSDEPARTEMENTET (Ministry of Church, Education and Research) (1992) *Ressurser og Resultater i Norsk Skole, 1980–1990* (Resources and Results in the Norwegian Educational System, 1980–1990) (Oslo: Falch Hurtigtrykk, Academica).

KOMMUNALDEPARTEMENTET (Ministry of Municipalities) (1991) *Inntektssystemet for kommuner og fylkeskommuner. Hva er det?* (Oslo: Kommunalavdelingen).

LANGERUD, B. R. (1991) 'Sett fra utsiden' (Seen from the outside), *Bedre skole,* Norsk Lærerlag, No. 4, pp. 43–47.

LAUGLO, J. (1992) *The Populist Trend in Norwegian Education Tradition* (revised version of paper presented 11 November 1992 at the Institute of Social Research, Oslo, in honor of Natalie Rogoff Ramsøy).

LAUGLO, J. (1993) personal communication to the authors, Oslo.

MÆHLE, A. B. (1989) 'Endring av lærarrollen – ei komplisert og viktig sak (Changing the role of the teacher – a complicated and important task)', *Bedre skole,* Norsk Lærerlag, No. 4, pp. 37–41.

ORGANIZATION FOR ECONOMIC COOPERATION AND DEVELOPMENT (OECD) (1990) *Reviews of National Policies for Education: Norway* (Paris: OECD).

ROKKAN, S. (1981) 'The growth and structuring of mass politics,' in E. Allardt *et al.* (eds), *Nordic Democracy* (Copenhagen: Munksgaards Publishers), pp. 53–79.

ROSECRANCE, F. C. and HAYDEN, V. D. (1960) *School Guidance and Personnel Services* (Boston: Allyn and Bacon).

RUST, V. D. (1989) *The Democratic Tradition and the Evolution of Schooling in Norway* (Westport, CT and London: Greenwood Press).

RUST, V. D. and BLAKEMORE, K. (1990) 'Educational reform in Norway and in England and Wales: a corporatist interpretation', *Comparative Education Review*, 34(4), pp. 500–522.

SEAY, M. F. *et al.* (1974) *Community Education: A Developing Concept* (Midland, MI: Pendall).

SEPPANEN, P. S. and HEIFITZ, J. (1988) *Community Education as a Home for Family Support and Education Programs* (Cambridge, MA: Harvard Family Research Project).

SJØBERG, S. (1991) 'Norsk skole – verst eller best i verden?' (Norwegian education: worst or best in the world?), *Bedre skole,* Norske Lærerlag, No. 4, pp. 67–77.

ST.MELD.NR 35 (Parliamentary Report No. 35) (1990–91) *Om opplæring av barn, unge og voksne med særskilte behov*.

ST.MELD.NR 54 (Parliamentary Report No. 54) (1989–90) *Om opplæring av barn, unge og voksne med sæskilte behov*.

TOLBERT, E. L. (1978) *An Introduction to Guidance* (Boston: Little, Brown and Company).

TYACK, D. B. (1979) 'The high school as a social service agency: historical perspectives on current policy issues'. *Educational Evaluation and Policy Analysis*, 1(5), pp. 45–57.

UTDANNINGS- OG FORSKNINGSDEPARTEMENTET (Ministry of Education and Research) (1990) *Education in Norway* (Oslo: A/S Norasonde).

POLITICS OF EDUCATION ASSOCIATION YEARBOOK, 1993, 33–47

Discovering shared values: ecological models to support interagency collaboration

Hanne B. Mawhinney

Throughout North America there is a groundswell of interest in holistic approaches to overcoming structural barriers to the integration of services for children. It is generally agreed that these barriers have been created by the interactions of the myriad of agencies that comprise the interdependent complex of federal, state/provincial, and local levels of government. The resulting fragmentation across services is seen as contributing to the precarious conditions of the growing number of children living in poverty, who come from single-parent families and from minority or limited-English-proficient backgrounds (Gardner 1989; Kirst *et al.* 1990). It is increasingly recognized that many of the problems of the poor, 'and of high-poverty neighborhoods as a whole, are interrelated and difficult to separate' (Edelman and Radin 1991: 10). A synthesis of lessons from past efforts suggests that although such problems cannot be solved without money, money alone will not solve the problems. There is growing agreement that 'measures to make services more comprehensive, and better coordinated' are fundamental components of the structural agenda for the new community (Edelman and Radin 1991: 9). The calls for interagency collaboration and coordination that flow from this agenda stem from the realization that each agency deals with the 'same person, the same client' (Hodgkinson 1989: 25).

Proponents of coordinated services for children and families are developing 'a growing base of practical savvy about what works and what does not' by examining the current efforts at the collaboration (Crowson and Boyd 1993a: 141). Observers warn that the diversity of approaches that have emerged suggests that no single model of collaboration will ever fit all settings (Gardner 1992). Nevertheless, research is beginning to accumulate evidence that confirms the importance of holistic approaches to the provision of services (Jacobs and Weiss 1988).

Several strands of research have outlined the salient dimensions of a holistic approach. Researchers and policy makers acknowledge, however, that much more must be learned about the complexities and 'deeper organizational issues implicated in collaborative ventures' (Crowson and Boyd 1993a: 141). Although policy makers, practitioners, and researchers commonly speak of the need for holistic orientations to designing coordinated service delivery systems for children and youth, they often speak from intellectual perspectives which adopt different rationales. The resulting conceptual confusion is of more than theoretical concern; it has practical implications for collaborative initiatives. Confusion can arise in defining the difference between cooperation, coordination, collaboration or integration of services. The literature calling for holistic approaches to service delivery is not clear on the dimensions of these linkages. In practice, conflicts among collaborative stakeholders may occur because of differing views about what these linkages mean (Hord 1986).

This chapter addresses the need to clarify the dimensions of holistic approaches by examining collaborative initiatives currently under way in the Canadian province of

Ontario. The chapter begins by outlining the social and demographic trends and discusses the ecological perspectives which have added force to the movement toward greater collaboration. It then takes up the challenge of exploring what Crowson and Boyd (1993a) describe as the 'murky waters that coordinated ventures must navigate' (p. 141) by examining the collaborative initiatives currently being developed in Ontario. Finally, it will be argued that policy making to support this vision must acknowledge the power of public ideas and must incorporate processes that allow members of a community to discover shared values. The conceptual requirements for policy making to build communities is discussed in the concluding section of the chapter.

Forces giving impetus to school-linked service collaborations

The impetus for integration of services for children in Canada arises from similar problems to those that established the context of proposals for collaboration in the US. Estimates of the number of children and young people 'at risk,' and with special needs in Canada comprise from 30% to 40% of urban school populations and from 15% to 20% of rural school students. A recent study in one Canadian province reported that one in every six children in Ontario is in a family receiving social assistance. About three-quarters are children of single parents, the vast majority of whom are women. Child poverty in Ontario is also on the rise, standing at 15.3% in 1990 (Ontario Ministry of Community and Social Services 1992). A recent report by the Saskatchewan Ministry of Education on integrated school-based services for children and families summarized the alarming situation where: 'Children and young people are coming to school hungry, emotionally and physically abused and neglected, destructive and violent in their behavior, with physical and learning disabilities, with language and cultural needs, with health or medical needs and suffering from stress of family breakdown' (Saskatchewan Ministry of Education 1992: 1).

According to Schorr (1988) 'rotten outcomes' cannot be attributed to a single risk factor. Rather, they result from the accumulation and interaction of biological and environmental factors. Theories of child development that propose 'ecological models' of intervention recognize that development is a 'complex negotiation between external, contextual forces and innate capacities and temperament' (Jacobs and Weiss 1988: 497). There is growing agreement that in order to be successful interventions must recognize that the factors that put a child at risk tend to be interactive and cumulative. Risk factors often culminate in particularly dire conditions for youths who are in transition from adolescence to adulthood. In Ontario, for example, one-third of all adolescents drop out of high school and, according to a recent report, 'runaways swell the numbers of the homeless in our urban centers, in disconcertingly large and increasing numbers' (*Children First* 1990: 74).

Canadian and American critics point out that schools and other child and youth service agencies cannot alone overcome the debilitating effects of such conditions. On their own schools cannot effectively address the entangled problems of youth such as drug abuse, homelessness, and violence. Indeed, there is growing agreement that the poor education, health, and social outcomes for young people result, in part, from the inability of the current service systems to respond in a coordinated and comprehensive fashion to the multiple and interconnected needs of both children and youth. Critics of the American system such as Gardner (1989) conclude that the 'program mentality,' which has pervaded policy making for children's services, has resulted in fragmented responses that ultimately fail. A recent assessment of the trends in social problems in Ontario argues that a new approach is required because social services are 'too fragmented, overspecialized and over-burdened, and they have limited outreach capacity and are working in isolation from one another' (*Children First* 1990: 49).

Mirroring efforts to ameliorate the community problems through holistic approaches that integrate social services currently under way in the USA, several Canadian provinces have developed policies and programs for interagency collaborations. Provincial authorities in Ontario, for example, have recognized the need to coordinate services in order to meet the needs of children and youth, and have supported a number of initiatives in this direction. In 1990, a report of the Advisory Committee on Children's Services, entitled *Children First*, recommended that a new provincial authority be created to integrate the responsibilities and staff of five Ministries providing services to children: the Ministries of Community and Social Services, Education, Correctional Services, Health and Tourism, and Recreation. The report argued that Ontario needs a Ministry of the Child.

Ecological perspectives on child development and family services

Such collaborative proposals and efforts have been given impetus by the development of several ecological perspectives that have implications for the delivery of services for 'at risk' families and children. Support for collaborative initiatives has been influenced by at least three overlapping ecological orientations: in understanding child development; in developing family service interventions; and in understanding the relationship between families, schools and communities.

Child development

An ecological orientation to understanding child behavior and development assumes that relationships between individuals are constantly changing as they adapt to each other and to the broader environment (Dym 1988). Ecological theories, such as those proposed by Bateson (1979) and others, emphasize patterns of relationships that span the biological, psychological, and social spheres. They are based on assumptions of co-evolution, or what Bateson calls recursive relationships in which patterns of human behavior evolve in relation to the evolution of other patterns of relationships. From this holistic perspective, simple determinations of cause and effect in 'at risk' children are seen as 'arbitrary and misleading' because of the nature of the co-evolving symptomatic behaviors and family patterns (Dym 1988: 485).

Family service interventions

Early approaches to family service interventions were based on linear models of cause and effect. In practice they stressed the provision of 'low keyed services to individual family members, rather than services to families or communities as corporate, group entities' (Slaughter 1988: 462). Beginning in the 1960s, the focus shifted to providing special family-oriented intervention programs. Many were based on concepts of circular causality and closed-system feedback. Groups were treated as closed systems rather than as open systems 'where variety and change are as normal as stability' (Dym 1988: 486).

During the past decades research has identified a number of flaws in these intervention programs. It has been found that 'program goals may be frustrated or defeated because program designers know little of the cultural-ecological context of the families to be served' (Slaughter 1988: 465). Recent studies of African-American family life, have, for example, discredited the assumption that family structure is a reliable indicator of family functioning (Harrison *et al.* 1984). Although single-parent families may confront the risks associated with poverty, that does not mean that they are inevitably disorganized or weak. In the case of African-Americans there is growing evidence that even under conditions of exceptional stress the extended family may provide critical assistance and support. Family members often develop uniquely effective coping strategies which have enabled the group to survive culturally and historically (Slaughter 1988: 468).

A holistic approach to intervention that takes into account cultural background is supported by the ecological theory of human development proposed by Bronfenbrenner (1979) which stresses the influence of the larger social setting on the behavior of the developing child. In this ecological perspective the child and the context accommodate one another, and both are influenced by the broader setting. Critics have acknowledged Bronfenbrenner's influence on broadening the view of the developing child, but have also turned to ecological orientations to family systems therapy such as Minuchin's (1974) structural approach. Minuchin's ecological perspective emphasizes the influence on the family of 'cultural imagery, norms, institutions, and community networks' (Dym 1988: 481).

Variations of structural family therapy have been widely applied in family service programs, and have provided the foundation for the more recent developments of ecological theories of family interventions. Dym, for instance, extends earlier ecological perspectives by proposing a more dynamic, ecologically based theory of intervention which emphasizes the interconnectedness of the 'biological, psychological, family and cultural system levels' (1988: 490). Changes in the cycles of activity in any one of the systems influence cycles in other systems. The patterns in a child's school relations co-evolve with cycles occurring within the family and the community, and 'changes in any of these cycles reverberate throughout the ecosystem' (p. 492).

Relationship between families, schools and communities

Recent research on minority education by Ogbu (1992) also confirms the critical influence of the child's cultural community on success in school. In outlining a cultural-ecological framework of minority education Ogbu raises the paradox that although 'involuntary minorities', such as African-Americans, have high educational aspirations, they often demonstrate low school performance. The influence of community forces has historically been ignored as an explanation of the paradox. Ogbu's (1992) cultural-ecological framework proposes that a minority's cultural model defines the beliefs, assumptions, competencies or skills minority children have to learn in order to be viewed as competent by their community. According to Ogbu, the salient issue is whether what is defined as competent behavior by the cultural community matches what schools reward as competence. To be successful school-linked interventions must be based on knowledge of the minority student's cultural background.

Educational researchers such as Comer (1980) also emphasize that a child's development depends upon both home and school factors. Successful development of the child requires that there be no separation of 'academic from social, moral, and emotional development' (Crowson and Boyd 1993b: 147). It requires that the school, the family, and the community share a common focus on education and caring, and that services be designed so as to communicate mutually reinforcing messages to children (Ianni 1989). These arguments reflect a cornerstone of ecological theories: the recognition of the influence of contextual forces on the intervention programs.

Similar support for interventions that recognize the ecological relationship between schools, families and communities is found in the research on the 'new ecology of schooling' (Crowson and Boyd 1993a: 144). In the tradition of the early research on the interdependence of urban life, recent research has recognized the 'importance of ecological relationships between schools and neighborhood housing, economic development, transportation, library services, health services, and recreation programs' (p. 145). Although in the past there was little concerted effort to link these services, the following section suggests that the recognition of their ecological relationship has influenced current efforts to develop interagency collaborations.

Theories support collaboration

Successful interventions depend upon the capacity for a flexible response by professionals who share understanding of the ecological context of the child. Current research on collaborative efforts has confirmed that there is no single model for restructuring services that best enhances the capacity for flexible responses. Much must be learned about the design and implementation of successful collaborative initiatives.

Research does, however, provide some guidance to understanding the range of possible collaborative efforts. Hord (1986), for example, proposes that interagency interactions can be placed along a continuum of cooperation that ranges from coordination to collaboration. The coordination and collaboration models at polar ends of this continuum are both 'valued models, but each serves a unique purpose and yields a different return' (p. 5). There is some consensus among researchers that successful interventions require, at the minimum, the coordination of professionals who are providing services for children. Critics argue, however, that although coordination of services may enable more effective service delivery, a more expansive approach requires collaboration 'whereby organizations join to create improvements in children's services that are no single agency's responsibility' (Kirst 1991: 617). The term collaboration has been used to describe integrations that result from the 'blending of provider disciplines and usually involves several organizations working together in a unified structure' (Morrill 1992: 40).

The context of collaborative initiatives in Ontario

Under the Canadian constitution, the provincial governments carry major responsibility for the provision of health, education and social services to children, youth, and their families. Provincial government control resulted in some distinct regional differences in service systems and child welfare issues. Moreover, provincial and federal authorities are currently limited in attempting to identify common problems by the lack of a national system for collecting and analyzing child welfare information from all jurisdictions (Townsend *et al.* 1986). It is evident, however, that different jurisdictions share similar fundamental problems and have developed similar policies in response to those problems. The federal government has both directly and indirectly influenced the development of an integrated orientation to children's services in many Canadian provinces. It contributes very limited resources for elementary and secondary education, most directed at the development of bilingualism in schools. It does, however, sponsor programs in vocational and technical training, and it supports a number of other specific programs such as a recent initiative to encourage secondary school students to stay in school. The federal government has also indirectly contributed to the general shift in thinking about children and youth in Canada. There has been a 'move to treat children as rights-bearing persons with individual developmental needs rather than the objects of paternalism' (*Children First* 1990: 37). Federal-level legislation, particularly the *Canadian Charter of Rights and Freedoms* (1982) has focused attention on children's rights generally.

Another more indirect impetus for provinces to examine the specific needs of children and young people has come from the federal government's support of the initiatives at the United Nations to establish the *Convention on the Rights of the Child*. In November 1989 Canada played a lead role in the United Nations General Assembly in ratifying the *Convention on the Rights of the Child*. The Convention reaffirms the fact that children, because of their vulnerability, need special care and protection. Although it places special emphasis on the primary caring and protective responsibility of the family, it also reaffirms the need for legal and other protection for the child. The Convention charges countries to place special emphasis on the provision of primary and preventative health care, of accessible education, and of social services to enhance the social security of the child.

The Canadian federal government supported the Convention during the United Nations summit on the plight of the child in September 1990. At that summit, the Canadian Prime Minister announced that the federal government would develop a broad plan for all Canadian children. Subsequently the position of Minister Responsible for Children's Issues was created and a Children's Bureau was established within the federal government to coordinate federal policies on children. In December 1991, the Canadian parliament ratified the UN *Convention on the Rights of the Child*, and set out a policy directive requiring provincial governments to develop plans for the implementation of the Convention. The basic principles of the Convention have provided a guiding framework for changes in children's services that are being developed in provinces such as Ontario.

Demographic, social and cultural changes have also provided the impetus for provincial governments to change service delivery systems. The Ontario Child Health Study (1990) identified family circumstances related to poverty that are associated with outcomes putting children at risk of: developing psychiatric disorders; needing professional help with emotional or behavioral problems; and performing poorly in school. In the *Ontario Child Health Study* circumstances associated with the risk outcomes for children include coming from single parent families, being on social assistance, and living in subsidized housing. These risk factors are strongly associated with each other. For example, the rate of social assistance in one-parent families is 41% compared with the 2% of two-parent families who live on social assistance in the province. Similarly 50% of children living in subsidized housing in Ontario come from families on social assistance. Both risk factors reflect a condition of poverty. The study found that child and youth outcomes are also strongly related to each other. For example, 24% of children with psychiatric disorders also performed poorly in school (*Ontario Child Health Study: Children at Risk* 1990).

This finding suggests that services must be designed to take into account the needs of children and youth with problems that require resources from more than one ministry. Although it is clear that the educational system is implicated in these outcomes, there is also general agreement that the vulnerable state of families places additional demands on schools, demands that educators are not appropriately trained to address. Teachers are not trained to provide counselling, health and other social services for needy chilidren, and, in the past, they have not been required to do so. In fact, during the past three decades these types of social services came to be provided by an increasingly complex and loosely linked maze of agencies in Ontario. During the 1950s and 1960s Ontario's economic growth and expanding tax base led to the expansion of the range of social services for children and families. Services for children and youth grew more complex and specialized and led to the proliferation of agencies that are loosely linked to the Ministries of: Education and Training, Health, Community and Social Services, Correctional Services, Tourism and Recreation, and the Office of the Attorney General.

Calls for new strategies for delivering children's services

During the past five years numerous reports on children's services have suggested that the new ways of meeting the needs of children and youth in Ontario must be based on a holistic perspective that integrates a number of services provided by these ministries. The Ontario Advisory Committee on Children's Services argued, for example, that new social and economic realities mean that different kinds of supports are needed for children, youth and families. The report of the committee, *Children First* (1990) charges that 'the wide acceptance of the myth of the traditional family has inhibited the development of a broader network of supports to assist families that are experiencing difficulties as they strive to meet the needs of their children' (p. 11).

The authors of the *Ontario Child Health Study* (1990) argue that the ministries must 'overcome their jurisdictional and funding boundaries and cooperate in prevention and intervention' (p. iv). Key recommendations of the *Children First* report are that 'the provincial government should promote models of service integration and collaboration that simplify access to service and rationalize the roles of our limited resource of trained specialized service providers', and that schools should be considered as a 'major focal point' for coordinating a service response to children's need (p. 56).

From the top down

The recommendations for increased collaboration by the recent reports on services for children and youth in the province cited in the preceding discussion have had an impact on the policies of the current government of Ontario. The idea of integration is congruent with the emphasis on community activism and the social democratic philosophy of the New Democratic Party (NDP) which forms the current government of Ontario. The severe economic constraints brought about by the current recession have also provided an impetus for the government to provide policy direction to encourage collaboration among children's services. A recent government fact sheet on integrated services for children and youth states 'with fewer public resources, governments must ensure that public moneys assist clients effectively and that services work together in a concerted fashion' (Ontario Ministry of Education and Training 1992: 5).

The government has responded to these pressures by supporting a number of initiatives that attempt to meet the needs of young people through various forms of collaborative service delivery. Most of the initiatives are recent undertakings, and many are either just being developed or they are in the early stages of implementation. These initiatives vary in the degree to which they are based on collaborations among provincial ministries whose mandate includes services for children and youth. The initiatives also vary in the degree of integration they promote among local-level agencies. Some initiatives for integration were in place when the current NDP government took office. For example, the Ministry of Education and Training has, for the past five years, provided funding to construct child-care facilities for non-profit child-care centers as part of every new or replacement elementary school offering primary and junior programs that is built with provincial funds. Other provincially funded programs have involved long-term collaborations among ministries. For example, the Home Care Program of the Ministry of Health is responsible for assessing student needs, and for providing specialized services at the request of a school board.

More directly the recommendations contained in the *Children First* (1990) report, although not formally adopted as policy, have, nevertheless, provided guidance for the initiatives currently being developed and implemented by the government of Ontario. One of the key recommendations of the *Children First* report was that:

> Government must become the leading partner in creating a public agenda for children and in establishing an integrated framework that ensures that the entitlements of children are met through a holistic system of supports and services. (1990: 107)

In the past children's services in Ontario have been provided by several provincial ministries, hundreds of local authorities and over a thousand agencies, but with no governing framework to foster integration. The resulting multiple lines of accountability among local service providers are a major impediment to service integration at the local level in the province. Voluntary collaborations have occurred but have 'historically run into obstacles of protected turfs, conflicting values and confused accountabilities' (*Children First* 1990: 115). To overcome the constraints to collaboration created by these conditions, the *Children First* report proposed that a single children's authority be created in the provincial government to integrate 'responsibility for all major legislation, strategic planning, policy and program development, and funding of services for children' (p. 115). The report also recommended that local-level children's authorities be created to complement the provincial children's authority.

The government of Ontario has, so far, not created a provincial children's authority such as that proposed in the *Children First* report. It has, however, supported the spirit of the report by establishing in 1990 the Interministerial Committee on Services for Children and Youth. The purpose of the Committee, comprising assistant deputy ministers and representatives from nine key ministries and several other special policy groups, is to guide the integration of policies, programs and services to facilitate the healthy development of children, youth and families. One of the key goals of the Interministerial Committee is that members of the community should assist collaboratively in the healthy development and continuing well-being of children and youth.

Initiatives to support interagency collaboration in Ontario

In order to meet this goal the Children and Youth Committee has initiated a number of major activities which focus on the reduction of interministerial barriers to service integration (Ontario Ministry of Education and Training 1991). The Committee insures the interministerial coordination of several major community-based research demonstration projects that have been initiated during the past five years; insures the interministerial coordination of new reform initiatives; and promotes and supports the many local, inter-sectoral integration initiatives that are being developed throughout the province.

Better Beginnings, Better Futures

This project focuses on children (from birth to eight years) at risk of emotional, behavioral, social, physical, and cognitive problems who live in economically disadvantaged neighborhoods in several communities in the province. The interventions include pre-natal/infant development programs which integrate with a preschool, which in turn integrates with a primary school. They also include other family and community-identified programs such as recreation, breakfast/lunch, single mother support and literacy programs.

Created in 1989 through the initiative of a collaboration among the Ministries of Community and Social Services, Education and Training, and Health, the project predates the creation of the Interministerial Committee on Services for Children and Youth (Ontario Ministry of Education and Training 1991). This 25-year longitudinal prevention policy research project is currently funded by the Ministries of Community and Social Services, Health, and Education and Training, as well as by the federal government's Department of Indian and Northern Affairs, and the Department of Multiculturalism. The programs involve the participation of families, agencies, and school boards in 11 communities in the province. It is based on an integrated services model which links home, school and community programs together in the implementation of high-quality prevention programs. A high degree of parent involvement and community development characterize the programs which also involve the blending and uniting of programs, services, staffing, facilities and funding. Leadership in coordinating and integrating services varies in the communities and includes community agencies, community development groups, health units, and local schools and school boards. Implementation of the Better Beginnings, Better Futures project began in September 1992 and will continue until 1995, with follow-up studies of children, families and communities to be undertaken for 20 years to determine the effectiveness of the interventions.

Community systems

Lacking direct authority and resources to support local-level collaborations, the Interministerial Committee has linked with the Laidlaw Foundation, a private family foundation supporting initiatives in research, in policy, and in practices related to the child and family. The Committee has supported community-level integration efforts through its involvement in a strategy group for Community Systems formed through the initiative of the Foundation which has representatives of several key ministries. The aim of the Community Systems approach is to find new means of supporting families by working with communities to develop strategic ways of using local-level resources.

The Laidlaw Foundation provides one-time financial support for community-level collaborations among public and private agencies and groups to develop a detailed proposal for restructuring existing resources to achieve outcomes that promote healthy families and children. The caveat to the Foundation's support is that the programs proposed do not require new funding. The rationale is that most pilot programs that depend on add-on funding are rarely well integrated with other programs. Even programs such as Better Beginnings, Better Futures, which involve the collaboration of a number of agencies, rely on add-on funding provided by those agencies and do not articulate well with other programs. The community systems approach takes a different orientation, one that encourages communities to find ways to restructure existing resources to promote healthy young people. Community systems is an emerging concept; and the Laidlaw Foundation encourages local communities to document the processes they have gone through in developing such systems and what they learn from those processes. The intent is to create an inventory of the various community systems models that emerge. Currently there are four local networks that are developing community systems through the support of the Foundation. A 'senior' network in Toronto, known informally as the 'Best Practices Group' (with executive directors of three family service agencies, the United Way, and the Ministry of Community and Social Services as members), acts as a mentor for other local community systems initiatives that are being developed. These initiatives vary in the membership of the initiators, their focus, and the degree of collaboration already present in the community.

The Laidlaw Foundation provides seed money to initiate and develop detailed proposals for, and to consolidate local commitment to, reshaping the use of existing community resources to enhance collaboration. As such its role is that of an arms-length provocateur for community development. Foundation representatives describe this as a strategic approach to extending private support for practices that improve the conditions for families, children and youth in the province. In funding the development of locally generated community systems the Foundation is attempting to move beyond the kind of program or project funding that has resulted in piecemeal support for collaboration in the province. The Foundation acts as a linking agent, sponsoring meetings that connect community systems projects with each other and with representatives of the Ministries of Education and Training, Health, and Community and Social Services. Its goal is to enhance horizontal cooperation among local-level agencies and vertical communication between the local- and provincial-level actors concerned with services for children and youth.

Scattering seeds but not changing systems

To some extent the provincial government appears to take a 'Johnny Appleseed approach' of seeding the province with pilot projects focused on specific programs involving collaboration. At the same time provincial authorities are attempting to develop more comprehensive approaches through participation in the community systems initiative. This approach, although in its formative stages, appears to be different from the categorical-funding and special-project initiatives that characterize most of the current and past efforts to encourage collaborations. Such system change is rare, and most critics would agree that provincial mandates, requirements and sanctions are required to bring about true system change. The government of Ontario has in the past undertaken significant system change, and may in the future be prepared to do so again. At present, however, the initiatives to promote collaboration can hardly be viewed as significant attempts to change the system of service delivery for children and youth in the province.

Although the top-down initiatives of the provincial government in Ontario do not, as yet, appear to have had any significant impact on local communities and agencies serving youth in the province, interest in the ideas of cooperation and collaboration is widespread. Even though the structural and institutional constraints to cooperation in many communities appear overwhelming, some locally generated and provincially provoked collaborations have been successful.

At the ministry level an inter-ministerial committee drawing representatives from Community and Social Services, Health, and Education has been formed to investigate and support collaborations among these services. Although other initiatives are being developed that focus more directly on youth, none have been implemented at the scope of the Better Beginnings program. At the same time community development staff, health workers and teachers recognize that youth in many economically disadvantaged neighborhoods are often significantly 'at risk'. These front-line workers commonly develop a number of interventions to serve the needs of youth, sometimes in collaboration with other service providers in the community. More often linkages between agencies serving youth can best be characterized as fragmented, and collaborations that do develop are often short lived.

Some critical considerations on collaboration

Much of the current research and writing on interagency relations makes the assumption that collaboration will result in more efficient and effective services for the public. Yet, if past efforts at cooperation are taken into account, it is evident that sustained collaboration among organizations will raise complex and sometimes subtle issues of communication, control and power. Clearly a degree of skepticism must be maintained when proponents of the integration of services provide blueprints for overcoming barriers to effective collaborations. Townsend (1980: 499–501) argues that a skeptic would question the possibility and even the necessity of coordinating education, health and welfare.

Moreover, if the purpose of collaboration is to better serve the needs of 'at risk' children and youth, then a major underlying cause of risk, that is, poverty, cannot be ignored. Coordination or even collaboration cannot overcome poverty, nor will they resolve all the problems of fragile families. Skeptics, in Townsend's (1980) view, may criticize proposals for collaboration as 'overly abstract, rational, and panacea-minded', and may cite the failure of collaborative efforts during the past decades to produce improvements in outcomes such as student success in school (p. 499). More fundamentally, skeptics may object to the 'technocratic and centralist' bias implicit in many of these proposals (p. 499). This bias could result in centralized and inflexible services which are not responsive to the choices of young people and their families.

Valid though some of these arguments may be, it is also clear that 'community-wide strategies are necessary if most students are to escape pervasive environmental risks' in both Canada and the USA (Bruner 1991: 9). Ecological theories of child development that have gained increasing currency suggest that such strategies must recognize the potency of environmental influences such as 'extended family, non-family neighbors or community members, formal and informal community services, the values, beliefs, and adaptive patterns of ethnic and cultural groups' (Jacobs and Weiss 1988: 497). Echoing the ecological perspectives on family programs, proponents of such collaborations argue that 'there should be more emphasis on prevention and early intervention and a focus that extends to the needs of the entire family unit not just the child' (Morrill 1992: 32). The services should be more comprehensive and flexible, and more decentralized, placing decision-making authority within the community and at the school and neighborhood level (Farrow and Joe 1992: 58). Experiments in collaboration in both the USA and Canada confirm that effective collaboration must be based on 'a community wide planning process that is locally generated and includes broad citizen involvement' (Kirst 1991: 617). A community must develop an approach and 'tailor program design to capitalize on its particular strengths and opportunities and to respond to its citizens' unique combination of needs and expectations' (Levy and Shepardson 1992: 46).

Discovering shared values and building community

Successful efforts at systemic reform to overcome the failures created by fragmented services must adopt a holistic vision that emphasizes building nurturing communities (Coleman 1987; Comer 1987; Cunningham 1990; Heath and McLaughlin 1987; Ianni 1989; Schorr 1988, 1989). Crowson and Boyd (1993a) note that current initiatives for coordinated services 'emerge from an intersection of movements in a new, many-sided effort to strengthen community connections for urban schols' (p. 141).

The structural and institutional constraints documented in recent studies of collaborative efforts suggest that such reconstitution is far from being realized (see Crowson and Boyd 1993a, 1993b). There are 'deeper structural failings to confront' when attempting to provide more effective services (Edelman and Radin 1991: 9). These failings, in turn, stem from a normative problem: the loss of the idea that 'a significant social policy aim is embodied in the notion of community, of a social infrastructure that embodies stability and security and shared values' (p. 8). Critics argue that structural changes must be made that reflect the understanding that 'one role of government is to help rediscover and rebuild the sense of community that we have lost in too many places' (p. 9).

The conceptual problem is that the emphasis on building community inherent in such strategies for interagency collaboration contradicts the view of society as a market-place which underlies the predominant rational policy-making model. Under the contemporary 'rationality' concept society is 'viewed as a collection of autonomous, rational decision makers who have no community life' (Stone 1989: 6). In the prevailing philosophy of policy making the 'public good', or the 'public interest', is seen as the sum of individual preferences. The 'role of ideas about what is good for society and the importance of debating the relative merits of such ideas' is disregarded in the rational model of policy (Reich 1990: 3). Concepts of policy development and implementation drawn from market and rational managerial theories cannot account for the ideas that generate community building such as the idea of a reconstituted local government for 'well-being' proposed by Cunningham (1990).

What is needed is a model of political community which recognizes that 'both policy and thinking about policy are produced in political communities' (Stone 1989: 7). Conceptualizations of policy making, such as the model of 'polis' proposed by Stone, provide the basis for viewing public policy as focused on the efforts of 'communities trying to achieve something as communities' (p. 14). This model recognizes the unique problems that arise when self-interest and public interest are combined, such as occurs when the interests of various agencies in self-preservation and expansion entail social costs in duplication of services and in failure to meet the needs of their 'at risk' clientele. A model of polis suggests that the gap between self-interest and public interest can be bridged by 'some potent forces: influence, cooperation, and loyalty' (Stone 1989: 17). Influence promotes collective behavior through bandwagon effects, and even through coercion. Cooperation is a fundamental force in this model of polis which recognizes that conflicts usually unite some people, just as they divide others. Unlike two-person market models, the model of polis recognizes the possibilities for 'strategic coalitions and shifting alliances' (Stone 1989: 17) as well as joint effort, leadership and coordination. Such a model provides the conceptual basis for examining the potential for collaboration through mechanisms such as 'hooks' linking student participation in one program with participation in another, or 'glue' money which allows children to be assigned a 'case manager' able to link with other services, or joint ventures where 'several agencies create partnerships to raise funds for jointly operated programs (Gardner 1989: 25).

Those who 'seek to re-create and support nurturing communities' must use policy-making models that generate processes sensitive to the ecology of the community (Levy and Shepardson 1992: 54). Such policy models acknowledge the ways in which normative visions can shape how government services are structured and what people want and expect from government and each other (Reich 1990). In these models the power of public ideas, such as the concept of 'well-being' proposed as a guide to policy making for human services, are given legitimacy. Public policies that reflect the idea of well-being enable individuals in the community to 'feel secure, confident, competent, even comfortable with themselves, their friends, their co-workers and, most important, their families' (Cunningham 1990: 137).

Effective change to meet the challenges of the interdependent and value-laden nature of the adversities confronting children and families today requires policy-making models guided by ideas such as community well-being, not by assumptions of market-driven self-interest. Models of policy that recognize the dominant role of public ideas also acknowledge the importance of 'democratic deliberation for refining and altering such visions over time and for mobilizing public action around them' (Reich 1990: 3). Public debate over the broad goals that flow from ideas such as 'well-being' is essential to building a sense of community, and to defining the institutional structures and processes that will enhance community values (Cunningham 1990). Planning for institutional processes, such as school-linked services, is critical to successful implementation (Gardner 1992). Planning must, however, be guided by ideas that have been defined and affirmed through public deliberation and debate. The kind of large-scale social and structural changes many critics believe are needed to 'break the cycle of disadvantage' that captures many children can only emerge from debate and discussion about public problems.

The importance of debate on public problems was recognized by Dewey (1927) who called for improved methods for such discussion. Reich argues that the 'core responsibility of those who deal in public policy' (1990: 3) is not simply to determine what the public wants. It is also 'to provide the public with alternative visions of what is desirable and possible, to stimulate deliberation about them, provoke examination of premises and values, and thus to broaden the range of potential responses and deepen society's understanding of itself' (p. 4). Engaging the public in rethinking the delivery of services for young people represents a key challenge for those promoting structural changes. Such engagement is fundamental to discovering shared values and to building community.

References

BATESON, G. (1979) *Mind and Nature* (New York: Dutton).

BEHRMAN, R. E. (1992) 'School linked services', in R. E. Behrman (ed.) *Future of Children* (Los Altos, CA: Packard Foundation), pp. 6–18.

BRONFENBRENNER, U. (1979) *The Ecology of Human Development* (Cambridge: Harvard University Press).

BRUNER, C. (1991) *Thinking Collaboratively: Ten Questions and Answers to Help Policy Makers Improve Children's Services* (Washington: Education and Human Services Consortium).

CANADIAN CHARTER OF RIGHTS AND FREEDOMS, Part I of the *Constitution Act, 1982*, being Schedule B of the *Canada Act 1982* (U.K.), c. 11.

CHILDREN FIRST: REPORT OF THE ADVISORY COMMITTEE ON CHILDREN'S SERVICES (1990, November) (Toronto: Queen's Printer).

COLEMAN, J. S. (1987) 'Families and schools', *Educational Researcher*, 16 (August–September), pp. 32–38.

COMER, J. P. (1980) *School Power: Implications of an Intervention Project* (New York: Free Press).

COMER, J. P. (1987) 'New Haven's school–community connection', *Educational Leadership* (March), pp. 13–16.

CROWSON, R. L. and BOYD, W. L. (1993a) 'Coordinated services for children: designing Arks for storms and seas unknown', *American Journal of Education*, 101(2), pp. 140–179.

CROWSON, R. L. and BOYD, W. L. (1993b, April) 'Structures and strategies: toward an understanding of alternative models for coordinated children's services', paper presented at the Annual Meeting of the American Educational Research Association (Atlanta, Georgia).

CUNNINGHAM, L. L. (1990) 'Reconstituting local government for well-being and education', in B. Mitchell and L. L. Cunningham (eds) *Educational Leadership and Changing Contexts of Families, Communities, and Schools* (Chicago: University of Chicago Press), pp. 135–154.

DEWEY, J. (1927) *The Public and Its Problems* (Denver: Alan Swallow).

DYM, B. (1988) 'Ecological perspectives on change in families', in H. B. Weiss and F. H. Jacobs (eds) *Evaluating Family Programs* (New York: Aldine De Gruyter), pp. 477–495.

EDELMAN, P. B. and RADIN, B. A. (eds) (1991) *Serving Children and Families Effectively: How the Past Can Help Chart the Future* (Washington: Education and Human Services Consortium).

FACT SHEET: INTEGRATED SERVICES FOR CHILDREN AND YOUTH (1992, November 24) (Toronto: Integrated Services for Youth Secretariat, Ministry of Education and Training).

FARROW, F. and JOE, T. (1992) 'Financing school-linked, integrated services', *California Tomorrow: Our Changing State*, 4, pp. 56–67.

GARDNER, S. (1989) 'Failure by fragmentation', *California Tomorrow: Our Changing State*, 4, pp. 18–25.

GARDNER, S. (1991) 'A commentary', in P. B. Edelman and B. A. Radin (eds) *Serving Children and Families Effectively: How the Past Can Help Chart the Future* (Washington: Education and Human Services Consortium), pp. 16–20.

GARDNER, S. (1992) 'Key issues in developing school-linked, integrated services', in R. E. Behrman (ed.) *Future of Children* (Los Altos, CA: Packard Foundation), pp. 6–18.

HARRISON, A., SERAFICA, F. and MCADDO, H. (1984) 'Ethnic families of color', in R. Parke (ed.) *Review of Child Development Research, Vol. 7: The Family* (Chicago: University of Chicago Press), pp. 329–371.

HEATH, S. B. and MCLAUGHLIN, M. W. (1987) 'A child resource policy: moving beyond dependence on school and family', *Phi Delta Kappan* (April), pp. 576–580.

HODGKINSON, H. (1989) *The Same Client: The Demographics of Education and Service Delivery Systems* (Washington: Institute for Educational Leadership, Center for Demographic Policy).

HORD, S. M. (1986) 'A synthesis of research on organizational collaboration', *Educational Leadership*, 43(5), pp. 22–26.

IANNI, F. A. J. (1989) *The Search for Structure: A Report on American Youth Today* (New York: Free Press).

JACOBS, F. H. and WEISS, H. B. (1988) 'Lessons in context', in H. B. Weiss and F. H. Jacobs (eds) *Evaluating Family Programs* (New York: Aldine De Gruyter), pp. 497–505.

KIRST, M. W. (1991) 'Improving children's services', *Phi Delta Kappan* (April), pp. 615–618).

KIRST, M. W. (1992) 'Financing school-linked services', in M. W. Kirst (ed.) *Rethinking School Finance: An Agenda for the 1990s* (San Francisco: Jossey-Bass).

KIRST, M. W., MCLAUGHLIN, M. and MASSELL, D. (1990) 'Rethinking policy for children: Implications for educational administration', in B. Mitchell and L. L. Cunningham (eds) *Educational Leadership and Changing Contexts of Families, Communities, and Schools* (Chicago: University of Chicago Press).

LEVY, J. E. and SHEPARDSON, W. (1992) 'A look at current school-linked service efforts', *The Future of Children*, 2, pp. 46–55.

MINUCHIN, S. (1974) *Families and Family Therapy* (Cambridge: Harvard University Press).

MORRILL, W. A. (1992) 'Overview of service delivery to children', *The Future of Children*, 2, pp. 32–43.

OGBU, J. U. (1992) 'A cultural-ecological approach to the study of minority education: a framework', paper presented at the Annual Meeting of the American Educational Research Association (San Francisco).

ONTARIO CHILD HEALTH STUDY: CHILDREN AT RISK (1990) (Toronto: Queen's Printer for Ontario).

ONTARIO MINISTRY OF COMMUNITY AND SOCIAL SERVICES (1992, May) *Time for Action, Towards a New Social Assistance System for Ontario* (Toronto: Queen's Printer of Ontario).

ONTARIO MINISTRY OF EDUCATION AND TRAINING (1991, November 21) *Better Beginnings, Better Futures Project* (Toronto: Integrated Services for Youth Secretariat).

ONTARIO MINISTRY OF EDUCATION AND TRAINING (1992, November 24) *Fact Sheet: Integrated Services for Children and Youth* (Toronto: Integrated Services for Youth Secretariat).

REICH, R. B. (1990) *The Power of Public Ideas* (Cambridge: Harvard University Press).

ROGERS, R. (1990) *Reaching for Solutions: The Report of the Special Advisor to the Minister of National Health and Welfare on Child Sexual Abuse in Canada* (Ottawa: National Clearing House on Family Violence, Health and Welfare Canada).

SASKATCHEWAN MINISTRY OF EDUCATION (1992, April) *Integrated School-Based Services for Children and Families* (Regina: Office of the Deputy Minister of Saskatchewan Education).

SCHORR, L. B. (1988) *Within Our Reach: Breaking the Cycle of Disadvantage* (New York: Doubleday).

SCHORR, L. B. (1989) 'Early interventions to reduce intergenerational disadvantage: the new policy context', *Teachers College Record*, 90 (Spring), pp. 362–374.

SLAUGHTER, D. T. (1988) 'Programs for racially and ethnically diverse American families: some critical issues', in H. B. Weiss and F. H. Jacobs (eds) *Evaluating Family Programs* (New York: Aldine De Gruyter), pp. 461–476.

STONE, D. A. (1989) *Policy Paradox and Political Reason* (Glenview: Scott, Foresman).

TOWNSEND, R. G. (1980) 'Is the local community an ecology of games? The case of schools relating to city agencies', *Education and Urban Society*, 12(4), pp. 486–507.

TOWNSEND, T., LETHBRIDGE, G., ALCOCK, R. and CALLAHAN, M. (1986, June), *A Proposal for the Development of a National Child Data Welfare System* (Toronto: Queen's Printer of Ontario).

PART 2
State and local perspectives

POLITICS OF EDUCATION ASSOCIATION YEARBOOK, 1993, 51–62

The politics of policy making for children

Julia E. Koppich

In December 1992, 25 people gathered in a conference room in Sacramento, California. Each individual attending the meeting represented a different children's advocacy group. Some were concerned particularly about preschoolers and child care arrangements; for others, professional interests revolved around children's health issues. Still others focused their efforts on child nutrition or elementary education programs.

These people met in Sacramento as members of a state-appointed task force to design the implementation strategy for a new law which all of their organizations had supported in its formative stages. The statute authorized additional funding to provide free milk for young children, from preschool age through grade three.

Once past the initial introductions and expressions of pleasure at being part of this collaborative activity, the group got down to the business at hand, or at least tried to settle into its task. What quickly became apparent, however, was that each task force member represented not only a different organization, but a different organizational agenda.

Organizational interests would shape task force discussions. In other words, individual organizations' conceptions of the parameters of the task, the boundaries within which it might be accomplished, and the particular role individual organizations might play framed the ensuing conversation about how the expanded free milk program would be implemented.

The individuals gathered around the Sacramento conference table were attending the meeting to accomplish the same public purpose, to insure that the milk reached the children. Yet this seemingly simple, straightforward undertaking quickly became enmeshed in interest-group politics and issues of turf protection. Who would be 'in charge'? What group might gain precedence in this activity? Who, ultimately, might claim credit if the program was successful?

The example cited above illustrates a fundamental challenge in the task of policy making for children. Bringing together representatives of various interest groups, even different groups with ostensibly the same interest, namely, developing and implementing a new program for children, causes the conventions of interest group politics to become standard operating procedure. Organizational interests tend to eclipse larger policy concerns. Yet the example of the California milk program does not even begin to approach the complexity of the far larger task of crafting comprehensive, coordinated public policy for children and their families. This bold undertaking, spanning numerous traditional policy boundaries, has come to travel under the umbrella of developing integrated, or coordinated, children's services.

The topic of integrated children's services has come to occupy an increasingly prominent place on the political and public policy agenda. The reason seems relatively straightforward: 'Report cards' for children and families, whether examined from national, state, or local levels, reveal a steady decline in the life situations for many of the USA's young people. Moreover, a growing body of research points to the conclusion that conventional policy making for children, which typically results in fractionated governance – multiple programs in multiple agencies – and unconnected funding streams – targeted dollars for specific programs – may be exacerbating rather than alleviating the problem. Thus, added emphasis is being placed in policy-making circles on the need for a comprehensive children's policy which brings together the now disparate elements of fragmented efforts.

Consonant with increased policy talk about comprehensive children's policy and integrated services, the number of children's advocacy groups is burgeoning. Some of these groups promote broad-based, encompassing agendas designed to lead to broad-scale policy for children and families. Most groups, however, work within long-established categories, targeting their activities to particular areas of children's policy, such as health, child care, foster care, or juvenile justice. Resulting policies typically mirror the fragmented and categorical nature of interest-group activities.

In addition to the growing band of children's advocacy groups, conventional education interest groups, particularly teacher unions and administrator and school board associations, continue to occupy their usual, and often influential, places on the policy-making scene. Yet these organizations, too, increasingly have become part of the children's policy-making mix with the spiraling recognition that children's ability to succeed in school is highly dependent on a complex web of family and environmental circumstances that shape children's lives.

This chapter is a preliminary exploration of the politics of policy making for children. It represents an effort, in other words, to begin to 'unpack' the political dynamics surrounding the development of children's policy. As such, it is an examination of the recent past, the present, and prospects for the future.

While this chapter aims to explore dimensions of the politics of children's policy, it also promotes a particular point of view. The chapter advances the argument that the development of integrated children's policy is necessary, but that the creation of such policy requires a conscious shift away from traditional, and conventionally incremental, interest-group approaches to policy development.

The chapter begins by offering a working rationale for the development of a comprehensive children's policy, then proceeds to a review of the recent history of efforts to initiate programs for children and families. It then places the discussion in context by briefly exploring the politics of children's policy in one state, California. The chapter concludes by asserting that, in order to open the policy doors for broad-based integrated services for children, the current political paradigm must be fundamentally altered.

The context for policy change

Multiple factors shape children's lives. These include level of family income, status of physical and mental health, existence of family support systems, availability of quality education, opportunities for healthful recreation, and racial and ethnic background.

While life for most children in the USA is healthy, happy, and productive, many children in this land of plenty face desperate existences. Today 20% of this nation's children live in poverty (Kirst and McLaughlin 1990), and the income gap between the richest families and the poorest continues to widen.

The largest segment of the population living in poverty in the USA is children; 40% of the nation's poor are young people under the age of 18 (Hodgkinson 1989). While some children fare well in low-income households, studies have shown that children from poverty backgrounds have a greater likelihood of succumbing to illness in infancy and early childhood, of becoming pregnant during the teenage years, and of dropping out of school (Kirst and McLaughlin 1990).

Poverty in America continues in large measure to be a function of race, gender, and family status. While one-fifth of children overall live in poverty, nearly half of the nation's black children (43.1%) are poor and more than a third (39%) of Hispanic children live in poverty.

Family structure greatly impacts on children's lives. The so-called traditional American family, with a stay-at-home Mom serving as the children's prime caregiver and a go-to-work breadwinner Dad is fast disappearing. In fact, only one-third of American families fit this once typical family profile. Increasing numbers of children live with just one parent, and large numbers live with a mother who has never married. While many single mothers are able to provide adequately for their children, the majority of children who reside in female-headed households live in poverty.

Nearly half of US children (46%) live in homes in which both parents or the only parent is working (Kirst and McLaughlin 1990). Yet even being employed is no shield against poverty. Four million Americans, most of whom work in the low-end service economy at minimum-wage jobs, remain eligible for poverty benefits (Hodgkinson 1989).

A combination of changing economic circumstances, which require large numbers of women to work, plus increased numbers of women who choose to work outside the home, has, perhaps permanently, altered the family, the fundamental structure for caring for children. No new social structure has yet taken its place.

Medical issues, too, are a concern to children and families. Medical care in the USA for those who can afford it is the best in the world. But 37 million Americans, including 12 million children, have no health insurance. One in four pregnant women in the USA receives no prenatal care (Hodgkinson 1989).

In addition, increasing numbers of preschoolers are not immunized against once deadly diseases, threatening a return of the very illnesses once thought to be eliminated in the USA. The percentage of fully immunized children is less than half the proportion in the UK, Canada, Spain, France, Sweden, and Israel (Hodgkinson 1989).

Other needs of children and families could easily be detailed. Increasing numbers of youth find themselves on the wrong side of the law. Reports of child abuse are on the rise. Many children are homeless.

What has become abundantly clear to professionals who deal with young people on a daily basis is that children have multiple needs. Many are not only poor *or* in fragile health *or* lacking sufficient family support. Children's problems often are severe and almost always are interdependent.

The locus of responsibility for children traditionally has been the family. But government, too, has assumed a responsibility for children. This governmental responsibility does not supersede the authority of the family, but serves as an important, sometimes crucial link in a complex family support system.

The next section of this paper describes the nature of governmental assistance to children and families during the 1960s, arguably the most intense period of efforts at broad-scale social reform in the USA since the Great Depression.

Into the 1960s: the categorization of care

Beginning in the mid-1960s, the federal government enacted a series of new programs designed to address the problems of the nation's poor, including children living in poverty. Many of these new policy thrusts were part of President Lyndon Johnson's Great Society Program and the accompanying War on Poverty. New programs in education, health, welfare, manpower training, and urban development were authorized and established. Poverty was used as the benchmark for federal financial assistance.

This broad expanse of policy initiatives was the product of a new national attitude, fostered by President John Kennedy and enlarged by President Johnson. Congress in 1964 and 1965 expressed the national purpose in bold and concrete terms – to outlaw racial discrimination, improve educational opportunity at every level, eradicate poverty, assure the provision of health care, and create jobs for the unemployed (Sundquist 1968).

This was a new national agenda. In effect, the federal government crafted social goals for the nation through the creation of new federally funded programs. These new policy initiatives also laid the foundation for a new conceptual premise, namely that the purpose of government was not simply to insure against economic loss, as had been the thrust of New Deal programs, but to promote social as well as economic gain (Anton 1989).

This was a time of great national optimism, the 'anything was possible' decade in which citizens believed in the capacity of government to enact initiatives that were capable of engineering social justice (Kirst and Gifford 1990). (Of course, feelings of euphoria were destined to be relatively short-lived as the escalation of the war in VietNam in the late 1960s began to eclipse attention to domestic issues.) During this period the federal government launched a broad series of policy salvos which created or expanded a vast array of social programs. Among these were the Elementary and Secondary Education Act (ESEA), the most massive program of federal financial assistance to schools in the history of the nation. Title I of ESEA targeted special assistance directly to students living in poverty.

Programs for disadvantaged children and youth also were created under the Department of Labor and the Office of Economic Opportunity. These included Head Start, the Job Corps, Comprehensive Health Services, Medicaid, and the Women Infants and Children (WIC) program. Existing efforts in the areas of prenatal care, food stamps, and public housing projects were expanded as well (Kirst and Gifford 1990). These new federal initiatives were woven into the fabric of a program of large-scale social reform; in effect, the governmentally created and sanctioned expansion of what constituted human services and the redefinition of who was eligible to receive them.

Great Society programs of the 1960s were also employed as a means to achieve a new cooperative arrangement among levels of government. National grants to state agencies which disbursed funds to local communities created an intergovernmental link.

Dollars were distributed to states and local jurisdictions in the form of categorical grants. These were targeted funds for special programs and particular populations. Federal strings followed federal dollars. Specific conditions were to be met if the money was to continue to flow.

Social programs of the 1960s reinforced the separateness of existing policy categories. Programs were targeted to specific, defined problems. Dollars were linked to strategies designed to meet particularistic, identified needs. Constituencies began to develop around individual programs and policies. Interest groups formed to lobby for these constituencies.

As the 1960s gave way to the 1970s, a changing political landscape would intensify the fragmented nature of policy and the categorical approach to funding. Interest-group politics would intensify as well.

The 1970s and 1980s: from consolidation to retrenchment

The decade of the 1970s represented a period of consolidation and slow growth (Kirst and Gifford 1990). The Nixon administration did not choose to focus on policies for the disadvantaged. Instead, this was a period of what many proponents of broad-scale social policy change believed to be 'backsliding'. Advocates of change feared losing the gains they had made in the 1960s.

Federal efforts to aid the disadvantaged were not entirely lacking, however. Congress in 1973 enacted the Education for All Handicapped Children Act (P.L. 94-142). This new statute required that all physically and mentally handicapped children receive a 'free, appropriate public education'. Handicapped children in many communities had, to this time, been an invisible segment of the population, hidden away at home or in public or private institutions, often being denied even rudimentary education. P.L. 94-142 was hailed as an additional, and until now missing, component of achieving civil rights for a forgotten segment of the American populace.

The Education for All Handicapped Children Act also created another entitlement and another categorical program, this time for expanded special education services. The number of interest groups, often focused on particular aspects of education of the handicapped or on specific types of handicaps, began to mushroom.

During this period as well, some advocacy groups, frustrated by their inability to secure legislative relief, sought redress through the courts. The cause of bilingual education was advanced in this manner. The 1973 US Supreme Court decision in *Lau* v. *Nichols* made school districts responsible for assisting limited- and non-English-speaking students. Congress added Title VII to the Elementary and Secondary Education Act to allocate funds through the states to local districts for bilingual instruction. Federal dollars, however, were more symbolic than vast.

Many states responded to the *Lau* decision by enacting new categorical aid programs aimed at bilingual and English-as-a-second-language instruction. As quickly as categorically funded bilingual education programs developed, advocates seeking to insure targeted dollars were indeed devoted to limited- and non-English-speaking students formed program-specific interest groups.

During the Nixon era, the federal government undertook some efforts to consolidate proliferating categorical grants. However, this move was resisted by the interest groups which had developed around particular categorical programs and feared that the elimination of targeted programs would become a governmental excuse for diminution of the service.

Programs such as Title I (now Chapter I) of ESEA, the Education for All Handicapped Children Act, and bilingual education programs that resulted from the *Lau* decision had developed well-defined constituencies, and these constituencies had bred interest groups whose principal focus was preserving and protecting 'their' targeted programs. Each group confined public and political activities to the narrow programmatic sphere it had carved out for itself. Advocates' professional responsibility, as they saw it, was to protect the program, or set of programs, now embedded in policy. Interest groups' line of sight focused specifically on the categorical programs they now identified as 'their' policy domain and funding province. As a result, policies, programs, and dollars remained categorical.

The Carter administration in the late 1970s revised the Nixon strategy and attempted once again to strengthen the categorical programs. But these efforts generally failed in Congress not as a result of diminished legislative interest in the categorical approach, but because few strong, politically viable links existed between legislators and the White House. In addition, there was a growing public perception that poverty, the foundation of many categorical entitlements, was fading as an urgent social issue (Kirst and Gifford 1990).

The 1980s, when Ronald Reagan assumed office, marked a period of retrenchment (Kirst and Gifford 1990). This was the era of limited government, particularly where domestic issues were concerned.

The Reagan administration attempted to consolidate a number of categorical programs, including many education categoricals, into block grants. Most of these efforts failed to win Congressional approval. Interest groups argued, largely successfully, to legislative policy makers that the Reagan administration's block grant proposals were simply a thinly veiled political ruse to enact wholesale domestic program cuts. White House-proffered budget cuts in numerous social policy areas added fuel to the interest groups' fire. Completing the 1980s, the policies of George Bush were more moderate, but reflected basically a Reaganesque policy stance and tone.

One result of the federal social policy thrust of the 1970s and 1980s was that interest groups circled the policy wagons. Few inter-interest coalitions were formed. Rather, the general stance of categorically based lobbies was to protect and defend established categorical programs. Political emphasis focused on securing incremental advances, or preventing backward slippage, for specific, defined programs.

How did this political and policy scenario, from the 1960s to the 1980s, play itself out in the states? For one perspective, we turn now to a brief review of social policy development in California.

Categorical precedence in the golden state

California's response to the Great Society programs of the 1960s was to develop and implement targeted services for children and their families. Categorical programs in the areas of health, child welfare, protective services, compensatory education, and alcohol and drug abuse prevention were widely promoted throughout the state (Smrekar 1988). Thus the categorical approach to funding at the federal level resulted in incremental, and fragmented, policy making at the state level throughout the 1960s.

California experienced boom economic times for much of the decade of the 1970s. The state's economy continued to expand, new Californians were added to the state's rolls, and even larger numbers of categorical programs in education, health, welfare, and juvenile justice became part of the budget and policy process. Then tax reform fever hit the state.

On June 6, 1978, California voters enacted the Jarvis–Gann Tax Limitation Initiative, popularly known as Proposition 13. A state constitutional amendment (Article XIIIA of the California Constitution), Proposition 13 was the first major salvo in the California taxpayers' revolt. The measure limited property taxes to 1% of the 1975–76 assessed valuation and limited assessment increases to 2% a year. (Property can be reappraised upon the sale or transfer of ownership.) It also severely curtailed the taxing power of local government by prohibiting municipalities from enacting new property taxes. (The single modest exception is that jurisdictions can levy taxes on parcels – square feet of living space – if two-thirds of local voters approve.) State taxes could be increased only by a two-thirds vote of the state legislature. Proposition 13 effectively transformed California into a system in which the state would henceforth provide the bulk of financing for local governments (Goren and Kirst 1989).

Californians' appetite for tax reform was not satiated by Proposition 13. Just one year later, in 1979, the Gann spending limitation (Proposition 4) was enacted. The Gann limit restricts growth in state spending to the rate of increase of the state's population and the lower of either the United States Consumer Price Index (CPI) or California personal income. In other words, state spending growth is pegged to changes in population and inflation. The measure further requires that unexpended dollars be returned as rebates to taxpayers.

Proposition 13 had restricted local municipalities' ability to pay for social services. The Gann limit crippled the state's ability to fund new, and even many existing, programs. State-level interest-group politics were destined to intensify.

The 1980s marked a period of consolidation and realignment in California. With federal regulatory and fiscal influence reduced, and the state now the keeper of the vast majority of public resources, the state role assumed a new prominence in terms of both funding and delivery of children's services. California lawmakers created additional state-specific programs, performance standards, and guidelines which were then translated into local agency actions and decisions (Smrekar 1988). Funding remained categorical, programs targeted, and policy thrusts splintered. Shrinking budgets did not encourage inter-interest coalitions to form around comprehensive children's services. Quite to the contrary, advocacy groups did their best individually to define themselves for policy makers and thus grab 'their' share of a shrinking fiscal pie.

To be sure, many of the categorical programs, designed to assist children in need, produced beneficial effects. Some additional number of children received more, and likely, better care. However, categorical funding translated into a program-by-program, service-by-service, problem-by-problem policy approach which took little notice of a coherent vision of children and their lives. One primary result was that little attention was paid to these programs' collective impact on children (Smrekar 1988).

The consequences were threefold: (1) underservice – too many children slipped through the social service cracks, (2) limited focus on prevention – the state adopted a triage approach to children's services, treating problems as episodic rather than continuous, and (3) service fragmentation – little or no interagency collaboration (Kirst 1989).

By the late 1980s, California boasted 169 different children- and youth-serving programs overseen by 37 separate entities located in seven different state-level departments. Separate, unconnected funding streams flowed to and from this complicated maze of children's services. State leadership in children's services scattered over politicians' special interest projects. And legions of lobbyists, representing a plethora of variously defined child-oriented groups, were to be found working the halls of the state capitol in Sacramento.

In November 1988 California voters struck again, narrowly enacting Proposition 98, a state constitutional amendment which guarantees to public education in kindergarten through community college (K–14) approximately 40% of the state's general fund revenues. In other words, before programs in policy areas other than public education would receive their financial allocations, 40% would 'come off the top' for schools.

Proposition 98 was passed in the wake of burgeoning school budget needs. Enrollments were climbing by more than 200,000 students per year. (By 1990, one out of every eight children in the USA would be enrolled in a California public school.) Many of the newcomers were immigrants with little or no facility with the English language. With the state unable to shake the recession, school revenues continued to decline. Frustrated Californians, seeing the dollars for education diminish, enacted yet another constitutional measure.

Advocates of Proposition 98 assured their supporters that the amendment would stabilize school funding and provide a steady and increasing stream of revenue for education. But Proposition 98 did not solve California's school budget crisis. In fact, even after Proposition 98 took effect, per pupil expenditures in the state, pegged to California's revenue intake, continued to decline.

Proposition 98 also did not, as promoters had promised, insulate schools from the pull and tug of state politics. Instead, the constitutional measure became the eye in a storm of controversy surrounding the financing of public services.

Those who had labored long and hard for the passage of Proposition 98 – principally the education interest groups – quickly became strict constructionists on the issue. Little policy-wiggle room was to be found. Two years after the enactment of Proposition 98, the first lawsuit was filed.

The state's largest teachers' union, the California Teachers Association (CTA), an affiliate of the National Education Association, sued over the state's efforts to partially fund preschool education out of Proposition 98 revenues. These dollars, the CTA agreed, were targeted to the kindergarten through community college education system. Preschool was not to be included. The CTA won the suit. The state would need to find a means other than earmarked Proposition 98 education dollars to fund preschool services.

In California, then, interest-group politics culminated in 'the mother of all categoricals', Proposition 98. While education interest groups' desire to secure adequate, or at least what they hoped would be relatively predictable, funding for one policy domain is on one level understandable, the situation sets in bold relief the dilemma inherent in developing coordinated, comprehensive policy for children and families. As long as politics as usual prevails, as long as the political system continues to reward fragmented policy and segmented funding, then status quo will be the order of the day.

Overcoming the politics of categorization and incrementalism

Policy formation is a political process. New legislation is proposed, new laws enacted, and new policies implemented on a daily basis. Some policies make news; most do not.

The policy system cannot handle every issue which seeks to call attention to itself. Thus, only a finite number of issues achieve political agenda status (Easton 1965, Cobb and Elder 1983); in other words, are considered for policy action. But of those issues that reach the political agenda, most are handled via routine political channels.

Generally, special interests capture policy via 'iron triangles' – interest-group representatives, minor government officials, and small groups of legislators that have a particular interest in the issue. Interest groups, in effect, control the policy process, and government acts to 'freeze' the status quo and retard innovation (Lowi 1969). Policy evolves by accretion, in a system of 'partisan mutual adjustment' (Lindblom 1977) as government agencies and interest groups adjust their behaviors to each others' intentions and relative power.

Self-interest plays a central role in policy formation (McFarland 1988). Groups of elites (organized special interests), in essence, co-opt special public policy arena which serve their particular organizational self-interests. Policy, then, is the product of the action of competing interest groups which vie for control and policy precedence in a continual political game of bargaining and compromise (Dahl 1956).

Resulting policy changes are incremental. Coalitions may form to enact policy, but even coalition policy generally is *incremental* and neither jars the status quo nor threatens the authority of established interest groups.

The conventional political picture, then, is represented by a system in which a set of organized self-interests determine the course of political action and the shape of policy outcomes. Pluralism, policy making by bargaining among competing interest groups seeking to advance their own aims, dominates. Policy is the summed product of these competing interests. Organizational preservation, rather than client interest, becomes paramount. Incremental change, or no change at all, is the result.

This description of the political scene is perhaps somewhat overstated, or at least unduly cynical. To be sure, many interest groups represent clients who need a strong voice to speak for them in legislative halls and executive branch offices. Advocates are often passionate and sincere about those whom they represent. Moreover, the policies and programs which are the result of advocacy efforts might have been slower to emerge, or might never have emerged at all, if not for the political pressure exerted on behalf of specific groups or individuals. Whether the nation's public school systems would have opened their doors to handicapped children or initiated programs to meet the needs of limited- and non-English-speaking pupils in the absence of legislative and judicial action cannot be known. What is indisputable is that programs for these populations of students resulted largely from the actions of advocates.

However, fragmented policy, which is the natural result of interest-group bargaining within the political system, has a self-reinforcing quality. Strong particularistic constituencies and tightly bounded interest groups become protective of 'their' policy turf. They come to view often narrowly conceived policy domains as objects of near-personal property. They lobby aggressively to maintain the policy boundaries within which they are comfortable operating. And they come to see any action that threatens established political territory or sovereignty as an attack on their purpose and mission.

The political system rewards this behavior. The group that shouts the loudest, distinguishes itself most clearly from the interest group pack (or, alternatively, strikes the quickest bargain with its lobbying compatriots), and defines its demands in the most politically palatable increments is likely to reap the greatest benefits. There simply are few incentives for groups to coalesce around broad-based issues because the political system typically rewards fragmentation and categorization.

Recall again the California scenario. Much attention was paid to developing and enacting policy for children and families beginning in the 1960s. Myriad highly specialized interest groups divided up the fiscal and policy pie into categorical component parts. A wealth of policy and a wide array of programs resulted. While those programs represent substantial interest-group trophies, the segmented approach to social policy has, arguably at least, only marginally benefited those individuals whom it was designed to assist.

Changing the policy focus by changing the political paradigm

As long as fragmentation is rewarded, the status quo will prevail. Creating coordinated, comprehensive, integrated policy for children requires breaking the mold of political convention, changing the current political paradigm, and dramatically altering the rules of the political game. More specifically, such a change entails revamping the system of political rewards and incentives so that it accrues to interest groups' material advantage to cooperate rather than compete, to merge their efforts rather than to maintain separateness. A system which offers fiscal incentives for decategorizing dollars and focuses on achieving results, rather than simply on providing services, would significantly advance the cause of integrated services.

California has begun down the path toward such a system. The state still has a considerable distance to travel, and the road to coordination is likely to be laced with political landmines. Nonetheless, steps the state has taken, and is currently contemplating, are both significant and instructive.

California, in January 1992, enacted the Healthy Support Services for Children Act (Senate Bill 620). Commonly called Healthy Start, the program provided an initial $20 million state appropriation for competitive planning and operational grants to establish locally based systems of integrated children's services. The Act targets those children generally assumed to be in greatest need – those whose families receive Aid to Families with Dependent Children (AFDC) support, those who are limited-English-proficient, and children who are eligible for schools' free or reduced meals.

S.B. 620 money can be used to assist schools and social service agencies collaboratively to provide a wide range of services, depending on local need. Such services can include general health care, immunizations, vision and hearing testing, family support and counseling, drug and alcohol abuse treatment and prevention, and prenatal care. Emphasis here is on interagency collaboration. Agencies combine programmatic efforts toward the goal of creating a seamless web of services for children and families.

All, however, has not been political smooth sailing for Healthy Start. As it made its way through the legislative process, the bill encountered little or no organized opposition. Children's advocacy groups applauded the proposed statute and lobbied actively for its passage. Education interest groups, however, were considerably more restrained.

The majority of the state's education interest groups greeted the proposed measure with an air of resigned acquiescence. On the one hand, they feared additional responsibilities would be heaped on schools' already overflowing plate of obligations. On the other hand, education interests were concerned that as the state's fiscal situation became increasingly grim, the relative 'security' of funding they believed schools had achieved with Proposition 98 could be threatened by a Healthy Start-type approach to program and policy.

The state's largest education interest group – the California Teachers Association – in fact initially voiced its opposition to Healthy Start. This position, if it had remained unchanged, had the potential dramatically to alter the fate of the bill. CTA each year contributes millions of dollars to legislative campaign coffers, and thus wields enormous political influence in the state. In the end, CTA was moved from an oppose to a neutral stance. But neither CTA nor the other education interest groups actively campaigned for the bill's passage.

Healthy Start is now on the books in California. Funded collaboratives involving school districts and social service agencies are working their way through the often wrenching process of coordinating programs and developing interprofessional teams. Of particular significance is the fact that the statute has been refunded twice. Despite California's dire fiscal straits (the state experienced an $11 billion budget shortfall in 1992–93, and must close an $8 billion budget gap in 1993–94), the legislature appropriated $14 million for Healthy Start's second year of operation and has tentatively approved $19 million for the third year.

It is too early to judge the relative success of the Healthy Start program. A formal state-supported evaluation is currently underway. To be sure, Healthy Start legislation, by itself, is unlikely to shatter state policy boundaries. Nothing in the statute speaks to pooling existing categories of funds at their source, state government. Moreover, the law delineates no set of specified, desired, comprehensive outcomes for children. Yet it is important to view Healthy Start in context, as a first step in a more comprehensive state policy strategy. That strategy, which has the endorsement of a range of policy and special-interest organizations, focuses clearly on flexible funding and client outcomes.

The California School Boards Association, California State Association of Counties, and the League of California Cities joined forces in 1992 to address the need for coordinated services for children and families. The organizations jointly sponsored a series of 'summits' around the state to discuss relevant policy coordination issues and to 'develop a whole new vision for children's services' (California School Boards Association *et al.* 1992). The resulting plan strongly recommends increased flexibility in the use of categorical funds, allowing the 'blending' of funding streams, and moving toward an outcome-based system of program assessment.

In a similar vein, a report by the Washington, DC-based Center for the Study of Social Policy asserts that California's service system must 'become outcome-oriented, not process-driven, . . . and must lessen the categorical restrictions in funding and program operation' (Center for the Study of Social Policy 1993). Interestingly, that report was commissioned and paid for by a set of California philanthropic foundations which have made integrated children's services among their funding priorities.

A February 1993 status report on integrated services by the state's Assembly Office of Research targets the categorical nature of service delivery programs and the segmented approach to funding. Acknowledging that developing a comprehensive system of integrated services requires 'the technical expertise of a CPA, the dexterity of a juggler, the creativity of an artist, the patience of Job, and the faith of the truly committed' (DeLapp 1993), the report comes down firmly on the side of pooled funding and decategorized programs toward a goal of a more holistic, integrated system. Finally, the state's non-partisan office of the Legislative Analyst also has taken up the twin policy cudgels of decategorized funding and client-based program results, asserting that the restrictive nature of program funding must be altered and greater attention devoted to outcomes of government social service programs (Hill 1993).

These reports and recommendations may find policy voice in a measure now before the legislature. A.B. 1741 (Bates) would establish the Youth Pilot Program. The program, designed to fund comprehensive, integrated services for high-risk children and families, would allow designated counties (i.e., those that are selected to participate in the pilot program) to transfer into a combined child and family services fund using dollars currently appropriated for various categorical services, such as health care, foster care, and drug and alcohol abuse prevention. The measure would also allow local school districts to transfer funds for purposes such as recreation or juvenile justice to the county child and family services fund.

The county would develop a plan for use of the newly blended funds and would be required to evaluate the effectiveness of coordinated programs on the basis of a set of annual performance outcomes for the children and families who receive the services. At the time of writing, the bill has passed the Assembly and moved on to the policy committee in the Senate.

California's emergent focus on pooled funding streams and program outcomes offers the potential for changing the political paradigm, for concentrating political energy on comprehensive rather than fragmented policy, by changing the system of political rewards and incentives *vis-à-vis* children's policy. California, to be sure, has embarked on a monumental political undertaking. Yet this is also the type of political challenge that must be considered and embraced more widely. Changing the political paradigm for the development of social policy calls for no less dramatic a shift than altering the way politics is done in this nation. But unless we are able to succeed in this, we surely will fail to meet the more critical human challenge of developing and implementing social policies that actually work for children and families.

References

ANTON, THOMAS J. (1989) *American Federalism and Public Policy: How the System Works* (Philadelphia: Temple University Press).

CALIFORNIA SCHOOL BOARDS ASSOCIATION, CALIFORNIA STATE ASSOCIATION OF COUNTIES, LEAGUE OF CALIFORNIA CITIES (1992) *Cutting Through the Red Tape: Meeting the Needs of California's Children* (Sacramento: California School Boards Association).

CENTER FOR THE STUDY OF SOCIAL POLICY (1993) *Improving Outcomes for California's Children: A Strategy to Build Comprehensive Community Services* (Washington, DC: Center for the Study of Social Policy).

COBB, ROGER W. and ELDER, CHARLES D. (1983) *Participation in American Politics: The Dynamics of Agenda Building* (Baltimore: Johns Hopkins University Press).

DAHL, ROBERT (1956) *A Preface to Democratic Theory* (Chicago: University of Chicago Press).

DELAPP, LYNN R. (1993) *Putting the Pieces Together: A Status Report on Integrated Child and Family Services* (Sacramento: Assembly Office of Research).

EASTON, DAVID E. (1965) *A Framework for Political Analysis* (Englewood Cliffs, NJ: Prentice-Hall).

GOREN, PAUL D. and KIRST, MICHAEL W. (1989) *An Exploration of County Expenditures and Revenues for Children's Services* (Berkeley: Policy Analysis for California Education).

HILL, ELIZABETH G. (1993) *The (1993)–94 Budget: Perspectives and Issues* (Sacramento: Office of the Legislative Analyst).

HODGKINSON, HAROLD L. (1989) *The Same Client: The Demographics of Education and Service Delivery Systems* (Washington, DC: Institute for Educational Leadership).

KIRST, MICHAEL W. (ed.) (1989) *Conditions of Children in California* (Berkeley: Policy Analysis for California Education).

KIRST, MICHAEL W. and GIFFORD, BERNARD R. (1990) 'The political outlook for federal programs for the disadvantaged', paper presented at the conference on Accelerated Schools, Stanford University, Stanford, California.

KIRST, MICHAEL W. and MCLAUGHLIN, MILBREY W. (1990) 'Rethinking children's policy: implications for educational administration', *Policy Bulletin* (Bloomington, IN: Consortium on Educational Policy Studies).

Lau v. *Nichols*, 483 f2nd. (9OR., 1973), 94S. C.7786 (1974).

LINDBLOM, CHARLES E. (1977) *Politics and Markets: The World's Political-Economic Systems* (New York: Basic Books).

LOWI, THEODORE (1969) *The End of Liberalism: Ideology, Policy, and the Crisis of Public Authority* (New York: W.W. Norton).

MCFARLAND, ANDREW S. (1988) 'Interest groups and the theories of power in America', *British Journal of Political Science*, 17, pp. 129–147.

SMREKAR, CLAIRE (1988) 'Governmental organization: the impact on the delivery of children's services' (Berkeley: Policy Analysis for California Education) (unpublished paper).

SUNDQUIST, JAMES L. (1968) *Politics and Policy: The Eisenhower, Kennedy, and Johnson Years* (Washington, DC: Brookings Institution).

POLITICS OF EDUCATION ASSOCIATION YEARBOOK, 1993, 63–73

State full-service school initiatives: new notions of policy development

Patricia F. First, Joan L. Curcio and Dalton L. Young

Introduction

Movement in the states towards human service integration into the school setting is a growing trend nationwide. A bill was introduced in the United States House of Representatives in June of 1992 that would have created a means for states to receive money to develop full-service programs. The bill did not pass. However, many states are taking the initiative to develop their own plans to serve students to the fullest extent at school sites. Statutes and policies are being developed regarding the integration of services into the public schools. In this chapter we discuss views of the policy development process and analyze the full-service schools movement in relation to those views. We discuss examples of these new state policies as scattered and vulnerable reforms but with promising interaction of state and local initiatives. We analyze the Kentucky and New Jersey movements in terms of the strength of state role and we call for time before stringent evaluation in order to allow this policy movement to mature and influence positively the lives of all our children.

Views of the policy process

Traditional views of the policy development cycle are summarized as a process that starts with the recognition of a problem followed by the formation of a study group, the development of policy recommendations, political decisions in the legislative and budgetary processes, implementation, and evaluation (Gramlick 1981, Schultz 1968, Stonich 1977). Critics have long argued that this rational view of policy never really happens, even when elaborate and systematic public decision strategies – such as planning, programming, and budgeting systems (PPS) or zero-based budgeting (ZBB) – are implemented (Baybrooke and Lindblom 1963, Lindblom and Cohen 1979). These critics argued that the policy process is disjointed and incremental (Baybrooke and Lindblom 1963) and that it can be influenced by expert analysis targeted at important policy issues (Lindblom and Cohen 1979). St John (1992) has written of the dichotomy between these two positions:

> These two points of view leave us with the impression that the educational policy process is either rational and it can be shaped by objective policy research, or it is nonrational and can be shaped by policy analysts who take an advocay position. Neither of those positions leave much room for the educational practitioner, and both assume that the political arena is the best – if not the only – place to influence the policy process. (St John 1992: 96)

In St John's (1992) alternate view of the policy cycle the most important actors in the educational policy process are the educational practitioners. 'Innovations by educational

0268–0939/93 $10·00 © 1993 Taylor & Francis Ltd.

practitioners have a major influence in the formation of educational policy' (p. 97). We argue that the full-service school movement is defying traditional, rational views of policy development and conforms closely to St John's alternative model.

The full-service schools policy process

Alternatives pioneered at the local level do seem to be influencing the policy-making initiatives at the state level in the area of full-service schools. The federal level has been virtually silent on the issue. According to Wirt and Kirst (1989) the modes of affecting federal policy change in education are general aid stimulation through differential funding, regulation, discovering knowledge and making it available, providing services and 'moral suasion.' Only 'moral suasion' is at all evident regarding the development of policy for full-service schools and that evidence must be inferred from the needs which must be addressed in numbers one and six of the National Goals for Education:

> Goal 1: By the year 2000, all children in America will start school ready to learn. ... Children will receive the nutrition and health care needed to arrive at school with healthy minds and bodies, and the number of low-birth weight babies will be significantly reduced through enhanced prenatal health systems.
>
> Goal 6: By the year 2000, every school in America will be free of drugs and violence and will offer a disciplined environment conducive to learning. ... Every school district will develop a comprehensive K–12 drug and alcohol prevention education program. Drug and alcohol curriculum should be taught as an integral part of health education. In addition, community-based teams should be organized to provide students and teachers with needed support. (US Department of Education 1990)

It should be noted that, with the popularity of the philosophy of communitarianism in the Clinton administration, federal interest in the full-service school movement may grow (Etzioni 1993). The communitarian emphasis on our responsibility toward each other and the inherent stress on cooperative modes of action express well the nobler values underlying the full-service schools movement. Less noble reasons driving the full-service school movement are the enormity of the problems of both the schools and the social service agencies and the lack of money in the separate agency budgets to address the problems.

Examples of state policy

The Oregon Educational Act for the 21st Century, passed by the Oregon Legislature in 1991, requires that 'schools provide alternative learning environments, services, and intervention strategies for students requiring assistance.' The bill also provides for 'the integration of health and social services at or near the school sites to assist students and families' (Oregon State Department of Education 1991).

One of the purposes of the Colorado 2000 project is to involve the community and business with education in order to improve the service to the students. In the early 1990s the Colorado Governor's Policy and Research Office was studying the possibility of implementing a plan for an integrated service delivery system that emphasized early intervention. A Governor's Cabinet Council has also been convened to develop comprehensive family centers in the schools (National Governor's Association 1991).

In a publication called *Missourians Prepared* (Missouri Department of Elementary and Secondary Education 1990), the Missouri State Board of Education stated that, in the 1990s, schools should become the focal point for delivering coordinated services that contribute to the well-being of students and their families (education, health, child care, etc.). Missouri has also instituted two pilot programs called 'Caring Communities.' The Board did not assert that schools should become the primary providers of such services, but that through coordination with other agencies, the services could be provided more conveniently for high-risk families.

Some states have legislated more specific and smaller scale cooperative ventures between the schools and the social service agencies. For example, Maryland law mandates that schools incorporate a youth drug-abuse and suicide prevention program.

In California the Governor has called for the coordination and integration of health and social services for all children through SB 620, Healthy Start which provides grants to schools where a group of collaborating agencies provide school-linked social services. Georgia has also stepped up efforts to develop full-service schools by offering incentives to schools which will set up health and social service centers. Illinois is looking into more family services integration into the schools (National Governor's Association 1991).

Indiana schools can receive a block grant of state and federal monies to develop comprehensive programs targeted to families (National Governor's Association 1991). In Mississippi comprehensive services exist for families with students who are developmentally delayed. The Mississippi Governor's office offered a $1 million dollar grant to the school that has the most promising strategy to increase student learning through interagency cooperation.

A scattered and vulnerable reform

That the states are moving on initiatives of various types and intensity can be seen from these examples. The intensity or level of state action is as important as its content because nominally identical policies with varying levels of commitment, such as resource allocation, behind them have very different impacts on school operations (McLaughlin 1981). The movement in the states is a scattered one which is not unusual. 'States vary tremendously in both intensity and expansiveness of activities concerning educational policy' (Mitchell 1988: 454). Mitchell lists the following reasons for this variance:

- State policy systems are vulnerable to pressures from a wide variety of forces in and out of the state.
- State systems are quite vulnerable to the influence of charismatic leadership by a governor, chief state school officer, or key state legislator. Thus policy activity varies between long periods of relative inactivity interrupted by bursts of highly visible change.
- Educational policy systems are vulnerable to the actions of well-organized or well-financed interest groups.

These vulnerabilities are operating in the full-service school movement and are further complicated by the overlap between in-state and out-of-state interest groups. For example the Danforth Foundation, an out-of-state influence, is funding projects in New York, Ohio, Oklahoma and Texas for the generation of coalitions to bring needed services to all children. When out-of-state coalitions form, they encourage the participation of in-state interest groups.

There are always blurred boundaries around state educational policies, making them difficult to analyze, and nowhere has this been more of a problem than in the full-service schools movement. Because schools undertake programs and perform a wide variety of functions that are very difficult to separate from community services and social welfare services, state and local school policies are hard to summarize and analyze. It is difficult to say precisely where educational policy leaves off and other state policies begin (Mitchell 1988). If the full-service school movement achieves its collaborative goals the boundaries around the policies of many state agencies will be intentionally blurred.

Because of this blurring, impact studies will need to focus on the overall values and goals of programs resulting from the full-service school movement and the results in children's and families' lives rather than on the impact of specific intervening statutes and policies. It is likely that in order to be successful with these new initiatives states will have to make use simultaneously of all the state policy mechanisms listed by Mitchell and Encarnation (1984):

- school organization and governance (powerful weapons used to allocate powers and responsibilities among interest groups);
- school finance;
- student testing and assessment;
- school program definition (what special programs or ancillary services should be available to children, the question at the very heart of the full-service schools movement);
- personnel training and certification;
- curriculum materials development and selection, and
- school buildings and facilities.

Political interaction model

The movement towards full-service schools tends to be one that is coming at the same time from the local district level as well as the state level. States may offer some incentives or general guidelines to local districts, but for the most part appear to be leaving local districts to develop the programs on their own. Thus in the full-service school movement we are seeing more of the political action model of implementation than we are of Timar and Kirp's (1988) other two models of implementation, rational planning and market incentive. In the political interaction model the state articulates broad policy goals but allows discretion and flexibility in local implementation. The purpose is to integrate state policy goals with local conditions and practices. Implementation becomes a process for problem solving instead of the imposition of a single best solution. Most of the new state initiatives regarding full-service schools can be described by the political interaction model.

However, some market incentives are seen in the movement such as the Georgia incentive program and the Mississippi grant competition. Policy development in these examples is concentrated at the state level but implementation is encouraged through fiscal incentives and compliance is decided upon at the local level. What has not yet materialized in the full-service school movement is the rational planning model of implementation with its top-down mandates, centralized authority and decision making, standardization, uniformity, and mistrust of local authority and local discretion.

Local initiatives – policy from action

In many cases policies in action are developing first at the local level and then being adopted by states after the benefits to students are demonstrated at the local level. For example, the Colorado 2000 project is being lauded as such a grass-roots phenomenon. Also, some innovative policies are being developed jointly by the state and a local district. The Volissia County Public Schools and the State of Florida launched a program under which students can obtain health insurance through a private insurer for under $60 per month (Soroham 1992).

The San Diego school system and partnership agencies began a program called New Beginnings. This program began at an elementary school with many 'high risk' families. The program was founded to provide integrated services to the community surrounding the school. The nucleus of the program's participants were the County of San Diego, the City of San Diego, the San Diego City Schools, and the San Diego Community College District. Other agencies have joined in the efforts as well. An initial report showed that 60% of the families at the school were involved with the County department of Social Services, the Probation Department, or the City Housing Commission. About 10% of the families were known to at least four programs with these agencies (Payzant 1992).

A comparison of the New Jersey and Kentucky policies

Major motivating factors are at work in the development of the full-service site. Budget, political, idealistic, and education factors interplay in the development of the full-service school. And though, as we have discussed, there has been no direct federal pressure, there has been in some states another key ingredient pushing for this type of reform: pressure from the courts. When New Jersey and Kentucky were both ordered to reform their education systems because of financial inequities among school districts the need for a variety of services for children and their families was addressed by the courts. New Jersey was ordered to reform its system with the *Abbott* v. *Burke* (1990) decision. Kentucky was ordered to reform following the *John A. Rose* v. *The Council for Better Education, Inc.* case (1989), in which the court actually set minimum standards for reform. In both decisions the need to reform broadly and to address the multiple needs of children were stressed (First and Miron 1991, Miron *et al.* 1992). The court pressure has resulted in state-wide attention to full-service schools in both states.

New Jersey

New Jersey's School Based Youth Services Program (SBYSP) began early in 1988 as the first statewide program of its kind in the nation. Each site provides the following core standards: health care, mental health and family counseling, job and employment training, and substance abuse services. Many sites also provide teen parenting education, transportation, day care, tutoring, family planning, and hotlines. All programs operate before, during, after school, and during the summer. Some programs are even open on the weekend.

The New Jersey plan was developed through collaboration and cooperation of the state departments of Education, Health, Human Services, Higher Education, Community Affairs, Labor, State, the Office of the Attorney General, and the Office of the Governor. These state agencies worked together to plan and develop the minimum standards and minimum service requirements for SBYSP. The planning began at a state conference which was attended by over 400 social service providers, and representatives from higher education and community groups as well as K–12 educators. Regional teams were then formed, followed by an interagency collaboration committee. Regional teams work with districts to meet specified needs.

Schools in the New Jersey plan are funded through grants ($250,000 maximum per year in the early 1990s). Communities must contribute a minimum of 25% either in direct funding or 'in kind' services and materials. (For a district in severe financial difficulties the percentage may be reduced.) To be eligible for the grant each applicant (or school) must demonstrate representation of a broad coalition of local nonprofit and public agencies. Applications must be filled jointly by the school district and one or more public or nonprofit agency. The Department of Human Services will contribute $6 million per year in state funds to establish 30 school-based programs. There will be at least one site per county. These funds may only be used to expand the current level of services, not substituted for services already offered (Altman 1991).

Kentucky

The Kentucky plan sets up a system of service provision very similar to the plan in New Jersey. The Family Resource Centers must include these minimum core components: full-time preschool child care, after-school child care (full day if schools are closed), parent and child education, support and training for day-care workers, and health services, referral to health services, employment services, summer and part-time job development, drug and alcohol abuse counseling, and family crisis and mental health counseling. A local needs assessment was mandated to identify needs and to identify resources for services to meet those needs.

Kentucky has established an interagency task force to oversee the operations of Family Resource Centers in the public schools. The 16 members are appointed by the Governor, one each from a spectrum of state agencies. The task force monitors implementation until December 31, 1995 when it will cease to exist. Each school site that maintains a Family Resource Center must also establish a local advisory board to collect needs assessment data, receive funds from and submit reports to the state interagency task force.

The Kentucky plan, while very similar to the New Jersey system, is much more specific in its requirements. For example, in Kentucky for schools to receive state grants for the service centers, at least 20% of that school's population must be eligible for free lunch. However, this requirement may be a reflection of the state economic situation, in that most schools can qualify for funding (Kentucky State Department of Education 1991).

Analysis of the strength of the state role

We have compared these programs on the basis of four general categories: funding requirements, actors involved, timetables for implementation, and data collection required. As did First and Cooper (1990), the authors assumed that a stronger state role would lead to a stronger commitment to solving the problem – here providing muliple services to students at the local level. Under each of the four categories the scale ratings range from very committed (3) to no commitment (0). The following scale was used to evaluate programs:

I. Funding Requirements: the funding requirements category speaks to the notion of what must be done for the site to continue to receive funding for the full service program.

0. Funding requirements do not exist.
1. Funding requirements do exist but are not stated in statute.
2. Funding requirements are clearly laid out in statute. Districts are informed of all application deadlines, but penalties were not stated in the statue.
3. Funding requirements are clearly laid out in statute. Districts were informed of all application deadlines. Districts were informed of the penalties of noncompliance with regulations.

II. Actors: this category addresses not only the number of actors involved but the variety of actors involved (i.e., not just legislators and state department personnel).

0. Legislators were the only actors.
1. Actors were limited to legislators and various state departments.
2. A smaller variety of actors excluding community members, parents, and business people.
3. A wide variety of actors including legislators, various state departments, school administrators, teachers, community members, parents, and business people.

III. Timetables Provided

0. No deadlines exist.
1. Deadlines were not addressed but do exist.
2. Districts were informed of the implementation deadlines but not the penalties for noncompliance.
3. Districts were informed of the implementation deadlines and the penalties for noncompliance.

IV. Data Collection

0. Data collection did not take place.
1. Evidence of data collection prior to writing of legislation. No data collection requirements for local districts.
2. Evidence of data collection prior to writing of legislation. Data collection required either before local districts begin programs or data collection required for reporting purposes.
3. Evidence of data collection prior to writing of legislation. Data collection is required before local districts begin programs. Data collection is required for reporting purposes each year.

Comparison of New Jersey and Kentucky

Using the categories and criteria listed above, both programs were analyzed. Table 1 summarizes these results, showing, with a score in the above four categories as well as a total score and a mean score, that these two state initiatives are indeed similar in terms of strong state role.

If this indicates, as it did in a similar study of state plans for homeless children (First and Cooper 1990), a greater likelihood of commitment to solving the problem, positive results may be seen long term in New Jersey's and Kentucky's full-service school

Table 1. Analysis of functioning integrated service programs

State	Funding requirements	Actors	Timetables	Data collection	Total	Mean
KY	3	3	3	3	12	3.0
NJ	2	3	3	3	11	2.75

movement. Interestingly, in the 50-state study of state plans for homeless children, the states showing the strongest state role over a variety of criteria were states where the issue was forced by court action. As mentioned, court action was the motivating force behind the New Jersey and Kentucky full-service school movements.

It is important to remember that a variety of social services are provided in the schools across the states whether or not an identifiable full-service schools movement has arisen in any particular state. In table 2 a checklist is displayed showing which types of service integration are currently underway in the states. A check [tick] indicates that a collaborative effort of some kind is taking place, which includes schools in providing this kind of service. The service may be provided at some school sites or the schools may only be brokering information to students and their families. The range and depth of the offered services also varies considerably. This list is not comprehensive, but it does provide an interesting snapshot of the scattered nature of the full-service reform movement.

Table 2. Checklist of services existing in each state

	Health	Mental health	Parenting skills and education	Family support services	Social services	Business community partnerships	Parent involvement	Teen pregnancy	Volunteers used	Preschool daycare
Alabama						✓	✓			
Alaska	✓		✓							
Arizona			✓				✓			
Arkansas					✓				✓	
California	✓	✓	✓		✓	✓	✓			
Colorado	✓		✓	✓	✓	✓	✓			✓
Connecticut			✓	✓	✓					✓
Delaware							✓			
District of Columbia			✓				✓		✓	
Florida	✓		✓		✓		✓			✓
Georgia			✓	✓						
Hawaii		✓	✓	✓		✓	✓			✓
Idaho		✓	✓	✓			✓			
Illinois	✓		✓	✓		✓	✓	✓		✓
Indiana	✓			✓	✓		✓			
Iowa	✓	✓	✓		✓	✓	✓			✓
Kansas			✓		✓		✓			
Kentucky	✓		✓	✓	✓					✓
Louisiana			✓				✓			

Table 2. Continued

	Health	Mental health	Parenting skills and education	Family support services	Social services	Business community partnerships	Parent involvement	Teen pregnancy	Volunteers used	Preschool daycare
Maine	✓					✓				✓
Maryland	✓	✓	✓	✓	✓	✓	✓	✓	✓	
Massachusetts			✓	✓	✓	✓	✓			
Michigan	✓		✓		✓	✓	✓			
Minnesota	✓		✓	✓	✓	✓		✓		✓
Mississippi										
Missouri	✓	✓	✓	✓	✓					✓
Montana										
Nebraska	✓	✓		✓	✓	✓				
Nevada	✓*				✓					
New Hampshire				✓						
New Jersey	✓	✓	✓	✓	✓	✓	✓	✓		
New Mexico		✓			✓		✓			
New York	✓		✓	✓	✓	✓	✓	✓		✓
North Carolina			✓			✓				✓
North Dakota				✓			✓			
Ohio	✓		✓	✓						✓
Oklahoma							✓			
Oregon	✓		✓		✓		✓			✓
Pennsylvania				✓	✓	✓	✓			
Rhode Island					✓		✓		✓	✓
South Carolina			✓		✓	✓	✓		✓	
South Dakota										
Tennesee			✓			✓	✓		✓	
Texas	✓	✓	✓	✓	✓	✓	✓			✓
Utah							✓			
Vermont			✓			✓	✓		✓	✓
Virgin Islands			✓				✓			
Virginia										
Washington										
West Virginia	✓		✓	✓	✓		✓			✓
Wisconsin	✓		✓	✓	✓		✓		✓	
Wyoming						✓				

Source: Compiled from the Kentucky *Interagency Task Force State Implementation Plan* (1991) and the National Governor's Association Report: *From Rhetoric to Action* (1991).

Conclusion

As the needs of students continue to increase, schools will need to come into a leadership role in service provision for students and their families. Students will continue to come to school with a wide array of problems and needs. Just as special education students had the

Education for All Handicapped Children Act in the 1970s, and homeless students had the McKinney Act in the 1980s, perhaps students in general will have in the 1990s a full-service school act to assure them of the education that is their right. In the meantime educational practitioners can shape meaningful educational change through their own actions. These actions can influence the policy development processes. 'In fact, bottom-up educational reform may be the most appropriate way in which meaningful educational change can eventuate' (St John, 1992: 98). In the full-service school movement practice may continue to lead policy rather than the reverse. If that is so the government's role at both the state and federal level will need to shift from control to facilitation. Officials will need to find more ways to foster and encourage bottom-up reforms, rather than trying to change the system with stricter controls from above.

In 1988 Mitchell described a reconceptualization of policy making as a process with several distinct phases: articulation, aggregation, allocation, regulation, implementation, and evaluation. The need for new ways to serve children and families has been long and well articulated (Edelman 1992, Davis and McCall 1990). The full-service school movement is at the stage of aggregation, both within states and across states. The process taking place is the aggregation of issues and the aggregation of interested parties into broad-based coalitions of support.

Some states, such as New Jersey and Kentucky, are already slipping into the allocation stage. The allocation of power and resources is taking place, but more important for the full-service schools movement will be the 'allocation of values' (Easton 1965). At the regulation stage, full-service schools will encounter a problem which has significantly slowed many reforms and which is especially problematic for full-service schools because of the complex web of relationships which makes them possible. 'Responsibility for regulation writing and the development of detailed organizational plans is frequently given to departmental functionaries who have been socialized to a bureaucratic world view alien to those who must implement the policy' (Mitchell 1988: 463).

Nationwide implementation has barely begun in the full-service school movement and it is too soon for meaningful evaluation of the only outcome which will ultimately matter, beneficial changes in the lives of children and their families. We fear that evaluation will be too demanding and will be done too soon. We raise our voices with those who ask for time for the meaningful development of this promising reform movement and patience in the quest for 'fair data' to substantiate meaningful results. Full-service schools need time to make a difference. They also need support, but not constant manipulating, probing and tinkering.

'The school reform movement is peopled at one extreme by hyperrationalists who believe that schools are infinitely manipulatable, and at the other extreme by romantic decentralizers who believe that if left alone schools will flourish' (Timar and Kirp 1988: 75). Both groups will be attacking full-service schools. But if given enough time, these new school configurations have the promise of making meaningful change in children's lives and less importantly, but certainly of interest, they may be a significant example of changes in the policy development process which should be closely studied.

References

ABBOTT V. *BURKE*, 575 A. 2d 359 (NJ 1990).

ALTMAN, D. (1991) *School Based Youth Services Program: Program Description* (Trenton, NJ: State of New Jersey Department Human Services).

BAYBROOKE, D. and LINDBLOM, C. E. (1963) *A Strategy of Decision: Policy Evaluation as a Social Process* (New York: Free Press).

DAVIS, W. E. and MCCALL, E. J. (1990) *At-risk Children and Youth: A Crisis in our Schools and Society* (Orono: Institute for the Study of At-Risk Students, University of Maine).

EASTON, D. (1965) *A Systems Analysis of Political Life* (New York: Wiley).

EDELMAN, M. W. (1992) *The Measure of our Success: A Letter to My Children and Yours* (Boston: Beacon Press).

ETZIONI, A. (1993) *The Spirit of Community: Rights, Responsibilities and the Communitarian Agenda* (New York: Crown).

FIRST, P. F. and COOPER, G. R. (1990) 'The McKinney Homeless Assistance Act: Evaluating the response of the states', *Education Law Reporter*, 60, pp. 1047–1060.

FIRST, P. and MIRON, L. (1991) 'The social construction of adequacy', *Journal of Law and Education*, 20(4), pp. 421–444.

GRAMLICK, E. M. (1981) *Benefit-cost Analysis of Government Programs* (Englewood Cliffs, NJ: Prentice Hall).

JOHN A. ROSE v. *THE COUNCIL FOR BETTER EDUCATION, INC.*, 790 S. W.2d 186 (KY 1989).

KENTUCKY STATE DEPARTMENT OF EDUCATION (1991) *Interagency Task Force State Implementation Plan* (Frankfort, KY: Author).

LINDBLOM, C. E. and COHEN, D. K. (1979) *Usable Knowledge: Social Science and Social Problem Solving* (New Haven, CT: Yale University Press).

MCLAUGHLIN, M. W. (1981) *State Involvement in Local Education Quality Issues: Interim Report Prepared for the Education Policy Development Center for Equal Educational Opportunity for Disadvantaged Children* (Santa Monica, CA: Rand).

MIRON, L., FIRST, P. and WIMPELBERG, R. (1992) 'Equity, adequacy and educational need: the courts and urban school finance', in J. Cibulka, R. Reed and K. Wong (eds) *The Politics of Urban Education in the United States: 1991 Politics of Education Yearbook* (New York: Falmer Press), pp. 181–193.

MISSOURI DEPARTMENT OF ELEMENTARY AND SECONDARY EDUCATION (1990) *Missourians Prepared* (Jefferson City, MO: Author).

MITCHELL, D. E. (1988). 'Educational politics and policy: the state level', in N. J. Boyan (ed.) *Handbook of Research on Educational Administration* (New York: Longman), pp. 453–466.

MITCHELL, D. E. and ENCARNATION, D. J. (1984, May) 'Alternative state policy mechanisms for controlling school performance', *Educational Researcher*, 13, pp. 4–11.

NATIONAL GOVERNOR'S ASSOCIATION (1991) *From Rhetoric to Action* (Washington, DC: Author).

OREGON STATE DEPARTMENT OF EDUCATION (1991) *Oregon Educational Act for the 21st Century* (Salem, OR: Author).

PAYZANT, T. (1992). 'New beginnings in San Diego: Developing a strategy for interagency collaboration', *Phi Delta Kappan*, 74(2), pp. 139–146.

SCHULTZ, G. E. (1968) *The Politics and Economics of Public Spending* (Washington, DC: Brookings Institution).

SOROHAM, E. (1992, March 31) 'Florida schools fill health gap for uninsured students', *Education Week*, pp. 1, 8.

ST JOHN, E. P. (1992) 'Who decides educational policy? Or how can the practitioner influence public choices?', in P. F. First (ed.) *Educational Policy for School Administrators* (Boston: Allyn and Bacon), pp. 96–103.

STONICH, P. J. (1977) *Zero-based Planning and Budgeting* (Homewood, IL: Dow Jones-Irwin).

TIMAR, T. B. and KIRP, D. L. (1988) 'State efforts to reform schools: treading between a regulatory swamp and an English garden', *Educational Evaluation and Policy Analysis*, 10(2), pp. 75–88.

US DEPARTMENT OF EDUCATION (1990) 'National education goals statement', (Washington, DC: Author).

WIRT, F. M. and KIRST, M. W. (1989) *Schools in Conflict*, 2nd edn. (Berkeley, CA: McCutchan).

POLITICS OF EDUCATION ASSOCIATION YEARBOOK, 1993, 75–91

Professional and institutional perspectives on interagency collaboration

Douglas E. Mitchell and Linda D. Scott

Changing public service economics and strong political support are stimulating a rapid expansion of collaboration between schools and other social service agencies. Available evidence indicates, however, that success in these new ventures will depend more on the development of appropriate institutional and professional cultures than on their fiscal or political appeal. Culture clash is the legacy of independent development among social service agencies. For more than a century, schools and other service agencies have been building their own unique institutional cultures and professional norms for defining and controlling staff work efforts. This chapter explores basic elements in the cultural systems of belief and expectation that empower, structure and stabilize existing social delivery systems. Through an examination of these cultural elements, we frame a basis for understanding how interagency collaboration might succeed in overcoming currently widespread problems of inefficiency and ineffectiveness in the way our society provides support to families and children.

A legacy of social and educational imperatives

The urgency of closing the gap between serious social problems and the organization of schools and other social service agencies is so painfully obvious that it has become headline material in the US daily newspapers. Before an effective response to these failures can be developed, however, it is important to diagnose their causes appropriately. The most serious problems are characteristically *systemic* in character, not *a priori* the result of personal failures on the part of teachers or other service agency staff workers. Once an organization stops working, it begins to encourage dull, routinized procedures, and individual staff efforts are hampered by the organizational structures within which they work. Problems we know how to treat are 'slipping between the tracks' of a system we do not know how to organize and manage.

Of course, individual staff workers vary widely in skill and dedication, but social service organizations are supposed to be designed to control the effects of individual staff differences. Program standards and supervision systems are supposed to catch individual failures and assure adequate attention to client needs. But contemporary service agencies appear incapable of compensating for the flaws of inept staff. Indeed, to many, they seem to be actually interfering with the performance of their most able workers. Still, systemic failures are not being engendered by violations of agency rules and norms or by the neglect of staff responsibilities. They are the result of the insensitivity of the systems themselves to the complexities of clients' actual life experiences and the holistic nature of client need. Solving agency problems becomes the driving force of agency management and organization. Once inside the system, the players lose sight of essential questions of

0268–0939/93 $10·00

deliberation; rules of evidence prevail (was the case 'proven'?), not the question 'Was justice obtained?'. Engagement in the logic of the system compels decisions rather than the logic of community need for the system. Los Angeles Mayor Tom Bradley expressed the problem clearly when he said of the verdict in the first Rodney King beating trial:

> Today, the *system* failed us. Today, this jury told the world what we saw with our own eyes wasn't a crime. Today, that jury asked us to accept the senseless and brutal beating of a helpless man. (*Riverside Press Enterprise* 1992: A1, emphasis added)

In this highly publicized case, we need to remind ourselves, the judicial system worked exactly as it is designed to work. It addressed the question: 'How much force can the police legitimately use to subdue a suspect?'. The logic of the system convinced the jury that the question was proper, the rules appropriately followed, and justice done. When the system was originally developed, the logic of the system worked. Yet this jury decision led to such a deep sense of alienation that it incited outrage and rioting.

At the heart of this tragedy lies the fact that our social system is not properly organized to answer deeper questions such as, 'How is it possible to make South Central Los Angeles a safe place to live?'. The primary issue is not excessive force but fractured communities and widespread alienation. People without a sense of place or participation in a community and who lack confidence in their ability to control their own lives lose their sense of compassion. They become vulnerable to fear and rage, strong passions that, demonstrably, have the power to rend the social fabric of civilized conduct and dissolve mutual tolerance and respect.

A legion of equally harrowing examples of systemic failure can be found across the full range of social service domains. These failures affect all economic classes and touch all cultural and ethnic groups. Moreover, the root causes of failures are not necessarily engendered primarily by political corruption or staff incompetence but spring largely from following the organizational design and service delivery logic that initially produced the greatest success.

Our social service systems achieved early successes by following the principles of *bureaucratic organization* and *scientific management*. Problems were identified as targets of action, specialized staff roles were created to focus resources and energy on the identified problems, and responsibility for various problems was distributed among staff specialists trained to apply sophisticated techniques to ameliorate or solve specific problems. Educators, psychologists, social workers, medical specialists and criminal justice workers divided the universe into problems and programs. As the system evolved, concern with problem definitions and service strategies gave way to an emphasis on qualifying clients and certifying needs. The result is a pulling apart of agency responsibilities and a fragmentation that weakens the power of specialization and destroys any sense of holistic support for families and children.

Operationally, the failures have two characteristics. First, clients cannot gain access to complex service bureaucracies because eligibility systems are preoccupied with statutory and regulatory specification of agency responsibilities rather than the clients' experienced needs. Second, service delivery strategies fail because they are based on responding to de-contextualized client 'problems' rather than on attacking the complex web of needs and conditions that have marginalized large numbers of families and children in contemporary society.

The links between initial success and ultimate failure are fairly easy to describe. Each agency develops logical service plans and assigns its own brand of professionals to work on identified problems or cases. Through statutory or resource constraints, agencies must limit the quantity and quality of services available to each client. But clients, already stressed by their needs, become so bewildered by staff specialization and agency regulations that they often do not even know how to seek services for which they could qualify. Their confusion about agency operations is further compounded by the existence of disparate physical service locations (with attendant transportation problems) and conflicts among service appointments and schedules. The result is a confusing array of inaccessible, ineffective, over-specialized and badly fragmented services. One juvenile judge describes the situation poignantly:

> You may have a 14-year-old girl who has been the victim of sexual abuse since the age of 9 who runs away from home. That makes her a child in need of supervision. She may steal clothing from a local merchant. That makes her a delinquent. Because she has been abused, she may suffer from emotional disorders – the jurisdiction of the Bureau of Mental Health. And because she's run away from home, she may be a charge on the welfare system. And, of course, she still needs to be educated. So here you have one child whose problems require the services of multiple agencies, sometimes even private agencies. Normally, the agencies themselves are not set up to address these multiple problems. (McGee 1991: 9)

One indicator of failure for educational, health, social service and justice systems is the effort they must devote to problem definition, eligibility certification and record keeping at the expense of actual service delivery. Increasingly, staff expertise is devoted to circumscribing agency responsibility, documenting compliance with regulations and protecting client rights. As a result, failing students, suspected criminals, drug addicts, welfare cheaters or incorrigible juveniles become mere 'cases' to be acted upon by appointed specialists: teachers, police, health care providers and social service case managers.

By focusing on defining and treating the problems that qualify a client for services, specialists develop a second indicator of systemic failure: the substitution of *specialization* for *professionalism*. By emphasizing targeted treatment of specific problems rather than energized emotional engagement with clients in need of help, agency staff can avoid their own sense of helplessness caused by client needs they cannot meet. Only if staff professionalism is characterized by *focused engagement* as well as skillful intervention will real needs be addressed. That is why failure among professional athletes is attributed to a loss of 'concentration' rather than a lack of skill. Professional work differs from skilled craft work by the fact that engaged concentration is required for success.

In the analysis that follows, we explore the proposition that interagency collaboration can relieve fragmentation and contain overspecialization only if three issues are properly addressed:

1. *professional* norms are developed to lift agency staff beyond skillful application of their expertise, focusing attention on the underlying character of client needs;
2. *inter-disciplinary* norms of professional cooperation are so sufficiently developed that they can guide consultation and decision making among professionals with different types of expertise; and
3. *institutional* norms and procedures are robust enough to guide both interagency case management and organizational resource allocation.

Analysis of these three culturally embedded aspects of service delivery provides a framework for evaluating the potential contributions of integrated social service delivery to improving overall support for families and children.

The development of new systems of service delivery, centered in schools and organized by educators has been widely touted as the best possible solution to systemic failures in social and educational service delivery. An early advocate of this approach was California's Committee for Policy Analysis for California Education (PACE 1989). Kirst and McLaughlin (1990) argue that a refashioning of children's services into a continuous and comprehensive system of care is needed to meet the needs of the current generation. Moreover, Kirst insists that under a new vision 'the school could become the site or broker of numerous services, such as health clinics, after-school child care, alcohol and drug abuse programs and organized recreation programs, although they need not be the only location of interagency collaboration' (Kirst 1990: 8). In such a collaborative model it is expected that narrow *problem-based* service delivery will be replaced by *neighborhood-based* comprehensive social programs. Within identified geographic regions – typically school attendance boundaries – health, welfare, education, criminal justice, recreation and other community services should be cooperatively planned and provided.

Empirical foundations: studies of professional and institutional norms

Three exploratory field studies conducted at University of California, Riverside, provide the empirical foundations for our analysis of the potential value of this type of interagency collaboration in overcoming contemporary social service delivery problems. Two studies examine the development of professional norms and cultures by teachers; the third examines the development of procedures and collaborative norms that emerge when educators undertake joint planning with other social service agency professionals.

Professional culture development is viewed from the vantage point of two different groups of teachers. The first is a cohort of new teachers who, during their first year on the job, reveal how individual professional norms are acquired (Goodlad 1990, Goodlad *et al.* 1990, Shulman 1986). The second is a group of experienced teachers involved in identifying, screening, supporting and eventually referring problem learners for assessment and assignment to special education. These experienced teachers demonstrate how well-established classroom teachers acquire collegial and inter-disciplinary norms for interacting with peer teachers and other professionals (psychologists, reading specialists, etc.), to define learning problems and plan service delivery. These two teacher groups illuminate critical tensions in the acquisition of professional norms and in the development of service delivery specialization that will have to be resolved in order for interagency collaboration to yield integrated service delivery.

The teacher studies

In 1988, compelled by recent statistics indicating that 30% of all new teachers leave the profession within the first two years, with another 10% leaving after three years, and over 50% leaving within five to seven years (California Commission on Teacher Credentialing 1992), California funded the 'California New Teacher Project' (CNTP). Over its three-year life span CNTP tested a variety of models for smoothing the entry of new teachers into the profession. One of these models, identified as an Extended University Supervision model, provided us with an opportunity to become participant-observers, facilitating new teacher socialization while we observed its development.

The Extended University Supervision model was based on the belief that, continuing into their first years on the job, the type of supervision given to preservice teacher candidates would substantially impact on new teachers' chances of successfully bridging the frequently devastating discontinuities between preservice teacher preparation programs and beginning teachers' experiences. This was accomplished by combining regular, on-site observations and structured interaction between first-year teachers and a university supervisor with a series of university-based seminars addressing their early problems of practice.

Data from this project include richly textured critical incident journals and self-reports from 12 first-year elementary-level teachers. The critical incident journal entries focused teachers' reflective attention on the 'what and why' of classroom-based problems and dilemmas. During the university seminars, small-group discussions helped new teachers develop skills in critical analysis, acquire heuristics for problem solving, and deliberate action applied to practice, and also encouraged collegiality and peer networking. The processes by which new teachers identify and acquire professional norms emerge from these data.

Our second field study of teacher professionalism was part of a three-year California Department of Education feasibility study. Aimed at validating a conceptual framework for describing how teachers handle the learning problems of ethno-linguistically diverse students, the study focuses on the critical period between initial identification of students with learning problems and their eventual referral for assessment as potential candidates for special education placement (Powell *et al.* 1991).

We conducted field observations of teachers and school-based Child Study Teams (CSTs) at two of the ten schools participating in this study and had access to data collected in the other schools. We observed and documented the work of 27 teachers and a number of parents, administrators, school psychologists, health care providers, special education teachers, resource teachers, officers of the court and appropriate other professionals. We occasionally observed, and comprehensively reviewed, the work of the school's CSTs to document how they defined learning problems, planned interventions and provided services for children and their families. During this process, the teacher and the CST relied on a variety of disciplinary specialties: educational, administrative, legal, psychological and medical, to identify student strengths and needs, plan interventions and develop techniques for monitoring progress.

The institutional study

Analytically distinct, but closely linked to the development of professional norms and practices, institutional structures and cultures also determine how interagency collaboration will develop in the schools (Kirst 1990, 1991, Kirst and McLaughlin 1990, Pollard 1990). Data guiding our analysis of the institutional context of collaboration came from a pilot study of experiences with California Healthy Start program planners who reveal the extent to which initial collaboration efforts demand patience, ingenuity and near-heroic staff efforts to overcome established norms and service definitions.

Healthy Start had its origins in 1992 when California adopted Senate Bill 620, legislation aimed at encouraging collaboration among a broad range of local agencies responsible for providing social services to families and children. Local school districts serve as the lead agencies in the development of integrated service *centers*. These centers are to bring into neighborhoods with large numbers of at-risk children direct access to various service delivery combinations of special education, social welfare, public health, mental health, juvenile justice, parks and recreation and other publicly and privately supported services. In most localities, 1992–93 was a planning year with coordinated services delivery to begin in 1993. For a small number of sites, operational grants of about a third of a million dollars per year began in 1992.

In one Southern California county having these school-based planning grants, an Executive Council for Children and Families has emerged in parallel with the 'Healthy

Start' grants program. This Executive Council consists of senior agency officials from a broad range of public and private groups who are expected to participate in the creation and operation of Healthy Start Centers. This council has been seeking advice about how to develop an appropriate monitoring and data system capable of documenting service needs and tracking delivery in order to document agency responsiveness and cost-effectiveness. We have participated in the planning processes with five local school districts (who have been designing three service centers) and tracking the activities of the Executive Council group. Our primary data sources are located within the county office of education which is providing staff coordination and support to both of these ventures. Additionally, we have had access to proposal and planning documents as well as contact with more than three dozen district and agency staff.

Our data collection and analysis in this study have focused on the motivations and strategies of the participating agencies. How, we have asked, do school districts expect to secure the attention and cooperation of other agencies? What are the motives of agency executives regarding collaboration? What are the implications for: need identification, case management, staff assignment, agency budgeting and allocation of public or private recognition of responsibilities? As described more fully below, this study provides basic insights and opens up critical questions about what can be expected when traditionally autonomous agencies with staff drawn from different social disciplines undertake to replace problem-based service planning with a neighborhood-based conception of their mission and tasks.

Theoretically, these data are interpreted from an institutional (as distinguished from an organizational) perspective. That is, our focus is on how the development of shared task conceptions, institutional norms, conceptual presuppositions and institutional rituals create and sustains structural patterns of interaction and reinforces particular programs and policies.

Novice professionals: acquiring norms

Data from the Extended Supervision Model of the CNTP illuminate the first prerequisite of successful collaboration, the development of individual professional norms. As Goodlad *et al.* (1990) note, professionalism 'describes the quality of a practice; it describes conduct within an occupation – how members integrate their obligations with their knowledge and skill in a context of collegiality and contractual and ethical relations with clients' (p. 226). This type of individual professionalism is not produced during preservice teacher training. It is brought into focus for the novice professional only when the 'baptism by fire' of regular classroom teaching responsibility is confronted on a daily basis. Anticipation of full professional responsibility does not give the novice teacher a full understanding of the context of his or her work. Moreover, 'Socialization into teaching is largely self-socialization; one's personal predispositions are not only relevant, but, in fact, stand at the core of becoming a teacher' (Goodlad *et al.* 1990: 244). Thus, novice teachers acquire professional norms only by finding ways of incorporating their personal aspirations and beliefs into the skillful practice of their craft knowledge.

Among the novice teachers we observed, professional work norms emerged as they reacted to initial feelings of inadequacy, lack of confidence and low self-esteem. These negative feelings are intense, sometimes overwhelming, during the early months of the school year. There is a painful newness to every experience, compounded by fear of the unknown, feelings of helplessness, and personal problems such as illness and homesickness.

In this context, interagency collaboration, even meaningful cooperation with other professionals, is beyond the reach of the new teacher. A kindergarten teacher sums up the novice's plight,

> I feel I cannot go to my principal or other more experienced teachers for help because I am afraid they will interpret it as weakness or, worse, incompetence. I learned this very quickly during the first few weeks of school.

Novice teachers are expected to be able to control and manage a classroom effectively and productively, that is, to develop for themselves those habits of mind and action characteristic of effective veteran teachers. Though they are frequently given the least desirable teaching assignments (large classes and culturally, linguistically or academically diverse students) novice teachers are expected to equate professionalism with personal success and to accept their initial feelings of inadequacy, isolation and helplessness as the standard context for induction into the profession. Not surprisingly, therefore, new teachers often become demoralized and dispirited, anxious about their own efficacy, personal character and capacity to cope with work responsibilities.

For the neophyte, professional norms can present themselves as marked land mines, not guides to professional practice. Why? In framing an answer we are reminded that the primary mission of schools is program delivery. The first study displays the evolution of professionalism in terms of programmatic focus and empowerment: new teachers must focus on learning the educational program and becoming empowered to deliver it to students. Like an initiation rite, this tumultuous period forces new teachers to attend to strategizing; failure to strategize equates with a failure of professionalism. Novices must somehow strike a delicate balance between strategizing the application of teaching techniques and depersonalizing their students in order to meet the most elemental demands of their work – to teach the class of children before them. Driving that need for balance are feelings of isolation and helplessness.

The novice teachers we worked with acquired their professional norms through the twin cultural processes of 'typification' and 'thematization' (Schutz 1967). Typification refers to the ways in which objects, persons and events are characterized as good or bad, important or trivial, relevant or irrelevant. Typification is the process by which instructional programs, work-role responsibilities, learning problems, test results, and the countless other details of teaching and learning take on conceptual meaning and become the objects of thought and action. Through typification, teachers develop a frame of reference for classifying problems and opportunities for action. The typification of instruction enables lesson plans to be distinguished from inter-office memoranda and text-books from other types of reading material. Typification distinguishes classroom lessons from teachers' 'lounge talk'. Typification tells new teachers 'the way things are' and signals how they will be evaluated. Typification of responsibilities, for example, says that sending more than three students at a time to the principal's office constitutes a crisis. Typification defines the taken-for-granted roles that explain what a teacher is supposed to do all day.

Whereas cultural typification populates the teachers' world with understandable processes and events and provides a basis for action upon that world, it is the companion process – *thematization* – that links sequences of events into a meaningful story of action, responsibility and purpose. This thematic structure gives action historical significance at both the personal and social levels. Schooling can be construed as a time of nurture and preparation or as an arena for testing and scoring. Teaching can be given instructional delivery or child sponsorship themes. Whereas typification tells the new teacher 'what things are', thematization tells 'how they work' and 'what they are for'. For the new teacher identifying work themes that elicit professional responsibility without overwhelming personal capacity is a critical developmental task. One young teacher confronted with a child abuse situation reported there was 'really no problem' with the procedures for reporting child abuse, but that there was great difficulty with 'the emotions it brings along. How do you get over the feeling of helplessness here?'

Confusion over idealized perceptions of the teaching role and anger over a sense of betrayal brought on by the dissonance between the 'real' and the 'ideal' interpretations of teaching life were not unusual among novices. Toward the end of the year, however, many of the novices began to work their way out of the first-year turmoil in positive ways. Work themes are recast in more limited and more connected ways. They report improved ability to get predictable results and learn to see themselves as 'not the only person responsible for the well-being of the child'.

Since it takes a long time to develop effective typification and thematization of teaching work, novice teachers cannot be expected to participate effectively in the joint planning and decision making required for interprofessional or interagency collaboration. Novice teachers' survival depends on their ability to meet the primary mission of the school – program delivery – and that struggle for survival demands all of their professional time, energy and focus.

Experienced professionals: interdisciplinary cooperation norms

While work with new teachers illuminates the acquisition of individual norms of professionalism, our study of special education pre-referral interventions shows how experienced teachers develop cooperative norms for working with other professionals. Once teachers have mastered the complexities of classroom management and educational program implementation, they are able to recognize the importance of innovative problem solving for hard-to-teach children. Interdisciplinary cooperation emerges as teachers are able to differentiate between their own capabilities and the special needs of various children. Until they can objectify problems and distinguish special cases from ordinary instructional problem solving, they cannot develop mechanisms for cooperative diagnosis and service delivery.

Our experiences gained from observing Child Study Teams (CSTs) as they interpret needs and plan special support services revealed that individually competent teachers still need to learn cooperative ways of typifying special problems and thematizing response strategies. Substantial cooperative experience is needed before common knowledge bases and cooperative problem-solving heuristics can be developed to allow for communication across professional language systems. As common heuristics develop, communication networks become institutionalized in the schools. These networks serve to coordinate problem attacks, define case management strategies and support the matching of problems with solutions. Within this context of interdisciplinary professional cooperation, special service problems elicit shared definitions and treatment plans.

Within the CST context, experienced professional teachers regularly interacted with parents, school-based resource teachers, school principals, psychologists and other professionals. While experienced teachers often provided their own response strategies, they also relied on the CSTs to identify and recommend an array of informal strategies for ameliorating the problems of the identified students and their families. These informal strategies frequently eliminated the need for formal referral and placement in special education.

In brief, the Child Study Team process displays the following form:

1. a teacher identifies a student with learning problems and refers the student to the school resource teacher who, in turn, notifies parents;
2. after an informal conference with the parents, the resource teacher may recommend that the student be returned to the classroom with a suggested list of interventions and an appropriate plan for monitoring developments;
3. if these interventions are successful, no further action is necessary, otherwise,
4. the CST takes up the case and determines whether to refer for formal special education assessment or develop a program of alternative responses,
5. if alternatives are developed and are successful, no further action is necessary, otherwise,
6. the CST reconsiders the case and makes a formal referral to district psychological services for assessment and placement.

Among experienced teachers the Child Study Team process was found to be a reasonably effective mechanism for cooperative identification of student learning problems and planning of appropriate interventions and services. Three aspects of the CST process stand out as central to its success. First, team members accept children's learning problems as subtle, complex and not amenable to easy diagnosis or formula-based treatment. Until formal evaluation for special education program placement is undertaken, solutions are seen as pragmatic adjustments based on professional judgment rather than technical diagnoses derived from formal tests and measurements. Second, service planning is seen as a matter of selecting from a repertoire of possible options, a repertoire that has been developed through professional experience with similar cases more than through theoretical analysis or research on the etiology or character of the learning problems being reviewed. Third, decisions are made as classroom teachers and other professionals develop shared language and a common vocabulary for classifying problems and service options. Taken together, these three features of CST decision making define the professional context of interdisciplinary cooperation.

The critical place of shared language in collaboration

Shared language is critical to collaborative success because rightful authority depends on language. This was vividly illustrated for us by a verbal engagement in the teachers' lounge between the CST coordinator and a classroom teacher. The classroom teacher announced to other teachers that she was frustrated with a student's behavior and progress and that he appeared to be 'so stupid I don't know what to do with him'. Immediately, the coordinator sternly corrected her publicly by saying 'We don't talk about these problems in that way. Please see me in my office today during your planning period.' Where common descriptive language fails, decisions lose their cooperative tone and begin to hinge on power relationships among team members.

The exceptional case: the dysfunctional school

Among the special education pre-referral study schools there was one notable exception to the generalization that experienced teachers are able to work productively in the interdisciplinary Child Study Team context. In this one school, interdisciplinary cooperation was woefully inadequate to the task of addressing children's learning difficulties. Over more than a year of observations, members of the research team working in this school judged it to be undergoing a dysfunctional systemic breakdown. The most obvious manifestation of this breakdown is the fact that substantially more than half the population of this school of nearly 1000 students was referred to Child Study Teams for consultation, and 50% of these were formally referred for special education assessment and placement. The field researcher sums up the situation observed in the school:

> Teachers are not only frustrated but overwhelmed by insufficient school administration, displacement of teachers, poor leadership from the principal and the politics of the school district. Most of the children cannot read and all academic measures are far below grade levels. When you combine the horrors of family and community life for most of these children with the school's inadequate 'babysitting' services, you get a situation that will, no doubt, produce complete rebellion among students, staff, administration and the community.

Within the context of this dysfunctional school, interdisciplinary cooperation has largely broken down. When 50% of the school population is being referred for special education services, it becomes clear that a process designed for problem solving and alternative service development for marginal students cannot produce either the quantity or the quality of services needed to replace the failed mainstream program. Again, the field researcher summarizes:

> The real issue is the chasm between the actual life experiences and backgrounds kids bring to school and what the schools are prepared to deliver based on unrealistic institutional expectations and inadequate resources. In these cases, the whole school needs to be restructured.

Interdisciplinary cooperation, no matter how expert it might be, cannot solve systemic breakdowns. It is a short step from this observation to the realization that interagency collaboration efforts are doomed to failure if they are merely 'pasted on' to an existing system which is failing to establish professional control over basic school program implementation.

The test case for interagency collaboration is the dysfunctional school. The CST is built on the premise that it works to solve the problems of a small number of children. However, when this number reaches a critical mass of the school population, the CST no longer treats cases that are exceptions to the rule. When problems become too large for the school to manage, interagency collaboration is needed. Yet, unless interagency collaboration systems provide mechanisms for reforming the core program of the public schools, they will likely become as hollow and resource-wasteful as the Child Study Teams have become at this dysfunctional school.

Moving back to the context of a non-dysfunctional school, Child Study Teams typically provide marginal support to a fraction of the school population. We see the shape and character of this marginal support for problem learners in that CST processes are not integrated into the induction and socialization of new teachers. When novice teachers in the California New Teacher Project were interviewed about their access to the Child Study Team process, all reported that they had begun the year without any orientation to how these special problem-solving processes are expected to work. Moreover, this lack of explicit orientation to the process continued throughout the first year. As a result, these new teachers had no way of accessing assistance for hard-to-teach students. They were reluctant to seek assistance, and lacked a language system for identifying problems that would be considered appropriate for consultation, even if they did figure out for themselves how the referral system operates. This situation helped to reinforce the novice teachers' belief that program implementation rather than individual student problem solving was their primary responsibility.

Professionalism expressed through interagency collaboration

To this point attention has been focused on how novice teachers acquire their own craft skills and norms of professional practice and then move on to develop interdisciplinary cooperation norms through working with other specialized school staff. In this section we turn to the problems of interagency collaboration requiring educators to cross institutional boundaries and generate an integrated approach to the needs of children and families. Involvement with California Healthy Start planners helped us identify six broad shifts in professional perspective that educators are likely to undergo in reaching out to work with other agency professionals. Similarly, our review of the organizational assumptions and operational concerns of a countywide Executive Council for Families and Children illuminated both the motives for their energetic support for interagency collaboration and the benefits for their own agency functioning that they expect to get through involvement with the schools.

Planning lessons

Observation of the Healthy Start program planners yielded six lessons about shifts in professional perspectives that are needed to support interagency collaboration.

1. Service planning begins with identification of a geographic region for service responsibility: Local educators recognize easily and immediately that the distinctive feature of school organization is its division of communities into school catchment areas with a separate school facility serving all families living within each attendance boundary. The use of catchment areas to frame the process of interagency collaboration provides an intuitively sensible basis for planning and organization. Frequently school planners decide to identify areas larger than that served by a single elementary school. When this occurs, however, they generally think in terms of combining multiple elementary schools, or selecting a secondary school attendance boundary to define their service region. In one case we studied, schools combined elementary school catchment areas from two adjacent districts.

Thinking geographically, educators can easily imagine comprehensive and integrated service delivery systems. A population is circumscribed, and the process of needs identification and service planning quickly takes on a tone of practical enumeration and organization. Other geographically organized agencies – churches, community centers, neighborhood groups, PTAs, etc. – are easily enlisted in the job of identifying needs. Additionally, the groups we worked with were genuinely excited about the prospects of using a computer-based geographical information system to cull potential need indicators from census data, school attendance rosters and the service data systems of collaborating agencies.

2. Schools enter the discussion of collaborative service delivery by undertaking a comprehensive assessment of the needs of families and children living within the identified service boundary: Where other social service agencies tend to define service needs in terms of the frequency with which problems covered by their statutory mandates are reported to various agency staff, educators easily grasp the concept of systematically scanning the entire population within their service region. Earlier experience with the special education 'search and serve' mandate of Public Law 94-142 has sensitized school planners to the possibility that many needy cases are not brought to anyone's attention. For this reason, educators seek to develop an 'intelligence network' to provide needs assessments. Teachers are surveyed, students are questioned about themselves and their families, and community leaders are asked to bring forth potential service needs. Some of the educators we worked with even planned house-to-house surveys of need.

This geographic approach has its shortcomings, to be sure. It is difficult to identify confidently the *most* needy neighborhoods for service; staff and historical factors easily dominate the selection of a specific area for concentration. Moreover, severe needs in areas with only a few cases are ignored as schools concentrate on high-incidence catchment areas.

3. In addition to funds channelled through schools by state policy, local schools provide resources to the collaborative venture in the form of a physical facility that can serve as a coordination and delivery center used by all of the collaborating agencies: Educators have a generally positive appraisal of collaborative efforts with other social agencies and assume these agencies have the most appropriate staff expertise and more adequate resources for handling non-academic student and family needs. As a result, they approach the planning process as a matter of identifying social service needs and facilitating the work of other agency staff in meeting the identified needs. Not surprisingly, therefore, they see creation of a physical center – a place where client conferences, small group meetings and delivery of such direct services as dental screening or immunization can take place – as their primary contribution to the collaborative process.

Close behind the physical facility comes educator belief that client advocacy, i.e., securing access to remote or unresponsive agencies, is a school responsibility. Educators are easily convinced that they have daily encounters with problems to which other agencies can and should respond. They have a tendency to believe that services are not provided because clients do not know that they are eligible or do not know how to get access to the agencies. A major exception to the generally positive appraisal of agency sensitivity and responsibility is the tendency for educators to believe that Child Protective Services are unwilling to act aggressively to protect children from abuse and neglect. If there is a general complaint, it is that most social service agencies act too slowly and then act too disruptively, creating a lot of unnecessary psychological pain and suffering for clients.

The physical center creation sought by California's Healthy Start program is seen by school people as a thoroughly promising response to characteristic social service delivery problems. Access can be guaranteed by school staff. Agency sensitivity to client needs can be monitored and, where necessary, improved. Above all, agency staff will be encouraged to see children and neighborhoods just as educators see them, as holistic systems rather than compartmentalized problems. The expected result: shared definitions of need and common priorities for responding.

4. Real collaboration begins when cooperating service agencies are prepared to identify and assign staff to the school center: Up to this point one may begin to wonder why schools have not initiated and advocated interagency collaboration more aggressively in the past. If all it takes to get services is to identify needs, create a center and advocate coordinated delivery of services, schools would long ago have developed interagency systems. What has been missing, of course, has been the willingness of other agencies to assign staff to school sites and to use school-based needs identification as the mechanism for setting service priorities.

There are notable exceptions to this generalization. In many communities police departments have assigned officers to work on school campuses. Also, school communication networks have been used to solicit participation in health and recreation programs. Occasionally, school sites have also been used to house clinics for family and health services. The development of broad-based systematic interagency collaboration begins in earnest, however, only when agency staff are explicitly assigned to work within a school neighborhood and need to develop their work agenda in cooperation with school staff. Three forces have made this prospect more attractive to a variety of service agencies in recent years. First, the agencies have become painfully aware of the extent to which problems converge in a single family and are exacerbated by neighborhood factors. Thus, there is a desire to develop joint planning and case management strategies. Second, many agency staff have come to recognize that intake screening helps exacerbate the very problems the agency services are intended to ameliorate. Forcing clients to prove they are destitute and helpless reinforces feelings of inadequacy and hopelessness. Finally, with tight public service budgets, traditional problem-focused service planning systems are proving too weak to raise overall neighborhood functioning. As a result, agencies are finding that the service needs are growing faster than agencies can solve them.

For these reasons, and encouraged by the broader political climate, agencies are now prepared to assign staff and begin collaborating with each other as well as with the schools. Significant collaboration begins when the staff are reassigned from traditional case and service responsibilities. Only then are significant resources made available to respond to neighborhood needs.

5. The first serious planning problem arises when collaborating agencies confront the need to develop an integrated case management system capable of both documenting a match between client need and service delivery and guiding decision making by service professionals as they plan needed interventions: Case management is the bedrock of improved social service delivery. Unless agencies agree to share information and rely on each other for coordination of services, there is little prospect that interagency planning will lead to more efficient or effective service delivery. There are three barriers to be overcome, however. First, since schools are program rather than case structured, educators tend to believe that each child or family should be looked at afresh every time there is a change in staff responsibility. As a result, school records are not closely studied, and many educators have little confidence that file data are a reliable measure of need. Second, case-oriented agencies tend to use case assignment as the primary basis for staff job definition. This means that expanding case responsibility becomes a work-load issue and that removing cases from staff members can easily threaten their sense of professionalism. Moreover, among case-oriented agencies, staff can easily believe that narrow case specialization is the best route to efficient service delivery. Finally, confidentiality regulations and norms make it difficult to share data on the most complex and difficult cases.

Educators are having to learn that there are two distinct levels of case management: 'brokering' and 'intensive.' At the first level, case conferences are confined to allocating responsibility and resources. Only at the intensive level do staff actually discuss the particulars of case histories, diagnoses and treatment strategies. It is this second type of conference that is protected by privacy regulations, and it remains to be seen how fully brokerage case management can operate if some staff are not eligible to know about diagnosis and treatment details.

6. Long-term comprehensive integration is possible only if planners are able to develop meaningful assessments of service impact: For the foreseeable future, interagency collaboration is going to require more complex and more expansive staff work by all of the professionals involved. Hence, if confidence in the virtue of this approach toward supporting families, children and neighborhoods is to be maintained, it will have to be on the basis of believable documentation that the effort has paid off in enhanced living conditions and improved life chances for those served. Such data will be hard to produce and will easily invite 'client shopping' to reach the easily helped or definition revision to make last year's failures this year's successes. Additionally, documentation is likely to compete for scarce resources with service delivery efforts and could threaten cooperation by unacceptably reducing overall system efficiency.

Executive Council lessons

From our work with the countywide Executive Council for Families and Children, two additional lessons serve to guide our thinking about the development or permanent service integration.

1. Resources: First, beyond the allocation of special incentive or start-up funds, resources can be garnered for collaborative work through one or more of three basic mechanisms: (a) identifying and eliminating duplication of cases and the resulting duplication of documentation and case management work; (b) reassignment to the school-based center of existing agency staff currently handling cases within the centers' identified geographic regions; or (c) using new data management systems to document service needs and delivery so as to strengthen the hand of the collaborating agencies in state and local budget battles.

2. Programs v. cases: The second insight provided by the Executive Council data is that public health agencies are most like schools in their conception of services in programmatic and community support terms rather than as case referrrals and reports. Criminal justice, social welfare, mental health, child protective services and most other special-purpose agencies rely on case-driven service systems and, therefore, tend to have rather different professional norms and institutional cultures. Since schools and public health agencies are program focused, they measure success in terms of engaging clients and reducing the incidence of such group indicators as communicable diseases or school dropout rates. Case management in the mental health and juvenile justice areas tends to be crisis driven and success is more narrowly measured. Social welfare case-oriented services are impelled by documentation of needs meeting specific criteria. These differences in viewpoint and priority are likely to place continuing stress on any collaborative effort.

Conclusions

Utilizing data from three studies of work norm development, this chapter has explored a framework for assessing the prospects for successful interagency collaboration between schools and other social service agencies. We began by noting that widely recognized social service failures are systemic in character, springing from the inappropriate use of work-role specialization and bureaucratic organization. Our data indicate that overcoming the resulting service fragmentation and client alienation will require close attention to three distinct levels of professional work-role development. At the individual level, teachers and other social service workers have to acquire a set of enabling professional norms – norms that define their responsibilities for client service while protecting them from a debilitating sense of helplessness because of client needs they cannot meet. For teachers (and, we suspect, for other social service workers) interdisciplinary cooperation with other professionals only becomes possible after individual level professionalism has become reasonably well developed. And interagency collaboration requires a still further development of professional and institutional work norms.

The single most potent threat to successful interagency collaboration lies in the historical division of client needs into distinctive 'problems' that are seen as amenable to treatment by the application of a given agency's staff energy and expertise. Once service agencies have been assigned unique responsibility for dealing with particular sets of client problems, the stage is set for systemic failure. Clients' needs are abstracted from their actual life circumstances, staff professionalism becomes defined narrowly in relation to their assigned problems, and screening for eligibility becomes a major focus of staff effort. As a result, client needs come to be defined in terms of an agency's capacity to respond.

From this perspective, the most important feature of recent interagency collaboration efforts is their capacity to redefine service responsibilities in terms of *geographic catchment areas* rather than unique *client problems*. While this shift in focus promises relief for the alienating fragmentation of current service arrangements, it also requires critical changes in institutional and professional work norms for staff members.

Even if geographic area responsibility is fully integrated into collaborative planning, there is a powerful tension between the *case-structured* work orientation of some agency professionals and the *program-structured* approach taken by others. Program approaches are characteristic of schools and other service agencies seeking to reach all members of a population group. Case-structured work predominates in those areas where delivery is targeted on individuals with clearly defined special needs. Income maintenance provided by social welfare and drug or psychological counseling for debilitated individuals are archetypical case-managed services.

While an initial distinction between case- and program-structured work helps account for agency differences with respect to such basic issues as careful documentation of client needs and concern with individual client privacy rights, we found substantial overlap. Agency differences reside more in attitude than in operation. Within traditionally case-oriented service agencies, program structures are used to organize services and specialize staff roles (family maintenance case workers, for example, take one set of child protection cases, while foster care has evolved as a separate program structure in the same agency). Schools are giving increased attention to case-based service delivery as a result of categorical program development and the Individual Educational Plan requirements for special education students. Case-structured education remains *at the margins* of school service delivery, however. The dysfunctional school we studied reveals clearly why this is so. Educators simply do not have the staff capacity or program flexibility needed to support a case-management approach to large numbers of children. Educators must define program operation as their first professional duty and must see case management as a device for responding to children who are problem learners, at risk of failure in the mainstream program. Contemporary interest in expanding case-managed schooling for problem learners is paralleled by a drive to make other social service agencies more efficient and effective by giving them a more programmatic character. Arguably, the principal source of the current crisis in health and welfare services is their inability to transcend traditional casework approaches in favor of holistic programs of family support.

While formulating a proper balance between case and program work structures is a crucial first step, two other institution-level issues will require development of new professional norms: managing the relationship between innovation and accountability, and developing appropriate information systems to monitor performance and document outcomes. While innovation is widely touted as the answer to ineffective social services, the simple truth is that when children are involved, social service innovation is difficult to produce. Innovative programs defy careful monitoring and confuse efforts to eliminate inadequate programs and staff. Neither parents nor policy makers are prepared to give social service workers broad latitude to use unproven techniques.

Information management problems abound because social service agencies rely on sharply different indicators of success and have very different systems for collecting, interpreting and reporting institutional performance data (Guthrie and Kirst 1984). This whole area is undergoing dramatic transformation as new data collection and analysis techniques are developed. Indeed, a rapidly expanding interest in data use in planning and managing service delivery is responsible for the recent upsurge of interest in Deming's 'Total Quality Management' system (Deming 1986, Gitlow and Gitlow 1987). Interagency collaboration can be successful at the institutional level if agencies can manage and share information that acts as data for a system of checks and balances, assuring accountability while documenting the effects of innovation, on the one hand, but also serving to verify program quality and guide case management, on the other.

In sum, interagency collaboration is supported when institutional norms allow geographic service regions to replace social problem-defined agency roles. This support is strengthened when these geographic centers establish an effective integration of program- and case-structured service planning, when they provide for a balance between innovation and accountability, and when information systems provide documentation of service impact as well as guidance for service planning.

Institutional collaboration cannot produce these characteristics without adequate development of both personal and interdisciplinary professional work norms. Our analysis of interdisciplinary cooperation among experienced professional teachers reveals that the needs of problem learners are too complex and subtle to permit simple solutions or single strategy responses. Teachers who have acquired enough professional skill and confidence to shift their attention from program opertions to the diagnosis of individual student problems look to colleagues and other professionals to expand their *repertoire* of useful strategies, not to identify a specific treatment strategy. Even when diagnostic information produces a singular definition of student deficiencies, Child Study Teams view program planning as a matter of *pragmatic judgment* rather than *scientific treatment*. As a result, professional cooperation depends more on a *shared sense of responsibility for student outcomes* and the development of a *common language for classifying problems* and *choosing solutions*, than on matching 'treatments' with 'diagnoses'. Thus, we conclude that interagency collaboration will only be successful if it is grounded on an interdisciplinary consultation system characterized by pragmatic decision making, an expansive repertoire of program options, and a well-developed language system for describing student problems and service program options. Even with a well-developed consulting language, interdisciplinary cooperation becomes impossible when basic programs are dysfunctional, as our pre-referral study reveals.

We end, therefore, where we began. Interagency collaboration can supplement competent individual-level professionalism but cannot replace it. We fully expect that, just as in the case of individual norm acquisition by novice teachers, there will be a period of confusion, anger, helplessness and frustration, this time agonized by the belief that other professionals are not listening, cooperating or understanding. As schools seek to establish formal interagency collaboration projects, educators will seek to reach beyond program-structured services and embrace case-structured attention to children and their families. As this happens, a reorientation of professional norms becomes a paramount consideration. This redefined professionalism can facilitate collaboration only if it redefines the mission of schooling, focusing education on family empowerment and integration, and treating the full range of other social services as resources for fulfilling that mission. The nascent potential of interagency collaboration resides in its promise of healing community alienation by overcoming systemic failure in our social service systems.

References

CALIFORNIA COMMISSION ON TEACHER CREDENTIALING (1992) *Success for Beginning Teachers* (Sacramento: California State Department of Education), p. 5.

DEMING, W. E. (1986) *Out of the Crisis: Quality, Productivity and Competitive Position* (Cambridge: Cambridge University Press).

GITLOW, H. and GITLOW, S. (1987) *The Deming Guide to Quality and Competitive Position* (Englewood Cliffs, NJ: Prentice-Hall).

GOODLAD, J. (ed.) (1990) *The Moral Dimensions of Teaching* (San Francisco: Jossey-Bass).

GOODLAD, J., SODER, R. and SIROTNIK, K. (eds) (1990) *Places where Teachers are Taught* (San Francisco: Jossey-Bass)

GUTHRIE, J. and KIRST, M. (1984) *Data-based Accountability in Education* (Berkeley, CA: University of California, Berkeley, Policy Analysis for California Education).

KIRST, M. (1990) *Rethinking Children's Policy: Implications for Educational Administration* Policy Bulletin No. 10 (Bloomington, IN: Consortium on Educational Policy Studies), p. 8.

KIRST, M. (1991, April) 'Improving children's services', *Phi Delta Kappan*, 72(8), pp. 615–618.

KIRST, M. and MCLAUGHLIN, M. (1990) *Improving Policies for Children: Proceedings of the 1989 New York Education Policy Seminar*, Rockefeller Institute Special Report No. 29 (Albany, NY: State University of New York, Albany; Nelson A. Rockefeller Institute of Government).

MCGEE, C. (1991) 'Link-up: a resource directory. Interagency collaborations to help children achieve', in *Children's Cabinet*, Project No. 63 (Alexandria, VA: National School Boards Association), p. 9.

POLICY ANALYSIS FOR CALIFORNIA EDUCATION (PACE) (1989) *Conditions of Children in California* (Berkeley, CA: M. Kirst).

POLLARD, H. (1990) 'School-linked services: so that schools can educate and children can learn, part 3', *Insights on Educational Policy and Practice*, No. 23 (Washington, DC: Office of Educational Research and Improvement).

POWELL, R., RAJAN, K., REED, D. and SCOTT, L. (1991) *The Impact of California's Special Education Pre-referral Interventions and Alternative Assessments on Ethno-linguistically Diverse Students: A Technical Report on the Feasibility Study* (Riverside, CA: California Educational Research Cooperative, University of California).

RIVERSIDE PRESS ENTERPRISE (1992, April 30) ' "Today the system failed us" L.A. Mayor says', byline Linda Deutsch, p. A1.

SCHULMAN, L. (February 1986) 'Those who understand: knowledge growth in teaching', *Educational Researcher*, 15(2), pp. 4–14.

SCHUTZ, A. (1967) 'The phenomenology of the social world', in G. Walshand F. Lehner (trans.), Series title: *Northwestern University Studies in Phenomenology and Existential Philosophy* (Evanston, IL: Northwestern University Press).

POLITICS OF EDUCATION ASSOCIATION YEARBOOK, 1993, 93–106

Resource issues: a case study from New Orleans

James R. Garvin and Alma H. Young

Fischer Elementary School in New Orleans is surrounded by three things. It is surrounded by a chain-link fence which encloses a two-story un-airconditioned building, a bare rectangular slab of blacktop used as a playground, and walls covered with the graffiti that symbolizes the contorted and complex world of its neighborhood. Beyond the fence, it is surrounded by a public housing development which is home to almost 5000 people, where the unemployment and functional illiteracy rates both approach 80%. Finally, Fischer is surrounded by a sea of indifference. It is after all a place where 'they' live; and if 'they' would just change, 'they' wouldn't have to live there any longer. Notably, it is this kind of school and this kind of neighborhood that presents urban America with its biggest challenge. That challenge exists not only for those who live there but for every city where such neighborhoods are reproduced.

The kinds of problems that permeate this particular school and too many others just like it are both myriad and overwhelming for the teachers, staff, children and parents. What to do and where to turn for assistance are questions that come at a dizzying pace. Unfortunately, a tremendous amount of time and a significant amount of resources have been spent on trying to find the one best solution, with little to show as an end result. Weiss (1985) makes an excellent point when she states that, 'It is now apparent, for example, that no one-way, simple, base-superstructure model will do to explain what goes on in schools' (p. 7). The issue now must be to consider not only what goes on inside schools but also what goes on in the communities surrounding schools.

The worlds of the parents and of their children, the worlds that now comprise the communities in which they live, have grown increasingly more complex, more violent, and all too frequently, more resistant to intervention by outside forces. A significant portion of that resistance may lie in the piecemeal attempts to mitigate the vast array of problems. As approach after approach was developed, put into place and institutionalized, specific territory was defined and barriers erected as to what each program could do and could not do and who was eligible and who was not. Rather than developing a holistic approach, schools and social service providers compartmentalized the lives of those they were intended to serve. The gradual evolution of that process made those compartments ever smaller. The net result of such a process is that each succeeding reduction becomes further removed from the reality of a person's life. It is a phenomenon of the functioning of bureaucratic institutions, such as schools, that the interconnectedness of the diverse elements of any human life appears to be ignored (Illich 1971). The time-consuming process of obtaining a particular service only becomes exacerbated when it is understood that to seek remedy for the whole of a problem means repetitive trips down the same pathway again and again and again and again. Ultimately, given enough hurdles to jump and gates to pass through, the likelihood of services either being used or being effective diminishes (Comer 1980).

Separation of cities and schools

It is important to realize that there are two kinds of politics impacting on education; the first is the kind that is endemic to the profession itself, while the second concerns the separate and distinctive policies and policy-making process within the community that surrounds educational institutions. The first is one that most educators and those in educational research know a great deal about. It is the second which appears to present particularly daunting problems.

Tyack (1974) lays out the historical account of the decoupling of the institutions of education from that of city and mayoral politics. In a move seen as progressive at the turn of the century, education was turned over to professional educators and removed from the influence of the world of city politics. Not only was this the decoupling of schools from city government, it was also the harbinger of schools being decoupled from the rest of the community. This decoupling led to a restructuring of the concept of the neighborhood school. Such schools had often served as the hub of activities that were characteristic of particular communities and particular groups of people. Schools became residential anchor points, serving not only as places of learning for children, but as focal points where community health care could be given, political meetings could be held, and information deemed essential to the body politic dispersed. The neighborhood school served as an important element of the social glue that gave adherence to the concept and reality of community (Silberman 1970).

As towns grew into cities and cities into large metropolitcan urban centers, schools also grew. As the schools grew in size, they were moved from neighborhoods to central locations that served wider and more diverse population bases. Schools slowly dissolved from the center of neighborhood activity into places of perceived efficiency and efficacy where performance was measured based on volume and numbers (Kaestle 1973). Now the students were no longer from the neighborhoods where the schools were located and neither were the faculty nor the staff. More often than not, teachers lived throughout the city, assigned to a particular school through a centralized system. Thus teachers and students were meeting in an artificially constructed institutionalized setting with the only thing in common between them being the legal obligation to be there (OECD 1983, Katz 1976). Schools no longer served the function of community, they served the bureaucracy of education (Hoy and Miskel 1982). What occurred was a shift from schools being an interwoven participant in community affairs to being an institutionalized compartment – a compartment into which children would disappear for a number of years and then return when it was time to rejoin the 'real' world (Katz 1983).

Schools now serve a large number of children and parents who need a vast array of social services. However, a great many of those services are under the control of local political leaders, the very people that educational progressives, both in the past as well as today, have been so opposed to having involved in education. As the progressives, at the turn of the century, disconnected education from the politics of local government, they also disconnected those social services controlled by local government from education. The belief that corruption ruled the day was the justification for severing the bonds between education and local government. Additionally, in the name of good government, education was also separated from the local community or neighborhood (Katz 1975). And to keep local politics from encroaching on its terrain, public education erected and maintained bastions of organization and bureaucracy as an encapsulating perimeter (Hoy and Miskel 1982). Thus, education and social service agencies now have very distinct power bases. How, then, to bring these separate and diverse forces together?

Necessity, more than reason, it seems, is serving as a catalyst for cooperation. Dwindling resources, legislative mandates, and communication have all served as one or more reasons for cooperation (Gage 1976, Lippitt and Van Til 1981, Warren 1973, Weiss 1991). Additionally, the pressures mounting from equity issues have served this same function (Kozol 1991). In state after state, the legal challenges to how resources are distributed from district to district are causing entire school systems to reconsider linkages across multi-agency boundaries.

One city's beginning

Over the last several years, New Orleans has slowly made some efforts to link public schools and social services. The genesis of the local effort discussed in this chapter centered around the involvement of the mayor. Initially, in May and June of 1991, a series of private discussions were held between the mayor and researchers from the University of New Orleans about the role of city government in improving public education. Those discussions focused on the possible avenues of reconnecting city government to public education. The problems plaguing public education had assumed high visibility in the metropolitan area and the body politic was beginning to coalesce around the issue. The business community had formed a task force, MetroVision, whose function was to lay out a plan for the city's entry into the 21st century, a plan that included correcting the presumed ills of the present educational system. Comprising business and civic leaders, the group had high visibility with the media as well as with the general public. Meanwhile two dynamic and very active city-wide parent groups (the Parents Network and Save Our Schools) had come into existence, both rallying behind ousting the members of the current school board and electing new members they felt would be more responsive to the 'real' problems of urban education. (Five of the seven school board members were defeated in the 1992 school board elections.) With all this activity the mass media was finding it had a cause *de jure*.

In New Orleans, as in many other large urban systems, the Mayor's Office does not have formal input into the operation of the school system nor is there any direct line of political responsibility. However, the problems that were mounting needed attention and the mayor and his staff were considering what his options for getting involved were. In the midst of their discussions, a meeting of the National Conference of Mayors was held at which education was a focal issue and the Mayor was a major participant. The residual effect of these discussions was to move the mayor to call a local summit conference on education in September of 1991.

The decision to call that conference laid the groundwork for much of the collaborative work among various agencies, both public and private, that was to follow. The first of what turned out to be a series of meetings, held over the course of a year, had almost 70 individuals in attendance. Attending the meeting were representatives of the local public school system (including the superintendent's office and the school board), the Chamber of Commerce, the local archdiocesan school system, the city's office of health, the Private Industry Council for the Jobs Training Partnership Act (JTPA), Even Start, Head Start, the local police department, the juvenile court system, the local universities (public and private), the governor's office, and the parent organizations (Parents Network and Save Our Schools).

The initial outcome of the first meeting was not conclusive, but it was historic in a sense. Within the city's recent memory it was the first time all of these agencies had met in one place at the same time to discuss the same agenda. Everyone agreed there was a serious problem in education: problems of curriculum development and implementation, problems of resources and resource management, problems with facilities and aging physical plants, problems with providing appropriate services to parents and children, and problems with developing a coordinated strategy to begin to deal effectively with all the issues. The group continued to meet once a month from October of 1992 to the following March. Each time they met the dialogue became a little more focused and the need for greater collaboration became clearer.

Collaboration or the linking of services was a serious item of discussion from the very first meeting. However, there was the amazing admission that the various groups had been building turf for so long that no one really knew how to work out a collaborative agreement to which large numbers of the participants could agree. Imagine a room full of people whose professional lives began with the notion of providing services to those in need, who acknowledged that the best way to meet those needs would be to work together, and yet admitted that they had no idea how to come together and operationalize the partnership!

This was the backdrop that served as a catalyst for a research team from the University of New Orleans, comprising members from three different colleges (Urban and Public Affairs, Education, and Science) at the University of New Orleans, to explore the possibilities of a collaborative effort which would attempt to bridge the gap existing between schools and social service agencies. One of the desired outcomes was the development of a process of community involvement that would enable parents, along with teachers and other community leaders, to negotiate their way through the maze of social service agencies. In particular, the team was interested in developing effective strategies that would begin to construct a collaborative network of agencies and services which could work with the public education system, particularly in inner-city schools. The researchers expected the end result to be enhanced community development for the neighborhoods in which these schools are located.

Use of grant funding

With the collaboration process beginning to evolve, the research team from the University of New Orleans (UNO) in January of 1992 decided to apply for a grant from the National Center for Family Literacy. The grant was to be used to create a family literacy program in three public school sites in depressed neighborhoods. The aim of the program was to have parent and child learn together: parents who had left school prior to scheduled dates of graduation and now had preschool-age children, would return to school to complete their high school education, while their children received preschool education. While family literacy was not the original focus of the UNO team, two items worked together in helping to crystallize their decision to pursue this grant. First was the ability to discuss with the potential funder the team's broader view and the possible role this particular grant could play in that vision.

That vision centered around using this specific program as a foundation for rebuilding and hopefully revitalizing the neighborhoods where these families lived. The hypothesis was that community development could be nurtured through family education (Hill *et al.* 1989, Ogbu 1991). The funder was struck by the concept and, while it was not within the grant's original guidelines, encouraged the team to submit the application. The funder agreed to visit the city to continue the discussion and also to meet some of the other possible participants in the program.

The second item that helped crystallize the decision to apply for the grant centered around the fact that within the school where the university was working and doing much of its research, the parents and principal of the neighborhood elementary school asked for assistance with parenting skills and job training. While the family literacy program was not traditionally thought of as a community development program, it had enough similar elements so that we were willing to give it a try. The key was to be flexible enough to recognize how available resources could be used and how those same resources could be leveraged across a number of disciplines and boundaries. Collaboration requires creativity, and the ability to focus on the opportunities present rather than on elements that we would like to have but do not (Bennis and Nanus 1985).

The first step in the application process was gaining the mayor's participation in a planned tripartite, which would apply for the grant. That tripartite would be composed of the University of New Orleans, the Mayor's Office, and the Orleans Parish Public School System. The mayor agreed that his office would serve as the focal point of the collaboration. In so doing, the mayor was pledging the support of city social service agencies that could be needed to make the program effective. The mayor was also helpful in getting the Citizen's Advisory Committee formed. The mayor invited representatives from the Chamber of Commerce, the local community foundation, the Superintendent of schools, principals of the three school sites, and a number of different social service agencies to serve on the Council. With the mayor serving as chair, the Council's role is to review the progress of the program and offer insights based on their experiences and knowledge. This participation by a broad range of individuals both within and outside the immediate collaborative continues to be a useful mechanism in building accountability into the process.

With the mayor's acceptance in hand, the next move by members of the UNO research team was to visit the three school sites where it was thought the program could be implemented successfully and to enter into discussions with the principals and teachers who would be involved. The schools were chosen on the basis of the research team's familiarity with the faculty and the staff. The discussions with teachers and principals also took place in February of 1992. It was extremely important that they make the decision to participate in the program for themselves, without any outside influence. It seems the lesson here is for people to decide for themselves what they want to do. This is an extremely significant point in any collaborative process – somewhere, almost always at the start, somebody has to invite all the other parties in, somebody has to lower the barriers and be willing to take the risk and accept the responsibility. These three principals and group of teachers, with a lot of courage and some concern and fear all mixed together, did just that and the invitation was made. With their consent obtained the team gained the support of the Superintendent's Office in early March 1992. The intention was to use personnel and resources already in place at the three sites and augment them with the resources from the grant.

The research team at UNO works under the umbrella of the Project for Urban Education and Community Development, which is housed in the College of Urban and Public Affairs at the University of New Orleans. This interdisciplinary team seeks to transform the process of education from being a 'punishing ordeal' into a lifelong resource. The project is constantly exploring that concept in the context of inner-city settings, especially in seeking ways to work collaboratively with the institutions of government, school systems, social service agencies, businesses and other private sector groups.

Application to the grantor was made in late March, and in late April word came that the collaborative effort was one of ten finalists from which, ultimately, five awards would be made. Part of the responsibility for being one of those finalists was to agree to an interview by the grantor of all the collaborative partners. There were a number of different ways to handle such a meeting, but the group decided to have those individuals who would be responsible on a day-to-day basis for implementing the program, across the various agencies involved, meet with the grantor. It was felt that this group could be specific about the realities, difficulties and possibilities of the proposed effort and could discuss those in the everyday context in which the program would have to exist.

It turned out to be a good strategy for two reasons. The first was that it impressed the interview team that a diverse group, who worked in different everyday arenas, could come together to build a case in such a unified manner. This no doubt helped secure the grant, which was awarded in May 1992. Second, the strategy helped to strengthen the collaborative bonds among the various agencies involved. They felt as though they had been instrumental in obtaining the grant as well as being responsible for implementing it on a day-to-day basis. Those bonds have served this particular effort extremely well. On a number of occasions when bureacracies have raised barriers, the team members have deflected and handled almost all of the potential difficulties.

Resource issues

The literature would suggest that the major resources needed for the implementation of programs are money and personnel. However, as money for social programs became tighter, due to changes in public policy (e.g., the federal cutbacks during the Reagan/Bush administrations) and the weakening economy, more attention has centered around finding ways to coordinate available resources and use them in more creative ways. This in turn has led to the need to respond to 'turfism' and to provide greater accountability for how resources are used. These issues surfaced in New Orleans as we worked on this collaborative effort. Thus, instead of money and personnel being our major resource issues, we found the following to be most important:

1. identifying one person with the vision and energy to pull the elements of the program together and to keep them together;
2. creating the time necessary for effective planning and implementation to occur (many programs, especially collaborative ones, need longer periods of time for the elements to gel sufficiently);
3. creating opportunities for effective communication among partners who had historically kept away from each other, thus lessening the felt need to protect turf from each other.

On another level we found other kinds of resource issues important. These included:

1. designing outcome assessments that were meaningful to our partners, including the grantor, the participants and the broader community, while still generating outcome measures that were specific to our program and faithful to the goals that we had set for the program;
2. having agencies agree to relinquish (or, at least give up day-to-day control over) resources necessary to the viability of the program; these resources included staff who were reassigned, and physical space;

3. creating an 'accounting' system internal to the program, that could be used to determine what was being expended on existing services, and whether (or, the extent to which) savings were resulting from the collaboration.

Anticipating as many problems as possible ahead of time helped, but keeping lines of communication open was essential to the efficient functioning of the collaboration. Many problems could only be resolved by talking them through among the partners. It also helped that there was an agreed standard of accountability that could serve as a measure of what we were accomplishing.

Implementation

In May of 1992, the grant was awarded and, after a summer of preparation, the program began that September. We began with three school sites: Fischer, the largest of the three with 15 adults and 15 children; Coghill, with 10 adults and 10 children; and Rosenwald, with five adults and five children. Enrollment in the program was on a first-come, first-served basis. On the day enrollment was opened at Fischer, over 100 parents stood in line in an attempt to fill one of the 15 available slots. This was impressive in a community where 100% of the families live below the poverty line; where 80% of the adults are unemployed; where 70% of the adults are functionally illiterate; and where 20% of the children who enroll in Fischer Elementary School drop out before the sixth grade.

During the first year of the program we had 37 families enrolled at one point or the other (seven families dropped out for various reasons), all of whom have been on public assistance. Thirty-two of the adults enrolled were women, and five were men. During the year, reading vocabulary increased by 2·1 grade levels; reading comprehension by 2·9 grade levels; mathematics computation skills increased by 3·0 grade levels; and the understanding of mathematics concepts and applications by 2·4 grade levels. When asked what they find most rewarding about the program, parents respond that it is the opportunity to work with their children in a safe and nurturing environment.

Each of the original partners in the collaboration has brought important resources to the program. The Orleans Parish School System has reassigned trained teachers (both pre-kindergarten and adult education teachers) to the program and has provided physical space within the three school sites. The principals of the schools consider themselves to be a part of the team. The City of New Orleans, through the Office of the Mayor, has provided funds to pay for two-thirds of the progam management staff and has facilitated (and staffed) the Citizens Advisory Committee. The Project for Urban Education at the University of New Orleans manages the program, facilitates the development of a team approach by the teachers in the program, and manages the research effort.

Because we were working with poor families that were in need of a number of services, it became necessary to broaden the scope of the program. Concerns centering around AFDC benefits, safe housing, and job readiness surfaced. As a result, the collaborative network expanded during the year. The Office of Family Services, especially through its JOBS component, agreed that participating parents who were welfare recipients were eligible for subsidies for child care and transportation. Parents could participate in a JOBS-required education program and still be close to their children. Perhaps more important, case workers and teachers are now in touch with one another. The Office of Family Services was interested in the collaboration because it could count the program's parents as JOBS participants without having to provide additional dollars for education or training. In Spring 1993 JTPA and the Office of Family Services' JOBS program began a collaboration of their own – sharing office space and case management. This makes it easier for JOBS participants to receive job training, which is very helpful to our parents.

The Department of Agriculture has made it possible for the parents and their children to be on free breakfast and lunch. (In the program, parents and children eat breakfast and lunch together at the school. For many these are the two most nutritious meals they have during the day.) The Louisiana Literacy Foundation used its contacts to get additional computers in the classrooms for the use of the parents and the children. They have welcomed this collaboration because it enables them to add another program to their list of accomplishments around the state.

The United Way has agreed to explore the possibility of sponsoring a number of their agencies to provide services on the school site. Fischer, the most impoverished of the schools, was the targeted site. Services would include health care, especially prenatal care, and drug intervention services. Discussions have also begun with the public housing authority in New Orleans for resident initiative programs. We are still at only the discussion stage with these two agencies because it has been harder to articulate for them what the benefits of collaboration would be to them, and because their bureaucracies are more arcane and effective points of entry are less clear.

Blending resource streams

The resource stream for this program is a blending of a number of sources, starting with the school system contributing teachers and physical space at an in-kind cost of approximately $300,000 per year. The university contributes by underwriting the costs of the research and management team. Through its Community Development Block Grant funds the city contributes approximately $42,000 per year for additional personnel needs. The National Center for Family Literacy (NCFL), through a grant from the Toyota Motor Corporation, provides funding ($225,000 over 3 years) for teacher training, computer hardware and software, and technical assistance. While none of these sources would be sufficient by themselves, collectively they are.

The school system by itself could not have launched this kind of pilot program; however, with the management assistance of the university and the training provided by NCFL, and the funds from Toyota and the city, they had the resources to do so. The Citizens Advisory Committee adds an essential element to this collaborative effort. The committee serves to broaden the perspective of the program from being one that has been captured by a single institution to one that embraces an entire community.

These groups have been willing to cooperate because someone took the initiative and talked to them about the possibilities of collaboration. This proved to be important: someone has to step forward and begin the dialogue. Social service agencies and other organizations are often locked into their own worlds and their own bureaucracies and rarely see what is going on anywhere other than immediately in front of them. When asked to help, and shown the program, their response has been to step forward. Communicating about what is going on and asking what they could do to help obviously makes a marked and positive difference.

Proximal benefits and proximal concerns

One of the largest problems that confronts collaboration is the perception of value, that is, the value or benefit of the collaborative activity to the individual participants involved. Urban arenas are traditionally venues where resources are shrinking and social problems are increasing (Wilson 1987). As a result, the sharing of resources, while it may be perceived as a positive concept, appears to be weighted by the considerations of proximal benefit and proximal concern. Wellington and Garvin (1992) diagrammed this phenomenon in their discussion on the difficulties that schools and communities have in working together. Their discussion centered around the perceptions of benefit or detriment of the activity to the parties interested in working together. Obviously, the perception that activities were not of benefit served as a hurdle to collaborative efforts. Perception is the operative word.

The issue of perception is related to proximity and is illustrated in a model called the Scale of Proximal Concern. The premise of the scale is that those who are closest to the problem are more likely to be involved in seeking a solution to the problem (see figure 1).

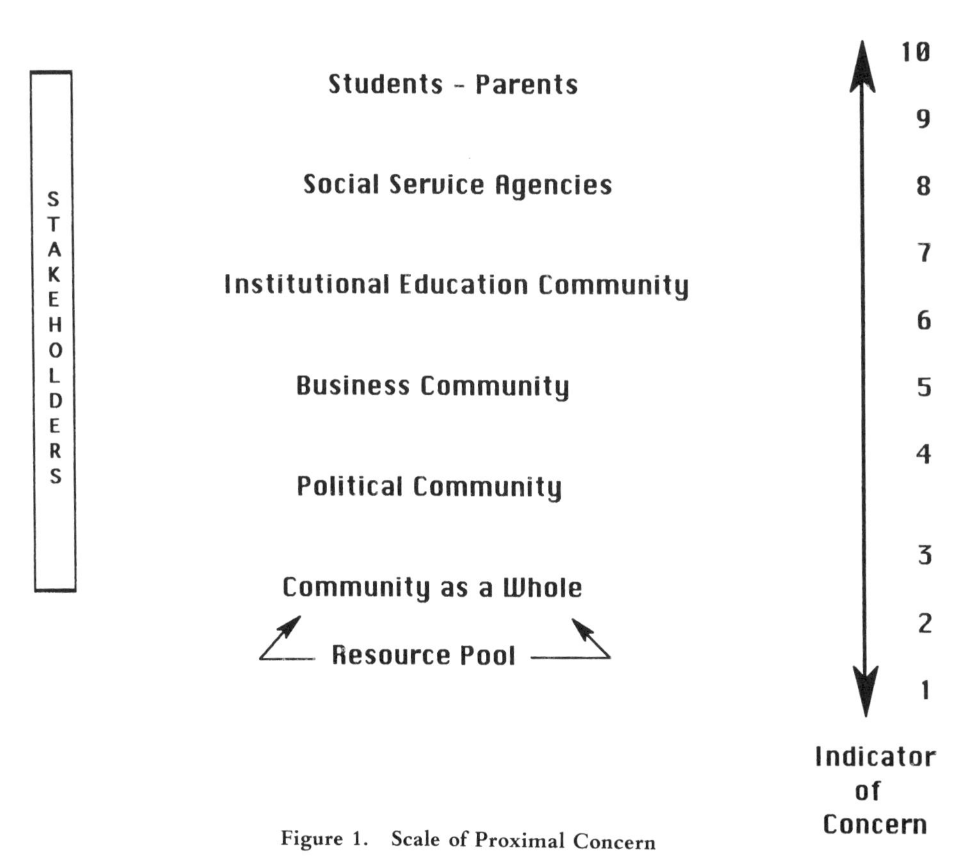

Figure 1. Scale of Proximal Concern

Source: Garvin and Young (1993)

However, while those closest to the problem may be more likely to want a solution, they may also have access to the least amount of personal and social resources to bring to bear on the problem. While they have the greatest personal interest in solving the problem, they may be least likely to be able to do so. Thus, we need to find ways of enhancing the interests of those with greater resources. Creating the understanding that this is a community issue, needing community action, should lead to more resources becoming available.

In figure 1, the parents and students are those closest to the problem while the community as a whole is the farthest from the problem. Accordingly, on the measurement of concern, with 10 being the highest level of concern and 1 being the lowest, the students and parents rate a ten. Obviously, the placement of the stakeholders moves as their perception of need changes. The problem is to get the various stakeholders of the collaboration as close as possible to the perception of need while simultaneously increasing their perception of benefit. Collaboration or linkage can only begin to truly function when those two proximal issues are in alignment. Any strategy which involves sharing any category of agency resources, in order to be successful, must start with an understanding of those concepts.

Getting prospective partners to appreciate the benefits of the program is necessary for collaboration to occur. All participants bring a perspective to the discussion, all participants are immersed in the values and culture of the arena of their particular organization. Finally, if resources are limited, and they are more often than not, participants are going to be reluctant to share resources without some acknowledged return (Yates 1989). Figuring out how to work together, to pool resources, did not happen overnight in the New Orleans collaboration.

Issues for collaborative efforts

Sponsorship

There were two issues that came to the forefront during our experiences. The first of these is sponsorship – somebody has to agree to sponsor the process in which all the diverse parties can gather and discuss what problems confront the agencies and the community. Additionally, someone needs to provide a neutral place for meetings. In this particular circumstance, the political presence of the Office of the Mayor carried weight in the discussions that led up to the implementation of the collaborative effort. Once the effort began, having the university act as manager of the collaboration is also important in terms of having a neutral sponsor.

Time

The second key point is time. There always exists a tremendous amount of pressure to cure problems and fix things with great speed and dispatch. Collaboration takes time and, in order to be successful, real time has to be built into the process. Not a year's worth of time perhaps, but certainly enough time to discuss real differences in perspective, real differences in methodology, and real differences in desired outcomes. Whoever acts as sponsor must know that sponsorship will require a sustained commitment to fostering the collaboration over an extended period of time.

Responsibility

One of the biggest obstacles that came up in the meetings over and over again was who was going to be responsible – not if things went right, but if something went wrong. It was the fear of being the responsible party that was the biggest concern. More often than not it was the perfect rationale for why things should not and could not be changed.

This is not a phenomenon that is uncommon to schools (Miron and Garvin 1992). Countless waves of reform have come and gone, yet resistance to change from the way things have been done continues to hold the high ground. Evidence shows that teachers get nervous about team teaching and that principals worry about letting strangers, much less parents, into their schools because of the notion of who would be responsible if something went wrong.

In this particular instance, the University of New Orleans was able to convince a number of agencies, including the Mayor's Office, the Superintendent of Schools, and the principal and teachers at three inner city elementary schools to try a pilot program. A pilot program does not entail a change in policy or a systemic shift in direction; it is one of those organizational phenomena that allows interventions and adaptations to occur without upsetting the larger 'apple cart.' It can be argued that by changing how resources are allocated (even on a temporary basis) new channels for funding are created that are more likely to be institutionalized later. If there are no changes in how resources are channeled, there is less likelihood that long-term changes will result.

Outcome measures and fiscal support

Pilot programs that function to minimize the initial expenditure of funds do, however, have serious financial repercussions. Three factors sit in the background when considering the financial parameters of collaboration in education and social services: (1) schools and most programs associated with schools carry the perception of not working and being dysfunctional; (2) schools and most programs associated with schools carry the perception of being bureaucratically top-heavy; (3) with the graying of America, fewer taxpayers and voters have children in public schools; and, as a result, they are increasingly resistant to any increase in tax dollars for education or services connected to education (see Kozol 1991). Returning to the Scale of Proximal Concern, pilot projects can be an appropriate methodology to evidence the need and the effectiveness of a proposed solution to that need, without the expenditure of large sums. Additionally, prior to changing policy formation or the intricate process of policy implementation, programs can be evaluated, tested, and developed without the need for large sums of money or the commitment of other large blocks of resources. The successful management of the pilot project approach can help coalesce the community as a whole into taking the desired action.

Those considerations converge into a political climate where accountability becomes a strategic imperative. With the separation of education from the community, along with its supposed depoliticization, business, government and education, while not being adversaries, certainly no longer perceive themselves as colleagues. In such environments where trust is apparently lacking, accountability becomes a central issue (Garvin 1991). Any attempt at collaboration needs to recognize this as one of the given realities.

Accordingly it is important not only to anticipate the demand for outcome measures, but also to attempt to anticipate outcome measures specific to the particular collaborative project. Here, the research team made the decision to set its own outcome measure criteria, making these a part of the collaborative negotiation, the rationale behind such an agenda being that internally generated bench-marks would present fewer programmatic hardships than ones which were external to the project. Additionally, it was more than just a symbolic gesture, for it indicated to the other collaborative partners that their concerns and constituencies were, in fact, being acknowledged. Outcome measures are extremely important as an evaluation tool – what has been learned, what can be duplicated – providing the necessary information essential for further public support and financial assistance (Weiss 1991).

Obviously, the need for establishing these outcome measures is heightened considerably as any program moves towards the allocation and use of financial resources. As this society has moved through the 1980s into the 1990s, resources for education and community service agencies have dwindled (Children's Defense Fund 1991). There are fewer textbooks, fewer supplies, fewer qualified teachers, and fewer case managers (Kozol 1991). The outgrowth of this shift is that the proverbial pie has to be divided many different ways. Fiscal constraint heightens the necessity for sound outcome accountability. Additionally, those outcome measures must be realistic in respect to the problems, resources and time constraints of any given setting.

It is more difficult to define these outcome measures than it may appear at first blush. Why? The reality is that the problems being faced are complex and intricate. Collaboration may not ask for additional funds from taxpayers, and certainly using existing funds more effectively is one of its primary goals; but even with concerted, holistic efforts, many of the difficulties being faced are not going to disappear overnight. Equitable solutions and difficult, complex problems that occur in the human arena take considerable amounts of both patience and time. It is an unfortunate occurrence that while monetary resources can be obtained, time often cannot, with the net result that hard fought for funds put into good programs never get the results everyone desires because of unreasonable time constraints. Thus, as time was an earlier concern in putting effective collaborations together, time also must be a significant part of the discussion with funders. Often very effective programs are in place, but in pieces scattered throughout the social service system in different agencies. Rather than initially asking for additional funds, a more appropriate strategy would be to make sure that current funding stays in place and that the only additional element being requested is that time be given in order to work out and institutionalize appropriate collaborative arrangements.

After that the real concern must be to make sure that existing funds continue to stay in place. As a result it becomes increasingly important that outcome measures be realistic given the parameters of specific collaborations. Goals and targets that are reasonable and obtainable are the success stories of policy makers and funders. Unrealistic goals and bench-marks of accountability doom collaborations to be horror stories rather than successes. There are few policy makers and few funders who have the kinds of political constituencies that allow them to continue to fund programs that fall below previously agreed standards of performance – regardless of the worthiness of the explanation. There are certainly far more policy makers and far more funders who will continue to fund collaborative programs that are considered successful by the bench-marks of accountability set at the beginning of the program.

This very important point is not just about measurable outcomes. All too often there is a failure to understand that collaborations serve very real people with very real problems. In order to be helpful, in order to change people's lives, hopefully for the better, in order to see children reach their full and best potentials, collaborative programs between education and social service agencies need to exist. They need to exist on an ongoing basis.

Having realistic bench-marks and negotiating obtainable and measurable outcomes increases multifold the possibility for successful outcomes – which increases the possibilities of continued funding. Keep firmly in mind that bench-marks attained result in continued opportunities and services for children and families. While the measurable outcomes are for policy makers, the services are for the parents and children who can only be served if the programs continue.

This is not to seek low standards or outcome measures which could be conceived as having little merit. Rather it is to note that setting unrealistic or unobtainable outcomes has a deeper price than just the failure of program or the demise of a collaborative arrangement. The real cost is in the loss of services to human beings who need them. The real cost is measured in a human equation, not a financial equation. Measurable outcomes, goals, and targets all need to be extremely sensitive to this fact.

One of the advantages of using a pilot program is that it may allow the agencies involved and the public at large to observe and see programs at work without significant fiscal risk to either, and it establishes an agreed amount of time to evaluate the effects of a collaborative arrangement and its set of measurable outcomes. Such was the case in the New Orleans program.

Conclusion

Collaboration allows for certain duplications of effort and expenditures to be avoided and that certainly is to be commended. Obviously resources saved in one element can be spent in other elements of the community that have need. However, the greatest strength of collaboration in our experience is to rebuild the concept of and context for community. One of the transforming experiences to come from this project was to have individuals say 'I thought those people in public housing were different, but they're not. They are just like me, they want the same things and love their kids in the same way as I do.' If collaboration can help individuals to see that everyone is the same then a certain amount of hope may exist for the future (Russell 1993). This project has been a tremendous aid in reconnecting education and family to one another and in reconnecting education and community.

References

BENNIS, W. and NANUS, B. (1985) *Leaders: Strategies for Taking Charge* (Cambridge: Harper and Row).

CHILDREN'S DEFENSE FUND (1991) *Annual Report* (Washington, DC: Children's Defense Fund).

COMER, J. P. (1980) *School Power: Implications of an Intervention Project* (New York: Free Press).

GAGE, R. W. (1976) 'Integration of human service delivery systems', *Public Welfare*, 34(1), pp. 27–32.

GARVIN, J. R. (1991) 'Education and evaluation', paper presented to the Louisiana Philosophy ofEducation Conference at its Annual Meeting, Lafayette, LA, November, 1991.

HILL, P. T., WISE, A. E., and SHAPIRO, L. (1989) 'Educational progress: cities mobilize to improve their schools' (Santa Monica: Rand).

HOY, W. K. and MISKEL, C. G. (1982) *Educational Administration: Theory, Research and Practice*, 2nd edn (New York: Random House).

ILLICH, I. (1971) *Deschooling Society* (New York: Harper and Row).

KAESTLE, C. (1973) *The Evolution of an Urban School System, New York City 1750–1850* (Cambridge, MA: Harvard University Press).

KATZ, M. B. (1975) *Class, Bureaucracy and Schooling: the Illusion of Educational Change in America* (New York: Praeger).

KATZ, M. B. (1976) *A History of Compulsory Education Laws* (Bloomington: Phi Delta Kappa Foundation).
KATZ, M. B. (1983) *Poverty and Policy in American History* (New York: Academic Press).
KOZOL, J. (1991) *Savage Inequalities: Children in America's School* (New York: Crown).
LIPPITT, R. and VAN TIL, J. (1981) 'Can we achieve a collaborative community? Issues, Imperatives, Potentials', *Journal of Voluntary Action Research*, 10(3–4), pp. 7–17.
MIRON, L. F. and GARVIN, J. R. (1992) 'Meeting national goals through community involvement', paper presented to the National Association of Elementary School Principals, New Orleans, March 1992.
OECD (1983) *Compulsory Education in a Changing World* (Paris: OECD).
OGBU, J. (1991) 'Minority Status and Literacy', in S. R. Graubard (ed.) *Literacy: An Overview by 14 Experts* (New York: Hill and Wang).
RUSSELL, J. (1993) 'Learning is a family affair', *Times-Picayune*, 25 January, A1 + .
SILBERMAN, C. E. (1970) *Crisis in the Classroom* (New York: Random House).
TYACK, D. (1974) *The One Best System* (Boston: Harvard University Press).
WARREN, R. L. (1973) 'Comprehensive planning and coordination: some functional aspects', *Social Problems*, 20(3), pp. 355–364.
WEISS, L. (1985) *Between Two Worlds* (London: Routledge and Kegan Paul).
WEISS, C. H. (1991) 'Evaluation research in the political context: sixteen years and four administrations later', in M. W. McLaughlin and D. C. Phillips (eds) *Evaluation and Education: At Quarter Century*. 19th Yearbook of the National Society for the Study of Education (Chicago: University of Chicago Press).
WELLINGTON, C. and GARVIN, J. R. (1992) 'Big stick, little carrot: Confronting compulsory school', paper presented to the Association for Supervision and Curriculum Development at its Annual Meeting, New Orleans, 1992.
WILSON W. J. (1987) *The Truly Disadvantaged: The Inner City, The Underclass, and Public Policy* (Chicago: University of Chicago Press).
YATES, D. JR (1989) 'Identifying and using political resources', in J. S. Ott (ed.) *Classic Readings in Organizational Behaviour* (Pacific Grove, CA: Brooks/Cole).

POLITICS OF EDUCATION ASSOCIATION YEARBOOK, 1993, 107–119

Using public policy to impact local practice: can it work?

Jacqueline A. Stefkovich and Gloria J. Guba

This chapter focuses on the restructuring movement in education and its relationship to school-linked social services. Schools are seen as 'open systems' which must elicit the support of the community and other service providers. Efforts in the change process to overcome the top-down mentality of prior reforms and to recognize the importance of the 'street-level bureaucrats' are explored. Issues of empowerment and autonomy are discussed using specific examples from restructuring efforts that have successfully recognized the importance of linking schools and social service agencies.

Addressing a state-sponsored symposium on preschool education, former surgeon general of the United States Public Health Service, C. Everett Koop (1992) admonished policy makers and educational specialists for failing to place the health and welfare of young people high on the national agenda. He called for collaboration between health care agencies and the education system in order to meet the critical and growing medical needs of children so that they might be better able to participate actively in the educational process. 'If we could bring health and education together,' urged Koop, 'they would strengthen each other.'

Koop envisioned a collaborative effort with curricular and clinical components, prevention and early intervention strategies, and stakeholders in health care and classrooms joining forces for young clients (Koop 1992). Orchestrating such collaboration poses clear implications for public policy and local practice. But can it work?

This chapter contends that not only can the kinds of changes that Koop proposed take place, but they *must* take place for educational, social service, and health institutions to meet successfully the needs of children and families. An important part of this change effort involves the restructuring of schools, an effort which would involve a dramatic shift in long-standing rules governing schools and their relationship to other child-serving bureaucracies. Such a shift calls for: a new conception of the relationships among service providers; empowerment of individual service providers; and a different view of the school's relationship to the community and its resources – one that is less fragmented and more collaborative.

The following discussion views this change process from four perspectives. First, it examines the problem. Second, it explores aspects of institutional restructuring particularly as they pertain to shifts in the roles and responsibilities of those providing direct service to students and their families. Third, it illustrates ways in which restructuring and school reform may empower service providers. Finally, it bridges the gap between theory and practice by providing descriptions of several nationally recognized initiatives which have demonstrated the potential for this type of massive change.

0268–0939/93 $10·00

The problem

Whether prepared to accept the responsibility or not, schools are the institutions most often seen as the centerpiece or linchpin for collaborative efforts among child-serving agencies (Davies 1991). Of all the agencies, they are the place where parents come, if only to register their children. And, while they do not bear the sole responsibility for collaboration, their input is essential. In order to assume their share of this responsibility, however, schools must take a critical look at both their purposes and structures.

American public schools, once viewed as democratic institutions emerging from local communities and reflecting parochial interests, are now often criticized as unresponsive, or possibly even oppressive, to their clients. The organizations as well as their personnel are often perceived as rigid, inflexible, bound by fixed rules and procedures, and loyal to the system first, client afterward (Seeley and Schwartz 1981). This alienation from community is further enhanced by adherence to a Weberian industrialized bureaucracy model which all but ignores authority based on professional expertise. This system places practitioners at the 'bottom' of the hierarchical system, thus minimizing their responsibilities and resultant contributions.

While school authorities attempt to operate bureaucratically, in reality, they are forced to operate as open, 'loosely coupled' systems characterized by flexibility, autonomy, and little 'connective tissue' (Weick 1976, Kirst 1983) which are embedded in the communities that they serve and subject to the demands and pressures of various interests and constituencies. Hence, school decision-making patterns often fall short of the rational deductive ideal, lacking established priorities, logical calculations based on data analysis, and synoptic approaches to solution selection. Instead, there persists the need to accommodate interests and to struggle with infinite variables in an open system replete with constant interactions (Lindblom 1980). In such open systems, initiatives that are only top-down, i.e., lacking collaborative efforts, are bound to fail (Berman and McLaughlin 1978, McLaughlin 1990).

Furthermore, schools, as well as other child-serving systems, are fragmented and crisis-driven. Their personnel are overwhelmed by the needs of their constituencies – the diverse challenges posed by dysfunctional families and ailing communities. While the efforts of these organizations are persistent and well-intentioned, they offer little in the way of constructive performance (Meyer and Tucker 1989). Coordination and collaboration are often absent. This situation results in a duplication of effort, inefficient utilization of resources, and an inevitable sense of frustration on the part of both service providers and their clients.

Moreover, as Edwards and Young (1992) point out, current strategies linking home, school, and community service providers lack an 'ecological approach' to addressing all aspects of the child's development. They question the adequacy of schools as meaningful social institutions, 'because they are built on outmoded assumptions about family and community' (Edwards and Young 1992: 78) which are based on the premise that the families can offer all the emotional, financial, experiential, and cognitive support that a developing child needs (Heath and McLaughlin 1991).

If schools have, or even share, the obligation to aid students with aspects of their lives that interfere with cognitive and social development, support services must be integrated. This kind of integration requires a new paradigm founded on the adoption of a holistic philosophy, a philosophy which blurs rigid boundaries between home, school, and community. School personnel at all levels must re-examine their purposes, strategies, and practices. Educators and policy makers must be called upon to alter social contexts and practices, redefine relationships, forge new alliances, and devise new strategies.

Such effective systemic coordination demands the involvement of all pertinent services such as health care, counseling, and education. Services and programs must be sequenced to ensure compatibility and delivered through cooperative relationships (Aiken 1975, Edwards and Young 1992). All aspects of the serving system must be deemed accountable for refining the service delivery both substantively and procedurally. Reflection in practice or frequent on-site monitoring and data gathering can yield additional strategies for meeting client as well as local systemic needs (Belasco 1989).

At the same time, public policy making and eventual implementation necessitates a thorough appraisal of the political culture which will be subject to expected changes mandated by the plan or program. The policy or activity should address the particular idiosyncracies of the local political culture and the organizational characteristics of the schools affected. Specific political realities, such as power distribution and degrees of centralization and decentralization, should be taken into account. Grass-roots participation must be enhanced and issues of concern to the clientele must be addressed (Davies 1981a). Responses to these and related queries are of critical importance if significant alterations of service delivery modes are to take place. If questions of efficacy and expediency are not addressed, resistance to change will be even more intense and prolonged.

In addition, certain key attributes of schools should be considered in the context of understanding their unique complexity. It must be recognized that in loosely coupled organizations relatively unprogrammed decisions become outcomes of the unpredictable interplay between problems, solutions, and options (March and Simon 1958, March and Olsen 1980). Choices, even in the most bureaucratic models, become resolutions arrived at through the interaction of variables operating relatively independent of one another.

Consequently, the paradigm sought must allow for programmed decisions, routine decision making and rationality; and yet it must encourage decision making founded on creativity, intuition, and spontaneity given the complexity and diversity of challenges facing schools and their needy clientele. This paradigm must incorporate the benefits of a bureaucratic system where it is easier to implement new policies with the benefits of a loosely coupled system that has the potential for giving greater power to the line worker (Berman and McLaughlin 1978).

Thus, the extent of public policy's impact on local practice resulting in effective, collaborative links between educational institutions and service providers will rest in large part on the implementation of changes at every level in these organizations. As Fullan (1991: 81–82) points out: 'A small number of dynamic themes in combination make a difference.' Therefore, altering organizational procedures, roles, and expectations in schools is critical to any responsive reform movement with restructuring of the system and empowerment of individuals of utmost importance to programmatic success (Louis and Miles 1990, Fullan 1991).

Power sharing and extending involvement and influence to direct service providers in the organization is crucial. Fostering an organizational climate which is collegial and establishing a work culture whereby the stakeholders interact and own viable decisions becomes indispensable. As Barth (1990: 159) points out: 'Changes in schools may be initiated from without, but the most important and most lasting changes will come from within.' Thus, while school restructuring does not, in and of itself, necessitate cross-agency collaboration and while cross-agency collaboration may be accomplished in schools that are not restructured, restructuring and the empowerment of service providers can bring to fruition those changes needed in order to strengthen school, community, and agency links.

As part of these changes, schools must also respond equitably to educational as well as other needs of their clients, particularly their at-risk pupil population. Historically, the public schools have met with difficulty when striving to meet even minimal standards for these students. Given the increasing numbers and acute needs of these students, however, schools must take the initiative to adapt and restructure in order to deliver necessary services. Schools have been, and will continue to be, asked to meet ever-increasing societal demands when determining a course of action. Such a commitment calls for a redefinition of schooling and a restructuring of the system.

School restructuring

School restructuring came out of a movement in the 1980s aimed at reforming schools. While it may take a variety of forms, in its simplest sense, restructuring means changing rules, roles, and relationships so that schools might better serve stated purposes or serve new purposes entirely (Seeley 1988, Schlechty 1990). Those who are involved with these organizations must unlearn previously applicable behaviors and be trained or socialized to new skills and abilities in order to meet new responsibilities (Timar 1989, Schlechty 1990).

Once the rationale for restructuring efforts is articulated, it becomes vital to identify what facets of the school are to be altered. These may include: patterns of decision making; policies, procedures, rules and regulations; formation of alliances or linkages; and staff development initiatives. Restructuring, in this way, distinctly changes the way schools deliver services or do business.

In restructured schools, a hierarchical arrangement may be replaced by one with bonded partnerships and collegial interactions. Hence, 'a new paradigm for school management' (Wise 1989: 303) challenges the Weberian, industrial bureaucratic model and replaces it with a more decentralized model.

In addition, restructuring may open up discussions about principles and values giving rise to questions about the purposes of schools and schooling; definitions of success in terms of outcomes as well as processes (Murphy and Hart 1988); and the implications of accountability for results (Corbett 1990). Responsibility for low pupil achievement is shifted from the student and his/her family to the school (Cuban 1989). This change in emphasis results in a need for schools to seek avenues, collaborative and otherwise, to provide for critical physical and emotional needs of young clients.

To facilitate school–community agency cooperation and collaboration, restructuring attempts to create a more viable partnership between the school and those outside resources that, if coordinated more effectively, could enhance pupil achievement. A restructured school would have formal mechanisms in place to coordinate with community agencies so that child and family services are available. Examples of such efforts include integration of health and welfare services for students and families and programs of youth employment (Newmann 1991).

As indicated earlier, training is vital to an endeavor which requires staff to accept new responsibilities and engage in new behaviors. This becomes even more essential given the nature of a restructuring effort affecting personnel in multiple organizations.

In some instances, opportunities for learning together might be offered more efficiently by a non-school agency. For example, in Massachusetts, the State Department of Education and the Office for Education of Homeless Children and Youth (OEHCY), in an effort to prepare school personnel to serve more effectively the needs of homeless children in their schools, conducted a series of in-service workshops across the state. These gatherings brought together school personnel, staff members of shelters, social workers, and formerly homeless parents to discuss ways to best serve homeless, at-risk youngsters. The forums varied with identified regional needs, and were followed by visits to specific schools and school districts which requested more intensive staff training (Linehan 1992).

In addition, all participating organizations must grapple with concerns about commitment as well as definitions of collaboration. As Melaville and Blank (1991) suggest, issues of commitment and the challenges of collaboration go beyond that of communication or cooperation to include: issues of power and control; decisions about leadership; agreements about group decision-making; patterns of accountability; understandings about the folkways of the other agencies involved in the process; and, above all, the establishment of a common vision with a joint mission statement.

Decisions to restructure in order to enable the schools to be more responsive to the needs of specified clientele carry with them certain concerns about the risks taken. For example, the relationship between pupil performance outcomes and restructuring efforts has not been clearly established. '[N]ot only is the empirical support for the structural components of restructuring weak, but also the theoretical foundations may be less firm than commonly assumed' (Murphy 1991: 76).

In addition to assessing pupil performance as a measure of 'in-school' outcomes, it may also be important to collect outcome data on other aspects of programs which may occur outside formal schooling. Few data have emerged to ascertain and compare the cost–benefits of alternative courses of action, information which could inform judgments about the acceptance of specific reform measures and the rejection of others (Murphy 1991). If society is asked to support resource allocation for collaboration, it is likely that justification for spending will be expected. Hence, it is important to consider a variety of types of outcome indicators.

Empowering stakeholders

Because educational organizations are nonrational, open systems (March and Olsen 1980, Weick 1976), changes in roles, expectations, policies and procedures do not emerge in a predictable, orderly manner. Tensions, contradictions, and conflict often characterize discussions of power, process, and responsibility. Such systems call for dynamic, transformational leadership and a willingness to share authority with 'grass-roots' level stakeholders.

The authors realize that the term stakeholder may apply to anyone who has a stake in the outcome of a program or initiative. In this chapter, however, the term stakeholder is used to apply to internal stakeholders, i.e., those persons who work at the grass-roots level of agencies providing services. It is our belief that, through empowerment of these internal stakeholders, external stakeholders, i.e., the clients they serve (students and parents) will also be empowered through receiving better services.

As early as 1980, Lipsky noted that 'street-level bureaucrats', those who work directly with public clientele, already make policy in at least two ways. First, they exercise wide discretion when arriving at solutions affecting citizens with whom they interact. Second, when taken collectively, 'their individual actions add up to agency behavior' (Lipsky 1980: 13). Thus, in loosely coupled organizations, 'street-level bureaucrats' achieve greater autonomy from authority when they establish routines and design shortcuts and simplifications in order to cope with work stresses (Lipsky 1980). In the most democratic sense, these stakeholders act as ombudspersons for their clients with whom they interact constantly and, thus, have a clear notion of needs to be satisfied (Lipsky 1980).

Successful programs, therefore, require stakeholder involvement and support, particularly in the planning and implementation stages. Individuals must converge for dialogue, issue resolution, and mutual appreciation and understanding (Belasco 1989). Access to power must be extended if local-level program changes are to take hold. The agencies' internal stakeholders, those 'street-level bureaucrats' including teachers, social workers, health care personnel, and agency employees, must have status and knowledge (Maeroff 1988) as well as flexibility to complete collaboratively the agenda they define.

As Schlechty and Joslin (1986: 159) note:

> The one element that cannot be centralized regardless of strenuous effort to do so is problem-solving capacity. Problems cannot be solved from the top down. They must be solved from the bottom up . . . problem solving is best left to those whose hands-on experience and expertise provide them with the advanced knowledge to invent novel solutions.

Consequently, there are new understandings about the dynamics of school improvement through restructuring, not the least of which is the realization that: (1) these stakeholders have the capability to resolve problems affecting themselves and their clients; (2) their efforts must be supported with resources; and (3) it is vital to engage them in leadership activities (Lipsky 1980, Lieberman and Miller 1986, Sarason 1990). In view of this recognition, it is imperative that decision making in the new paradigm be decentralized (Newmann 1991).

Designing and implementing an ecological approach, or what Fullan (1991) terms 'interactive professionalism', carries with it several advantages. It enables participants to share expertise at the level of direct service. This sharing of responsibility through multiple partnerships, school–community alliances, and school–agency collaboration, may, in turn, free educators to focus on pupil learning needs in a purely academic sense (Edwards and Young 1992). It may also allow service providers to network in order to satisfy non-educational needs in a holistic sense. Finally, sharing expertise can build trust as each participant begins to appreciate the contributions of the others while reaffirming his/her own unique contributions to the collective endeavor (Comer 1980).

Empowerment of stakeholders, however, must be an integral part of a process aimed at joint problem solving. As Comer (1980: 234–235) notes: 'No particular model, technology, method or person is as important to improved student behavior and learning as a process that places higher priority on flexibility, accountability, shared expertise, open communication, trust and respect.'

On the other hand, restructuring organizational practices and procedures and empowering personnel is not without pitfalls and concerns. The process of changing and developing can be an arduous one particularly if it necessitates that workers accept additional responsibilities (Silberman 1970). Educators need to 'navigate the difficult space between letting go of old patterns and grabbing on to new ones' (Deal 1990: 11).

This implies a call for transformational leadership where leaders and followers are united in pursuit of higher level goals common to both (Sergiovanni 1990). It also raises the question of who empowers whom. The assumption is that those who currently wield power transfer it to others. However, as Elmore (1991) notes, it is essential that those 'giving power' both see themselves as powerful and are clear about the conditions of transfer of power.

Inevitable tensions between 'autonomy and control, responsibility and accountability, collaboration and isolation, group goals and individual satisfaction' must be addressed in any inquiry into personnel empowerment (Rallis 1990: 194). Therefore, when empowering one segment of the organization, it is critical that such empowerment is not done at the expense of others in the organization and that factions within the organization are not disenfranchised (Zeichner 1989).

In sum, a successful collaboration must have clear goals, precise responsibilities, shared resources, mutual respect and trust, and an ecological approach which legitimizes coordination of educational and noneducational services. Despite any reservations about the efficacy of restructuring and the absence of empirical evidence to offer unmitigated support, these elements must accompany efforts to effectuate school–community agency linkages.

Nationally recognized initiatives

Several nationally recognized initiatives afford interesting illustrations of how these schema are played out. They include: the School Development Program (Comer 1980); the League of Schools Reaching Out (Davies 1991); The Philadelphia Children's Network (Smith 1992); and New Beginnings (Payzant 1992). These initiatives were singled out because they represent an interesting cross-section of the types of efforts that exemplify the principles of cooperation and collaboration set forth in this chapter and, thus, appear to be successful in bridging the gap between theory and practice. In essence, these examples provide models for rethinking and restructuring service delivery to students and their parents that also empower agency stakeholders as well as their clients.

The Yale Child Study Center's Development Program (SDP)

Dr James P. Comer, Director of the Yale Child Study Center, initiated the School Development Program in 1968. This program, which began as a collaborative effort between the Center and the New Haven, Connecticut School System, is now a nationally recognized model which has been adopted by a number of school districts throughout the USA (Comer 1987).

Funded first through the Ford Foundation and later through the Rockefeller Foundation, SDP is driven by the philosophy that all children can learn regardless of their backgrounds. Consequently, an underlying premise of this program is that the children, themselves, are not the sources of most learning and behavior problems. Instead, these problems stem from conflicts between the children's home and school environments and are often related to issues associated with differences in class, race, income, and culture. Therefore, successful schools must foster a climate of trust, cooperation, and caring among school personnel, students, parents, and the community. Because children gain the skills, attitudes, and habits that influence future achievement early on, this program focuses on learning and development at the elementary school level (Brown *et al.* 1991).

SDP has four goals: to address the causes, as well as symptoms, of school failure; to support the physical, emotional, and intellectual growth of all students; to bridge the gap between attitudes, values, and behaviors developed at home and at school; and to create a structured, predictable, school environment in which school personnel and parents communicate clear expectations for behavior and academic performance (Brown *et al.* 1991).

Comer's model stresses collaboration and team-building consisting of three groups:

- a school planning and management team (SPMT);
- a mental health team (MHT);
- a parent program (PP).

The SPMT which governs the school consists of the principal and individuals elected from their respective groups and represent teachers, parents, professional support staff (e.g., counselors, psychologists), and nonprofessional support staff (e.g., custodians, secretaries) (Anson *et al.* 1991).

Focusing on prevention and the building of interpersonal relationships between students and school staff, the MHT consists of support services staff including, but not limited to, psychologists, counselors, social workers, and special education teachers. The purpose of the PP is to use and expand on existing parent groups in an effort to increase dramatically parental involvement with the schools. Some members of the MHT and the PP also act as liaisons among these groups by serving on the SPMT (Anson *et al.* 1991). These groups are designed to foster among the participants a sense of shared ownership and to support a 'community' spirit that values educational performance (Anson *et al.* 1991).

Finally, SDP supports collaborative efforts by assisting students to perceive the school as a 'positive community' and facilitating this attitude in the students' and parents' interactions with other child-serving agencies. In this regard, SDP has a strong 'social skills' component that seeks to link students with institutions (e.g., religious, social, or cultural groups) that can help meet students' needs. Such organizations teach students social skills and expose them to opportunities that they might not otherwise experience (Anson *et al.* 1991).

The League of Schools Reaching Out

Housed at Boston University's School of Education, The League of Schools Reaching Out was established by the Institute for Responsive Education (IRE), a nonprofit public interest research and advocacy organization created to 'study, promote, and assist citizen participation in educational decision-making and school improvement.' Funded primarily through The Pew Charitable Trusts and the John D. and Catherine T. MacArthur Foundation, the purpose of the League is to demonstrate how partnerships between the school and families and the community can contribute to school restructuring (Davies 1991: 24).

The League conceptualizes school restructuring as a process aimed at increasing the academic and social success of all students, but particularly those who are labeled 'at risk' (Davies 1991). The League characterizes its work as:

> . . . an alternative approach to educational reform designed to demonstrate the potential effectiveness of a comprenehsive ecological approach to restructuring in which school reform is directly linked to family support and education, neighborhood social and economic development, integrated services for poor families, and means for family contribution to children's development. (Davies 1991: 6)

As indicated above, the League, in line with earlier concerns mentioned in this chapter (Edwards and Young 1992), stresses an ecological approach which involves all aspects of a child's development. As Davies, executive Director of the IRE, has pointed out: 'As with a natural ecosystem, what happens in one part of the child's ecology affects the child and affects the other parts or subsystems as well' (Davies 1991: 5).

The League's work, therefore, springs from the belief that the roots of educational failure lie in social and economic paralysis. Thus, the only viable approaches to improving the success of schoolchildren are by working through all the institutions that shape the child – institutions which deeply affect a child's social, physical, emotional, spiritual, and academic development. These include, but are not limited to, the family, the neighborhood, schools, day care centers, and churches as well as government agencies, civic organizations, and business and financial institutions (Davies 1991).

The League is based on an ideology which maintains that: all children can learn and achieve academic and social success; all institutions affecting the child are part of the problem of the social and academic failure of children; and the only way of solving this problem is through collaborative planning, coordinated programming, and partnerships that result in 'a new social contract for children' (Davies 1991: 8–9). Therefore, for the League's efforts to be successful, it is critical that a substantial number of stakeholders, including teachers, administrators, community representatives, and parents, share this ideology (Davies 1991).

The League envisions itself as a national network and a reform strategy as well as a collection of individual schools implementing their own plans for increasing student success through family, community, and school collaboration. Reform-oriented schools form the basis for the League's efforts which rest on several core tenets. These include a shared ideology; joint ownership of the need for change; and the necessity for constructive criticism and outside assistance on a regular basis from third-party reform agents and intervenors recruited and trained by the League.

League members are also expected to establish and implement a clear plan of action that includes parents' centers (i.e., 'a physical presence for parents in the school'), parent support workers to help connect parents with the school, and teacher action research teams. These teams accomplish what Davies characterizes as 'an all-important need to involve classroom teachers'. Within these teams, teachers study school–family–community issues and problems, and propose and implement solutions such as developing methods to improve classroom instruction and curriculum by involving families or collaborating with community agencies (Davies 1991).

The Philadelphia Children's Network

'Help the children. Fix the system.' This is the slogan of the Philadelphia Children's Network (PNC), a non-profit organization established in the spring of 1990 by Ralph Smith, professor at the University of Pennsylvania Law School, former chief of staff in the Philadelphia School District, and special advisor on children's issues to the city's mayor.

Funded in part through a grant from the Warren V. Musser Foundation, the Children's Network focuses on a system-wide audit, analysis, and redesign of the support systems provided to young children. Recognizing the need for both substantive and procedural changes, the Children's Network has two substantive objectives and one procedural, or what Smith calls, a 'strategic' objective (Smith 1992: 21).

The first substantive objective, to promote school readiness, is also one of the national goals set forth by the nation's governors and former President George Bush in the US Department of Education's (1989) America 2000 plan. Smith (1992) clearly points out the sad plight of so many children and how the schools can help; but doing so requires the assistance of other agencies.

> In schools across the nation, far too many children come to school weary survivors of the journey from birth to school, bringing with them undetected, undiagnosed, and untreated physical ailments, vision, and hearing impairments, developmental delays, and emotional scars. It is true that schools and teachers must be held accountable for teaching the students they have and not just those they would like to have. Nevertheless, their jobs could be eased significantly if the primary health care, day care, early education, parent training and family support systems worked together to ensure a child ready to learn and care givers prepared to support that learning. (Smith 1992: 21)

The second objective of the Children's Network is to re-engage young fathers with their children. Here, the Network, through peer support groups, intensive case management, and a 'fatherhood' curriculum with values-clarification activities, offers encouragement, support, and strategies aimed at enabling fathers to become and remain engaged with their children (Smith 1992).

Smith's third, 'strategic' objective is to: 'foster coordination among the child-serving systems'. To this end, the Children's Network has been involved in a variety of local capacity-building functions such as expanding Headstart and other early education programs, lending assistance to and training parents and other primary care providers, and connecting families with other services such as family literacy and day care (Smith 1992).

Underlying all the Children's Network's efforts is a philosophy which recognizes that the system is part of the problem and changing the system must be part of the solution. Empowering agency stakeholders is critical to these efforts. These stakeholders can improve the effectiveness and efficiency of programs in a variety of ways. They can educate students as well as provide information to parents that will facilitate student development and learning. They can identify specific problems (e.g., scarcity of resources) and link with other agencies and families to help resolve these problems. And they can provide and exchange information regarding specific approaches to addressing student needs. At the same time, these service providers, as well as all other aspects of the child and youth serving system, must be held accountable for making measurable progress towards improving service quality and accessibility and producing healthy, school-ready children (Smith 1992).

While change in the public sector is difficult, it is not impossible if challenges such as highly delineated agency boundaries and the absence of traditional incentives are confronted and overcome. Consequently, agencies must work together to improve family functioning, promote family self-sufficiency, and nurture supportive neighborhoods as a means of assisting children and youth, as well as develop viable and replicable strategies that empower stakeholders and facilitate system change (Smith 1992).

New Beginnings

Recognizing that its city's service delivery was inconsistent, wasteful, crisis-oriented, and fragmented, governmental agencies in San Diego, California joined forces 'to develop a long-term strategy for systemic change in the way services are provided to young people and their families' (Payzant 1992: 140). Having received funding for an initial study from the Stuart Foundation and subsequent funding, for evaluation purposes, from the Pew Foundation, this effort currently involves a number of San Diego family-serving agencies. These organizations include: the San Diego County Department of Social Services; the San Diego City Schools; the City of San Diego; the San Diego Community College District; the San Diego Housing Commission; the Medical Center of the University of California; and the Children's Hospital (Payzant 1992).

New Beginnings started in 1988 with an interagency forum to bring the leaders of various governmental groups together to exchange ideas about how they could jointly serve the needs of their constituencies which mostly comprised low-income children, youth, and their families. Early discussions focused on arriving at a consensual definition of collaboration – a task which was not only difficult, but deemed to be essential to the success of the program (Payzant 1992).

Thomas Payzant, former superintendent of the San Diego City Schools, mirrored the deliberations of the group when he stated that collaboration is 'more than simply talking to one another . . . learning about the services and resources of the other agencies, sharing data about clients, coordinating the delivery of various services' (Payzant 1992: 141).

Rather, collaboration is joint consensus and agreement to identify, and then to address, specific problems for service delivery.

As discovered in San Diego, collaboration as change requires that a single government entity cannot have the major responsibility for planning and implementing such an intensive effort. Collaboration, once defined by those involved, means adding 'partners' to the process and raising both substantive and procedural questions (Payzant 1992). Hence, current practices are no longer sufficient where an alliance replaces individual efforts.

Besides this definition of collaboration, participants in New Beginnings share a common set of assumptions about their work. These premises include:

- a recognition of the complex problems that the city faces including a large and growing immigrant (Indochinese and Latino) population, inadequate low-cost housing and public transportation, and high rates of family mobility;
- a focus on making the most of existing resources in light of serious financial constraints imposed on all public service agencies;
- emphasis on assistance early in children's lives;
- a recognition that the targets of effective programs must be family systems rather than individuals;
- an understanding that staff members in most agencies are either unfamiliar with, or mistrustful of, staff in other organizations; and
- the realization that interagency collaboration calls for leadership efforts and commitment from the executive level. (Payzant 1992)

The work of this alliance has involved the execution of feasibility studies consisting of: intensive interviews with families, students, and front-line service providers from participating agencies; comparisons of data sources indicating the types and levels of services and resources available from the participating agencies; an investigation of the mobility patterns of the families of school-age children; placement of social workers in the schools to work directly with families; and, finally, the institution of a system of inter-agency liaisons to make outside agencies more accessible to school staff (Payzant 1992).

Some of the most dramatic findings of these studies indicated that: most families are unaware of the services available to them; families see the school as a place to get help; differences in philosophy make cooperation among agencies difficult to accomplish; and most social service providers feel dehumanized in their jobs and frustrated by the narrowness and inflexibility of their work. The studies also confirmed the agencies' initial impressions that services were fragmented and often duplicated each other (Payzant 1992).

Participating agencies have officially adopted the recommendations of the feasibility study, one of which proposes to empower agency staff by allowing these persons to work more intensively with fewer families, and, in essence, become 'family advocates'. Another suggests that a common eligibility process be developed with one central contact point for families. This would avoid duplication of effort. Last, but probably most importantly, New Beginnings has established a demonstration site for interagency collaboration at a San Diego elementary school (Payzant 1992).

Conclusions

This chapter has characterized schools as 'open systems' which, if they are to remain viable, must elicit the support of the community and other service providers. Successful collaboration, however, demands that there be: clearly agreed goals; precise responsibilities; shared resources; mutual respect and trust; and an ecological approach that legitimizes and enhances the delivery of collaborative services. To achieve this type of organizational culture requires, in most cases, a rethinking of the rules that govern educational institutions as well as a new conception of the roles and responsibilities of school personnel. In this process, agency stakeholders, those 'street-level' bureaucrats who provide direct service to students and their families, must be empowered.

The authors acknowledge that this type of collaboration is difficult, but they do not believe that it is impossible. The four nationally recognized initiatives described in this chapter seem to bridge successfully the gap between theory and practice. While each of these efforts approached interagency collaboration from its own unique vantage point, common themes emerged. They included: a reconceptualization of the roles of schools; decentralization of agency control; empowerment of agency stakeholders; an ecological approach stressing development of the 'whole child'; an emphasis on family needs rather than individual student problems; and a recognition that agencies must share responsibilities in meeting the needs of their clientele.

References

AIKEN, M. (1975) *Coordinating Human Services* (San Francisco: Jossey-Bass).

ANSON, A., COOK, T. D., HABIB, F., GRADY, M. K., HAYNES, N. and COMER, J. P. (1991) 'The Comer school development program: practice resting on theories of society', *Urban Education*, 26, pp. 56–82.

BARTH, R. S. (1990) *Improving Schools From Within* (San Francisco: Jossey-Bass).

BELASCO, J. (1989) *Teaching the Elephant To Dance, The Manager's Guide to Empowering Change* (New York: Plume Books).

BERMAN, P. and MCLAUGHLIN, M. W. (1978) *Federal Programs Supporting Educational Change*, Vol. VIII: *Implementing and Sustaining Innovations* (Santa Monica, CA: Rand).

BROWN, R., PALAICH, B., LEDERER, M., and PAOLINO, A. (1991) *Restructuring the Education System: A Consumer's Guide* (Denver: Education Commission of the States), pp. 17–18.

COMER, J. P. (1980) *School Power – Implications of an Intervention Project* (New York: Free Press).

COMER, J. P. (1987) 'New Haven's school community connection', *Educational Leadership*, 44, pp. 13–16.

CORBETT, H. D. (1990) *On the Meaning of Restructuring* (Philadelphia: Research for Better Schools).

CUBAN, L. (1989) 'The at risk label and the problem of urban school reform, *Phi Delta Kappan*, 70, pp. 780–784, 799–801.

DAVIES, D. (1981a) 'Citizen participation in decision-making in the schools', in D. Davies (ed.) *Communities and their Schools* (New York: McGraw-Hill), pp. 83–119.

DAVIES, D. (ed.) (1981b) *Communities and their Schools* (New York: McGraw-Hill).

DAVIES, D. (1991) 'Testing a strategy for reform: The League of Schools Reaching Out', paper presented at the annual meeting of the American Educational Research Association, Chicago.

DEAL, T. E. (1990) 'Reframing reform', *Educational Leadership*, 47, pp. 6–12.

EDWARDS, P. A. and YOUNG, L. S. (1992) 'Beyond parents: family, community, and school involvement', *Phi Delta Kappan*, 74, pp. 72–80.

ELMORE, R. F. (1991) *Restructuring Schools* (San Francisco: Jossey-Bass).

FULLAN, M. G. (1991) *The New Meaning of Educational Change* (New York: Teachers College Press).

HEATH, S. B. and MCLAUGHLIN, M. W. (1991) 'Community organizations as family: endeavors that engage and support adolescents', *Phi Delta Kappan*, 72, pp. 623–627.

KIRST, M. W. (1983) 'Effective School: political environment and education policy', *Planning and Changing*, 14, pp. 234–244.

KOOP, C. E. (1992) 'Strengthening the bonds between health care agencies and communities in meeting the needs of young children', presentation to the Pennsylvania Department of Education's third annual pre-school symposium, Harrisburg, Pa.

LEVY, J. E. and SHEPARDSON, W. (1992) 'A look at current school-linked service efforts', in R. E. Behrman (ed.) *The Future of Children*, Vol. 2 (Los Altos, CA: Center for the Future of Children), pp. 44–55.

LIEBERMAN, A. and MILLER, L. (1986) 'School improvement themes and variations', in A. Lieberman (ed.) *Rethinking School Improvement* (New York: Teachers College Press).

LINDBLOM, C. (1980) *The Policy-Making Process* (New York: Prentice-Hall).

LINEHAN, M. F. (1992) 'Children who are homeless: education strategies for school personnel', *Phi Delta Kappan*, 74, pp. 61–66.

LIPSKY, M. (1980) *Street Level Bureaucracy* (Newbury Park, CA: Sage).

LOUIS, K. and MILES, M. B. (1990) *Improving the Urban High School: What Works and Why* (New York: Teachers College Press).

MCLAUGHLIN, M. W. (1990) 'The Rand change agent study revisited: macro perspectives and micro realities', *Educational Researcher*, 19, pp. 11–16.

MAEROFF, G. I. (1988) *The Empowerment of Teachers* (New York: Teachers College Press).

MARCH, J. G. and OLSEN, J. P. (1980) *Ambiguity and Choice in Organizations* (London: Oxford University Press).

MARCH, J. G. and SIMON, H. A. (1958) *Organizations* (New York: Wiley).

MELAVILLE, A. and BLANK, M. (1991) *What It Takes: Structuring Interagency Partnerships to Connect Children and Families with Comprehensive Service* (Washington, DC: Education and Human Services Consortium).

MEYER, M. and TUCKER, L. (1989) *Permanently Failing Organizations* (Newbury Park, CA: Sage).

MURPHY, J. (1991) *Restructuring Schools: Capturing and Assessing the Phenomenon* (New York: Teachers College Press).

MURPHY, M.J. and HART, A. W. (1988) 'Preparing principals to lead in restructured schools', paper presented at meeting of the University Council for Educational Administration, Cincinnati.

NEWMANN, F. M. (1991) *Issues in Restructuring Schools* (University of Wisconsin-Madison: Center on Organization and Restructuring of Schools).

PAYZANT, T. W. (1992) 'New Beginnings in San Diego: Developing a strategy for interagency collaboration', *Phi Delta Kappan*, 74, pp. 139–146.

RALLIS, S. F. (1990) 'Professional teachers and restructured schools: leadership challenges', in B. Mitchell and L. L. Cunningham (eds) *Educational Leadership and Changing Contexts of Families, Communities, and Schools* (Chicago: University of Chicago Press).

SARASON, S. B. (1971) *The Culture of the School and the Problem of Change* (Boston: Allyn and Bacon).

SARASON, S. B. (1990) *The Predictable Failure of Educational Reform* (San Francisco: Jossey-Bass).

SCHLECHTY, P. C. and JOSLIN, A. W. (1986) 'Images of schools', in A. Lieberman (ed.) *Rethinking School Improvement* (New York: Teachers College Press).

SEELEY, D. and SCHWARTZ, R. (1981) 'Debureaucratizing public education', in D. Davies (ed.) *Communities and their Schools* (New York: McGraw-Hill), pp. 59–81.

SERGIOVANNI, T. J. (1990) 'Adding value to leadership gets extraordinary results', *Educational Leadership*, 47, pp. 23–27.

SILBERMAN, C. E. (1970) *Crisis in the Classroom* (New York: Random House).

SMITH, R. (1992) 'Help the children. Fix the system', *University of Pennsylvania Law Journal*, 27, pp. 20–23.

TIMAR, T. (1989) 'The politics of school restructuring', *Phi Delta Kappan*, 71, pp. 265–275.

US DEPARTMENT OF EDUCATION (1989) *America 2000, An Education Strategy* (Washington, DC: US Dept. of Education).

WEICK, K. E. (1976) 'Educational organizations as loosely coupled systems', *Administrative Service Quarterly*, 21, pp. 1–19.

WIRT, F. M. and KIRST, M. W. (1972) *The Political Web of American Schools* (Boston: Little, Brown).

WISE, A. E. (1989) 'Professional teaching: a new paradigm for the management of education', in T. J. Sergiovanni and J. H. Moore (eds) *Schooling for Tomorrow* (Boston: Allyn and Bacon).

ZEICHNER, K. M. (1989) 'Preparing teachers for democratic schools', *Action in Teacher Education*, 11, pp. 5–10.

POLITICS OF EDUCATION ASSOCIATION YEARBOOK, 1993, 121–134

Implementing collaborative services: new challenges for practitioners and experts in reform

Stephanie Kadel and Dorothy Routh

Introduction

Implementing a new program in an organization is often a difficult matter. Changing the 'way we do things around here' is even more unsettling. Perhaps one of the most challenging changes of all, however, is implementing collaborative social service provision, because it requires changes in the way a variety of organizations do things and involves simultaneous and complementary reform across systems. Human service providers are currently facing this challenge when trying to offer integrated, comprehensive services to families. Fortunately, enough examples of school–social service relationships or other collaborative efforts exist to reveal some common elements of this implementation process. In order to help collaborators meet this challenge successfully, we will describe in the following pages eight practical stages through which most collaborative initiatives pass and highlight these with descriptions of actual efforts.

While interagency collaboration poses challenges for service providers, it can also serve as a new focus for researchers in the area of reform and change. In this article, we will look at the ways in which the reform literature can be helpful to collaborators but does not always address the complex changes required in collaborative service reform. We will conclude with recommendations for additional research focused on the change process involved in collaborating to integrate services.

The implementation process

Through a review of literature on developing collaborative relationships, visits to successful integrated service sites, and descriptions of efforts nation-wide, we have compiled the following eight stages of the development process. While the stages provide practical guidelines, they should not be viewed as a recipe for collaboration; each effort will have unique resources and needs. Also, collaborative efforts will have to be both flexible and organized; too much organization may prevent the bending and compromise that are necessary, and too much flexibility may delay tough decisions. These stages can also overlap, be repeated, or occur in a different order as collaborators refine their goals and expand their efforts.

Stage 1: getting started

A collaborative service effort typically begins when an individual or small group recognizes the need for collaboration to improve services for families, conceives of various

0268–0939/93 $10·00

options, perceives that the climate is right for such a collaboration in the community, and believes that success is possible. This initiation can come from any point in the community: a principal, parent group, social services administrator, school board member, medical clinic team, community advocacy group, or business. Initiation can also result from a state or federal mandate or new funding opportunity, but dynamic change agents at the local level are still important to take advantage of political and financial support.

Stage 2: developing a community collaborative council

The first charge of the initiators of collaboration is to develop a community collaborative council and plan the council's first meetings. This council should have diverse membership, representing human service agencies – including schools, social service providers, and health clinics – as well as community and parent groups, universities or colleges, and other interested parties. It is also important to seek the participation of key decision makers in the community whose input and conviction will be invaluable during planning and implementation and to invite possible local funding sources, such as businesses and foundations. Initiators may want to meet individually with agency administrators, practitioners, and community groups to discuss the perceived critical needs of the community and determine which service agencies should be involved at the start. To develop the council, initiators may find it easier to begin with a small council and a limited set of services and plan to expand over time. Whatever the size of the council, however, it is especially important to include practitioners – those who will actually provide the coordinated services – including nurses, social workers, counselors, and classroom teachers. Their input, trust, and feelings of ownership will be required for successful implementation.

The Networking Committee in Decatur, Georgia is one example of a community collaborative council. It began with a desire to provide more comprehensive services for students who attend Oakhurst Elementary School. In 1988, the director of the DeKalb County Teenage Pregnancy Task Force and the superintendent of Decatur City Schools brought together six agencies who met with Oakhurst's principal to discuss how to improve service delivery for specific students. The Networking Committee has since grown and now serves as an umbrella organization representing private business, social agencies, the court system, parks and recreation, churches, United Way of Atlanta, grant agencies, and community service organizations. Over 30 agencies currently work with nine schools, two of which serve as 'nucleus sites' and provide parent education, health care, staff development, after-school care, and service referral for families (Griffith 1992).

In order to recruit potential collaborators to the first meeting of the council, initiators may remind those who are invited of the social problems relevant to the work of their agencies which cannot seem to be overcome successfully using individualized approaches. At the meeting, agency representatives can discuss collaborative objectives and attempt to connect these to individual objectives (Gans and Horton 1975). Levy and Copple (1989: 16) suggest a similar strategy:

> At the beginning, when participants are still struggling to understand one another and get past their differences, it is useful to focus on issues whose mutual relevance and importance is readily apparent. Frequently, a prime motivator is systemic 'pain' – inefficiency, inability to carry out necessary tasks, undesirable impacts, or bad press. It is easier to garner support to fix tangible problems than to tackle abstract matters because 'it's the right thing to do'.

Collaboration may develop slowly. Gardner (1992a) recognizes four increasingly complex ways in which organizations interact: (1) sharing information about agencies and specific cases; (2) coordinating services through joint projects; (3) changing the rules of the system by redefining jobs and administrative policies; and (4) changing the system itself by continuously evaluating service mechanisms and promoting supportive public policy. New collaborative councils must recognize the likelihood of this gradual process and allow the necessary time for changes to build on themselves.

A crucial objective of the initial meetings of a community collaborative council is for members to get to know one another. They will need to build trusting relationships and become more familiar with each other's service agencies, professional positions, and priorities. Members will quickly realize the need to avoid professional jargon with which others will not be familiar, and the council will need to agree on the definition of some terms. Clear leadership will also need to be established. While a leader (or leaders) may naturally emerge early in the collaborative process, the council will need to make certain that all participants are comfortable with the leadership choice and that the leader can meet his or her responsibilities. Shared decision making can be encouraged by a leader who conveys trust in the participants' abilities, offers support, and shares the responsibility for failures as well as successes (Wilkes 1992).

Some conflict will be inevitable as the council begins its work. 'Turf' issues such as the need for autonomy or fear of job loss will arise, as well as conflicts resulting from poor communication, funding limitations, confusion over goals, and the natural uncertainties that result from breaking new ground. Liontos (1991) recommends that a new collaborative council begin its work by focusing on a problem which is not traditionally the exclusive responsibility of any one agency (such as teenage pregnancy), and Ayres (1984) suggests that groups in conflict should focus their attention on issues that will restore balance and remind collaborators of the group goal. Council members should also take time to review accomplishments achieved through collaboration. Of course, 'some group tension can be healthy and provide momentum for change and opportunities to reestablish commitment' (Ayres 1984: 17). It is important to encourage discussion of conflict which results from differing values and opinions; suppressing conflict in order to hasten progress toward a goal will hamper long-term success. Problem solving which allows collaborators to work through their differences and reach acceptable compromises will build trust between individuals and a feeling of ownership of the collaborative.

Other difficulties may be encountered during this stage. Guthrie and Guthrie (1991: 21–22) warn collaborators of these 'pitfalls and danger signs':

> 'NATO (No Action, Talk Only)' – New groups can spend a lot of time making assumptions, theorizing about solutions, and presenting information. Some of this is necessary in the beginning, but collaborators should try to determine goals early in the process in order to avoid wasting time and frustrating participants.
>
> 'Creating an interagency czar or a superagency' – Participants need to beware of establishing a new layer of bureaucracy through a collaborative council and remember that 'money is best spent on direct, front-line services'.

Another common constraint is the lack of available staff time to work with the council. Agency administrators at all levels will need to support the collaboration so that members of the council can make the necessary time and energy commitments.

The council will have many responsibilities in the collaboration. Its most important role will be to develop the collaborative initiative, but other tasks will also be required. The council can work to promote its efforts in the community and attempt to involve more participants. It can monitor success of collaborative activities and plan for evaluations. It can seek additional funding for the initiative and work with policy makers to encourage and support collaborative efforts. A large council may want to divide into advisory committees to deal with specific issues or responsibilities and to make recommendations for the whole group to consider (Heal *et al.* 1990).

Stage 3: identifying a shared vision and goals

One of the first tasks of the community collaborative council is to come to an agreement about a vision for integrated services and the goals of a collaborative venture. Participants will need a clear focus, early in the process, to justify time spent on the council's activities. In order to establish this vision, participants should focus on what is best for children and families as they develop a shared awareness of needs and desired outcomes. Successful collaborative efforts are characteristized by a family-centered approach, a preventive focus, comprehensive services, and flexibility (Guthrie and Guthrie 1991, Jewett *et al.* 1991, Melaville and Blank 1991).

Goals will necessarily be broad until a formal needs assessment is conducted, but goal-setting will be an ongoing process taking place before, during, and after the needs assessment. Ringers (1981) suggests setting intermediate as well as long-term goals so that council members can recognize some early accomplishments. By setting intermediate goals, collaborators are preparing to evaluate their progress throughout the development and implementation of the collaborative in order to make mid-stream adjustments and enhancements. Setting short- and long-term goals will inevitably lead to discussions on program evaluation and funding accountability requirements, thus preparing the council for later stages.

Stage 4: conducting a needs assessment

A needs assessment for a social services collaborative involves asking these questions:

- What services are needed in the community?
- What services are provided by the existing service agencies?
- Who is providing what services?
- What needed services are not being offered?
- Who can best provide these services?
- What personnel and services do agencies themselves need?

A needs assessment should be conducted early in the collaborative process and periodically repeated throughout the life of the program. Needs change over time, and the agencies which can best provide certain services will fluctuate with changes in funding and personnel. It is especially important to ask community residents to identify and clarify their own needs; they know their needs better than anyone.

Responses to some of the above questions may be gathered quickly by examining data already collected by schools and other agencies. Other effective methods of data collection include interviewing or surveying practitioners, parents, administrators, and clients; studying the demographics of the community (census and land-use planning data); and observing the current system at work. The community collaborative council may also benefit from a look at existing and past agreements between agencies that may serve as building blocks for collaborative work. Agency representatives can discuss other experiences working together and identify characteristics or types of agreements (e.g., mandated, informal, sharing of resources, sharing of personnel) that contributed to success or failure (*Planning for State Solutions* 1988). This also allows agencies to discuss their perceived roles further and to answer such questions as 'How do agencies know which children need help?' or 'How does one agency help families obtain services from another agency?' (Farrar and Hampel 1987).

The 'Center' in Leadville, Colorado, responded to child care and educational needs of an economically depressed community when it opened in 1988. Parents, who left in the early morning to drive to low-wage jobs at ski resorts, needed affordable, all-day child care. Statistics demonstrated that other services were needed as well: only 63% of students completed high school, just 30% went to college, and the teenage pregnancy rate was 12%. The superintendent of schools met with teachers and other practitioners to design the Center which offers Head Start and after-school programs, parent education, access to prenatal care, and other services. In the past four years, the Center has made significant progress in meeting the needs of parents, educators and children and has helped reduce the teenage pregnancy rate by half and double the percentage of students going on to college (Wehling 1992).

Stage 5: developing a plan of action

When a community collaborative council has determined the current status of service delivery in the community and agreed on a mission and goals, the next step is to develop a strategy for reaching those goals. Decisions will have to be made regarding many issues and activities such as the following.

Choosing a facility: While some collaborative initiatives may find that service provision can be improved without collocating services at a central site, many existing efforts have determined the need for such a hub. Choosing a location will largely depend on space availability, resources, and community demographics. A site should be easily accessible to the people who will use it and should allow for expansion. It should be perceived by parents and other community members as a safe and comfortable place to bring children and come for help. While a school may seem the most logical facility because it is the only place in the community where children come every day, arguments are made for and against collocating services at a school. Some benefits of developing a school-based collaborative include better communication between parents and schools; increased community involvement at the school; more comprehensive records of students' academic and other service requirements; and expanded use of existing school facilities such as libraries, auditoriums, gymnasiums, kitchens, and recreational areas. Also, student attendance may increase when students can get medical and other services at school and then return to class (Cohen, D. L. 1989a, Groves 1990, Kagan 1989).

However, some reservations about making schools the hub of service provision have also been voiced. First, schools have traditionally maintained a policy of separatism from other human services; some agencies may be skeptical of a school's willingness or ability to collaborate (Cohen, D. L. 1989a, Kirst and McLaughlin 1989). Second, schools can appear intimidating to parents or other family members – seeming unwelcoming or bringing back feelings of failure. Third, busing and desegregation policies confuse the relation between 'school' and 'community' when children are bused away from their neighbourhood to another area of town. If a community determines that the school is not the ideal location for collaborative services, it can investigate other options, such as a church, medical clinic, Head Start center, or community recreation facility.

The Family Servies Center of Alachua County, Florida is located between a middle school and an elementary school in a high-poverty area of Gainesville. The Center consists of seven portable buildings which house a medical clinic, an adult education classroom and computer lab, early child-care classrooms for infants to four-year-olds, a toy-lending library, administrative offices, and a reception area. On-site human service workers provide public assistance eligibility determination; vocational and employment guidance; health, mental health, nutrition, and substance abuse counseling; college admission and financial aid assistance; and more. Because the Family Services Center is located on city property and not directly affiliated with either school, the director believes both schools, and parents with young children, are more comfortable using its services (Cantrell 1992, *Family Services Center* 1992).

Establishing family eligibility: Councils need to decide who will be served by the collaborative. The question of targeting is not any easy one to answer, but Gardner (1992b) warns against avoiding this critical issue: 'Planners must address it explicitly. They should do so knowing that there will be substantial political resistance to saying that one group is more in need than another' (p. 90). Of course, program eligibility restrictions will impact on targeting decisions; while health clinics located at schools, for example, often serve the total school population, many programs funded by state or federal funds have narrow eligibility requirements. Varying eligibility criteria can pose problems in determining who can receive what available services. The National Commission for Employment Policy suggests instituting 'multi-purpose application forms' which include agency-specific questions as well as questions that apply to all service programs. This benefits families by reducing frustration and time spent filling out separate forms and may also save money in administration time and paperwork (*Coordinating Federal Assistance* 1991: 18). Collaborators may also want to rethink existing eligibility regulations that may be barriers to effective and comprehensive service delivery.

Meeting confidentiality regulations: Record sharing among service providers is usually necessary for providing coordinated services to families, but most agencies have confidentiality policies which restrict access to records. One way to overcome these regulations is to obtain parental consent to share information between agencies. Consent is also necessary to secure parental permission to provide services to children and can be used to inform parents of the services that are available to them and their families. Another recommendation for addressing confidentiality concerns is to maintain limited access to records of highly confidential information (such as mental health treatment) but to include broad statements about referral and recommendations in central files (such as school records) that are accessible to parents and practitioners (Cohen, D. L. 1989b). While local agencies will be limited in their control over confidentiality policies, members of the collaborative council may want to reconsider certain regulations and propose a new, coordinated record-keeping system. Such a system would allow records on a family to be compiled in one location, entered onto a computerized database if possible, and accessed by any service provider who signs an oath of confidentialilty. *Confidentiality and Collaboration: Information Sharing in Interagency Efforts* (1992) may be a helpful resource for collaborators facing this issue.

Assigning responsibilities: As part of the action plan, the council will need to decide which agency will offer which services and how existing staff will be integrated into the new program. Some of these decisions, such as that of leadership, may be made earlier in the process. Redistributing service responsibilities for school nurses, school psychologists, or counselors will need to be handled with practicality and sensitivity, especially if services are located on school grounds. As with other major decisions in the planning process, assigning responsibilities should be the result of shared decision-making among all council participants. New roles should be based on the strengths and wishes of individuals and should allow for flexibility as the collaborative develops and changes. Training and ongoing support for practitioners with new responsibilities will be necessary. While changing people's job responsibilities can cause conflict, practitioners will be more receptive to change and will find it easier to adapt if they have been involved with the council from the beginning and are consulted about the changes.

Making use of existing funds: Most collaboratives that begin at a grass-roots level bring together numerous agencies with various funding streams and attempt to pool resources. This is a sensible approach given that few new funds for social programs appear to be forthcoming and that coordinated administration and reduced duplication of services make better use of limited resources. However, as Melaville and Blank (1991) note, 'The administrative time and staff required to patch together and maintain accountability for multiple money sources inevitably takes away from organized development on other fronts' (p. 13), and it risks creating a collaborative which offers a smattering of programs that meet funding accountability requirements but do not meet the comprehensive needs of families. One suggestion is to create a multi-year 'master-contract' which redefines rules and accountability requirements by identifying performance criteria and a single, combined set of regulations (Melaville and Blank 1991, Gans and Horton 1975).

Stage 6: implementing the plan

Once collaborators have designed a plan for the collaborative, consideration should be given to the most effective means for informing the public and recruiting children and families who need the services. The opening of a Collaborative Service Center can be coordinated with the beginning of a school year or, if it is located at a school, with the school's 'open house' night. An official 'ribbon-cutting' ceremony will generate publicity for the Center and establish connections with political organizations and the media. Letters of invitation to families and announcements posted in local businesses, city buses, and churches may encourage use of the Center.

As with any stage in the process, implementation will present many challenges. Agency personnel will have to adjust to new responsibilities, policies and regulations, and interruptions. Seemingly simple scheduling can cause problems; for example, daily routines and monthly calendars for each agency may not coincide. In addition, families may require assistance with transportation in order to make use of the services. Since lack of transportation for families can be a significant logistical constraint to successful implementation, Hodgkinson (1989) suggests using school buses while school is in session or after school to transport parents to and from service providers.

Ongoing staff training will also be a necessary component of the implementation process. Because 'collaboration occurs among people – not among instututions', workers must be 'supported at each level of organization where collaboration is expected to take place' (Bruner 1991: 26). Training and support can focus on changing attitudes as well as building skills. Practitioners will benefit from guidance in why and how to share resources, refer clientele, maintain records, and make collaborative decisions. They will need knowledge about the array of possible services, the structure and requirements of each agency, and the culture of the community being served. Additional staff development on the vision of holistic service delivery and societal improvement will also be important for all participants in a collaborative effort (Melaville and Blank 1991).

Seeking financial and political support: Local-level collaborative initiatives can be greatly aided by local, state, and federal support such as improved policies and increased public and private funding. Support for integrated services can vary widely, and council members should be encouraged to seek such support. For example, technical assistance from experts can help a Collaborative Service Center acquire certification as a Medicaid provider or design a computerized database for record keeping. Regulation waivers offered by policy makers can simplify confidentiality or eligibility requirements or allow funding to be pooled more easily. Financial support and incentives from foundations or government depeartments can reward interagency collaboration through demonstration programs that 'balance specific objectives to ensure direction, with sufficient flexibility to match local needs and resources' (Melaville and Blank 1991: 19).

A collaborative council may want to use its combined clout to lobby, at the state or national level, for policy changes and funding allocations that will aid present and future collaborative activities. A council may also offer its assistance to national organizations that are currently involved in the effort to gain political and financial support for collaborative services. However, initial and more immediate assistance in implementing a collaborative may require other actions, including seeking in-kind contributions, organizing a team of volunteers, and writing grant proposals.

The Parent Center at Sudduth Elementary School in Starkville, Mississippi, relies on community volunteers and donations to support its activities. For example, the local newspaper runs a weekly column devoted to parenting and children's learning. The local television station allows parents, children, and school personnel to demonstrate and televise good parenting techniques and at-home activities on its leftover public service time. Fund-raising for family gatherings and materials was aided by an agreement with Coca-Cola and Mississippi State University's baseball team; parents sold concessions at the games and all the proceeds went to the school. In addition, the 'Coats for Kids' project provides Sudduth students with needed clothing. Because of such contributions, the Parent Center, which also offers social service referrals, evening workshops for parents (and child care for children), a toy/videotape/book library, mental health counseling, and a 24-hour parenting help line, costs the school district only the salaries of two para-professionals who act as home–school coordinators and who collaborate with other service providers (Butler 1992).

Stage 7: evaluation

As with any human service program, a collaborative effort will need to be evaluated. Plans for evaluation should be made while the collaborative is being developed: outcome measures should relate to initial goals, needs assessment data may be compared with results, and some data collection may involve record keeping over the course of development and implementation. A thorough evaluation looks both at whether the initiative was successful in meeting its goals and why it was or was not effective. Especially important for seeking financial and political support is identifying ways in which collaborating saves money over traditional service delivery practices. In addition, when designing both formative and summative evaluation strategies, collaborators will 'need to go beyond the traditional bean-counting of numbers of children served or contact hours' and ask meaningful questions about such issues as improved communication, policy changes, participant satisfaction, and reduced risks (Guthrie and Guthrie 1991: 21)

If collaborators have set short- and long-term goals, early improvements can be acknowledged and publicized while ultimate indicators of success – such as increased graduation rates or decreased welfare dependency – can be demonstrated over time. While many of the expected outcomes are easily quantifiable, including reduced teenage pregnancy rates and reduced numbers of children removed from their homes due to family problems, collaborators should not lose sight of additional outcomes that are more difficult to measure, such as improving children's self-esteem, empowering individuals and families to become independent, raising the expectations of community members, and improving the surrounding environment. These results can be gleaned from methods such as focus group meetings of community members, pre- and post-service attitude surveys, interviews with students and parents, and case studies of individual families.

Stage 8: publicizing successes and planning for improvements

Based on the evaluation results, the collaborative council will need to make decisions about how to improve or redesign the collaboration. Improvements will necessarily result from evaluation findings but may also include expanding the available services, developing new avenues for communication, setting up a centralised database of information, or opening Service Centers in different areas. It will take time to establish credibility for the collaboration in the community; but credibility should result from publicized improvements in service provision, participant satisfaction, and the potential for making a difference in the lives of children and families. Also, those who provide, or are considering providing, funds for the initiative will want concrete evidence of the collaborative's successes. Lastly, it is important for the council and staff to celebrate and publicize their successes so that participants can be recognized for their contributions and other communities may be inspired to try a similar strategy for improving services.

Understanding the implementation process

A review of the literature on program implementation and school reform or restructuring sheds some light on the implementation process as we have described it. Much of the literature identifies dual factors in the process of reform. Maher and Illback (1983) discuss structural/technological and functional/behavioral changes, and Fullan (1991) talks about key factors (such as roles) and key themes (such as vision) which must both be addressed. He also identifies types of change that teachers may encounter, including changes in structure and in beliefs (Fullan 1983). These dual challenges – focused on the organizations and the participants – are clearly relevant to collaborators; they should be aware that both kinds of change are involved in and necessary for the success of such a complex reform. Participants in reform must also consider the total set of goals involved in an innovation and need to realize that collaboration is just one of many ongoing changes in an organization; staff members are often involved in a number of simultaneous changes (Fullan 1991). The dynamic of multiple innovations in multiple organizations intensifies the challenges for those involved in the attempt to integrate services. These collaborators will also need to recognize that 'change is a process, not an event' and can take anywhere from three to ten years to be fully realized (Fullan 1991: 49).

A few researchers have addressed specific aspects of the reform process which may be especially useful to the implementation of collaborative efforts. Developing evaluation criteria early in the planning stages is recognized as necessary for looking at both the process and the outcomes of change (Fullan 1983, Maher and Illback 1983). Since collaboration is a relatively new venture, it is important to focus evaluation research on how people and agencies learn to collaboratate as well as on improvements in service delivery.

Fullan (1992) discusses important aspects of leadership which build collaborative work cultures. He suggests that the leader should be considered an enabler of solutions rather than the finder of solutions, help build a vision among participants, employ conflict-resolution strategies, encourage collegiality and respect for individuals, and provide ongoing professional development to practitioners. These are all aspects necessary for leaders – and collaborative councils themselves – in the implementation described above.

In discussing how reforms get institutionalized, Miles (1983) identifies some necessary components, including having leadership that supports the innovation, extending use of innovation to large numbers of people, and protecting the change from problems caused by personnel turnover. Harmony between practitioners and administrators is also important. Collaborators would be wise to pay attention to these guidelines. Effective leadership can be a significant challenge in multi-agency change, and supportive relationships among staff must be consciously sought and nurtured. Also, extensive participation – by service providers and families – should be characteristic of all collaborative efforts. Fortunately, a large and active collaborative council may ameliorate the problems of staff turnover that usually plague attempts at institutionalization.

McLaughlin (1987) echoes the need for political support as discussed in stage six. She suggests that policy making which puts pressure on agencies to change is important, but that the 'changes in attitudes, beliefs, and routine practices typically assumed by reform policies' cannot be effected without policies which support and enable such change (p. 173). Other researchers (Cohen, M. 1990, Pressman and Wildavsky 1984) also recognize the need to connect policy with implementation and to anticipate two-way effects and mutual adaptation of innovative initiatives. Efforts at collaboration need political support not just to help participants cope with change, but also to deal with the many technical and regulatory barriers to effective collaboration that are often caused by and can be remedied by policy decisions.

Despite these helpful suggestions for interagency efforts, factors which have been shown through previous research to lead to failed reform initiatives could discourage potential collaborators. In the reform literature, one of the most commonly mentioned characteristics of successful implementation is a small-scale project with a limited number of participants involved in the planning process (Huberman and Miles 1984, Pressman and Wildavsky 1984). This is obviously a problem for collaboration efforts which necessarily involve many people with differing values and priorities, and which are large scale by definition since they require policy and strategy changes within many organizations while seeking agreements on new approaches that involve all agencies. Fullan (1991) recognizes that many successful reforms do involve numerous participants, but that they most likely began as small groups of people who built momentum and encouraged later, widespread participation. Such a gradual expansion of a collaborative council is certainly possible, but truly comprehensive service delivery cannot avoid extensive involvement during the planning process.

In a landmark study of implementation, Pressman and Wildavsky (1984) expected failure of the innovations they studied when 'intense conflicts of interests were involved, if peopled who had to cooperate were expected to be at loggerheads, [and] if necessary resources were far beyond those available' (p. 87). They suggest that the chances for success are one in a million if participants must all agree on most of the decisions which are made during a planning process. These predictions for failure can be disheartening for collaborators who will inevitably face conflicts of interest, difficulties in making decisions, and even hostility during the beginning stages when 'turf-guarding' seems necessary and trust has not been established. Resource requirements are harder to anticipate with collaboratives, some of which may simply move existing service programs while others must seek additional resources to satisfy previously unmet needs. However, enough successful examples of interagency collaboration exist to suggest that all of these 'failure factors' can be overcome.

Fullan (1985) reveals another characteristic of the change process which seems incompatible with collaborative efforts when he says that 'changes in attitudes, beliefs, and understanding tend to *follow* rather than precede changes in behavior' (p. 393). Collaboratives depend on at least some surface changes in attitude before planning can even begin. Just bringing people together and telling them to 'do collaboration' is not enough at the outset; council members will have to believe (or be convinced) that working with others is necessary for improved service delivery and effectiveness, and they will have to develop trusting relationships with others before they can engage in collaborative behaviors. More study of the process of attitude change among participants in a collaborative reform is necessary.

Fullan (1985) calls for more research on the roles of teachers, parents, principals, and others in the change process. Collaboratives also need more information on this issue. How do roles of practitioners – such as social workers, teachers, and school psychologists – change; and what information will these staff members find helpful in adjusting to new roles? What roles can the principal assume in efforts at school-linked services? How do the local school district, administrative jurisdictions of other service agencies, and state offices fit into the plan? Successful collaboratives no doubt have varied experiences in dealing with role changes, but little research has surfaced on this issue.

A recent article by Fullan and Miles (1992) reveals a more comprehensive understanding of the complexity of systemic change as it may occur in interagency collaboration. They stress the importance to all participants of developing the following perspectives:

- understanding the process of change itself;
- having a clear 'map' of where reform is headed;
- realizing that solutions to complex problems are not easy or are yet unknown;
- recognizing that transition is not always comfortable for people but that reluctance or negative attitudes do not necessarily mean 'resistance' to the goals of the planners;
- viewing problems as an opportunity to be creative; and
- being prepared for the resource requirements and managerial needs of effective change.

All of these issues arise in the implementation process described above, but more research on how collaborators deal with these elements of successful change is necessary. Fullan (1991) also offers advice which is particularly relevant to service integration: 'Assume that changing the culture of institutions is the real agenda, not implementing single innovations. Put another way, when implementing particular innovations, we should always pay attention to whether the institution is developing or not' (p. 107).

Conclusion

Given the present emphasis in education and other social sciences on reforming, restructuring, and collaborating, the process of change and 'implementation planning' (Gardner 1992b) demand attention. Much research has been done on these processes as part of school reform studies, and the issues involved in developing and implementing collaborative services have received a lot of notice in recent years. However, understanding the change process as it unfolds in interagency activities is different from school reform efforts and would benefit from more research on its unique needs and difficulties.

The implementation process described in this article is meant to be a practical guide to potential collaborators. We compiled research on this process and advice from experienced collaborators into stages in order to help participants in a collaborative initiative prepare for many of the activities and constraints that would arise. But this is only one piece of comprehensive work that is necessary for interagency collaboration to become more widespread and easier to implement. Other issues discussed in this volume – including policy changes at the state and federal level and higher education programs to develop new interagency professionals and leaders – must be addressed concurrently. The potential for improved services and enhanced lives for high-risk populations has been demonstrated by successful collaborative activities nation-wide. The combined efforts, and collaboration, of researchers, practitioners, administrators, and policy makers can make services integration a reality for all those who need it.

Note

Parts of this chapter were previously published in Kadel, S. (1992) *Interagency Collaboration: Improving the Delivery of Services to Children and Families* (Tallahassee, FL: SERVE) produced with funds from the Office of Educational Research and Improvement, U.S. Department of Education, under contract no. RP91002010.

References

ASCHER, C. (1990) 'Linking schools with human service agencies', *ERIC Clearinghouse on Urban Education Digest*, 62. (ERIC Document Reproduction Service No. ED 319 877).

AYERS, G. (1984) 'Planning problems and issues with community use of educational facilities', *CEFP Journal*, 22(6), pp. 15–18.

BRUNER, C. (1991) *Thinking Collaboratively: Ten Questions and Answers to Help Policy Makers Improve Children's Services* (Washington, DC: Education and Human Services Consortium).

BUTLER, J. M. (1992, 13 May) Personal communication. Principal, Sudduth Elementary School, Starkville, MS.

CANTRELL, L. (1992, 26 February) Personal communicatiuon. Principal, Family Services Center, Gainesville, FL.

COHEN, D. L. (1989a, 15 March) 'Joining forces: an alliance of sectors envisioned to aid the most troubled young', *Education Week*, pp. 7–8, 10–11.

COHEN, D. L. (1989b, 15 March) 'New Jersey project: help close at hand', *Education Week*, pp. 9, 12.

COHEN, M. (1990) 'Key issues confronting state policymakers', in R. F. Elmore and Associates *Restructuring Schools: The Next generation of Educational Reform* (San Francisco: Jossey-Bass), pp. 251–288.

Confidentiality and Collaboration: Information Sharing in Interagency Efforts (1992) (Denver, CO: Education Commission of the States).

Coordinating Federal Assistance Programs for the Economically Disadvantaged: Recommendations and Background Materials (Special Report No. 31) (1991) (Washington, DC: National Commission for Employment Policy).

Family Services Center Brochure (1992) (Gainesville, FL: School Board of Alachua County).

FARRAR, E. and HAMPEL, R. L. (1987) 'Social services in American high schools', *Phi Delta Kappan*, 69(4), pp. 297–303.

FULLAN, M. (1983) 'Evaluating program implementation: what can be learned from Follow Through', *Curriculum Inquiry*, 13(2), pp. 215–227.

FULLAN, M. (1985) 'Change processes and strategies at the local level', *The Elementary School Journal*, 85(3), pp. 391–420.

FULLAN, M. G. (1991) *The New Meaning of Educational Change* (New York: Teachers College Press).

FULLAN, M. G. (1992) 'Visions that blind', *Educational Leadership*, 49(5), pp. 19–20.

FULLAN, M. G. and MILES, M. B. (1992) 'Getting reform right: what works and what doesn't', *Phi Delta Kappan*, 73(10), pp. 745–752.

GANS, S. P. and HORTON, G. T. (1975) *Integration of Human Services: The State and Municipal Levels* (New York: Praeger).

GARDNER, S. (1992a) 'The four stages of collaboration', in *Cutting Through the Red Tape: Meeting the Needs of California's Children* (West Scramento, CA: California School Boards Association), pp. 49–52.

GARDNER, S. (1992b) 'Key issues in developing school-linked, integrated services', *The Future of Children*, 2(1), pp. 85–94.

GRIFFITH, D. (1992, 24 April) Personal communication. Superintendent, City Schools of Decatur, Decatur, GA.

GROVES, L. (1990) *Full Service Schools: A Joint Effort Between the Department of Education and the Department of Health and Rehabilitative Services* (Paper presented to the State Board of Education, Tallahassee, Florida).

GUTHRIE, G. P. and GUTHRIE, L. F. (1991) 'Streamlining interagency collaboration for youth at risk', *Educational Leadership*, 49(1), pp. 17–22.

HEAL, L. W., COPHER, J. I. and RUSCH, F. R. (1990) 'Inter-agency agreements (IAAs) among agencies responsible for the transition education of students with handicaps from secondary schools to post-school settings', *Career Development for Exceptional Individuals*, 13(2), pp. 121–127.

HODGKINSON, H. L. (1989) *The Same Client: The Demographics of Education and Service Delivery Systems* (Washington, DC: Institute for Educational Leadership, Center for Demographic Policy).

HUBERMAN, A. M. and MILES, M. B. (1984) *Innovation Up Close: How School Improvement Works* (New York: Plenum).

JEWETT, J., CONKLIN, N. F., HAGANS, R. and CROHN, L. (1991) *Integration of Education and Human Services Project: Conceptual Synthesis and Review of Community-Based Integration Activity* (Portland, OR: Northwest Regional Educational Laboratory).

KAGAN, S. L. (1989) 'Early care and education: beyond the schoolhouse doors', *Phi Delta Kappan*, 71(2), pp. 107–112.

KIRST, M. W. and MCLAUGHLIN, M. (1989) 'Rethinking children's policy: implications for educational administration', *Florida Policy Review*, 5(1), pp. 1–8.

LEVY, J. E. and COPPLE, C. (1989) *Joining Forces: A Report from the First Year* (Alexandria, VA: National Association of State Boards of Education).

LIONTOS, L. B. (1991) 'Collaboration between schools and social services', in *At-Risk Youth in Crisis: A Handbook for Collaboration Between Schools and Social Services* (Albany, OR: Linn-Benton Education Service District, and Eugene, OR: ERIC Clearinghouse on Educational Management), pp. 19–22 (ERIC Document Reproduction Service No. ED 330 025).

MAHER, C. A. and ILLBACK, R. J. (1983) 'Planning for organizational change in schools: alternative approaches and procedures', *School Psychology Review*, 12(4), pp. 460–466.

MCLAUGHLIN, M. W. (1987) 'Learning from experience: lessons from policy implementation', *Educational Evaluation and Policy Analysis*, 9(2), pp. 171–178.

MELAVILLE, A. I. and BLANK, M. J. (1991) *What it Takes: Structuring Interagency Partnerships to Connect Children and Families with Comprehensive Services* (Washington, DC: Education and Human Services Consortium).

MILES, M. B. (1983) 'Unraveling the mystery of institutionalization', *Educational Leadership*, 41(3), pp. 14–19.

Planning for State Solutions to the Problems of Youth At Risk (1988) (Madison: Wisconsin Department of Public Instruction) (ERIC Document Reproduction Service No. ED 307 517).

PRESSMAN, J. L. and WILDAVSKY, A. (1984) *Implementation* (Berkeley: University of California Press).

RINGERS, J. (1981) *Developing, Managing and Operating Community Service Centers* (Charlottesville: University of Virginia, Mid-Atlantic Center for Community Education) (ERIC Document Reproduction Service No. ED 208 169).

WEHLING, C. (1992) 'Leadville's remarkable experiment', *Principal*, 71(3), pp. 10–12.

WILKES, D. (1992) *Schools for the 21st Century: New Roles for Teachers and Principals* (Tallahassee, FL: SouthEastern Regional Vision for Education).

PART 3
The role of the universities

POLITICS OF EDUCATION ASSOCIATION YEARBOOK, 1993, 137–151

University-based preparation for collaborative interprofessional practice

Michael S. Knapp, Kathryn Barnard, Richard N. Brandon, Nathalie J. Gehrke, Albert J. Smith, and Edward C. Teather

As interest in interprofessional practice grows, there is increasing recognition that this mode of service to families and children requires new forms of training, both for candidates first entering human service professions and on a continuing basis throughout their professional lives. Because the university is a central player in the preparation of human service professionals, the challenge lies squarely before it to devise and sustain preparation programs that will instill the skills, knowledge, and attitudes needed to guide collaborative interprofessional work. Please note that we use the term 'university' generically to include all institutions which prepare teachers, social workers, public or mental health workers, nurses, and other service professionals – not just the larger institutions occupying the first two categories of the Carnegie classification.

Universities are unlikely to accomplish this goal by adding an elective course in the school of education, social work, public health, or nursing. Rather, collaborative interprofessional practice challenges fundamental assumptions underlying professional education in the university. These challenges arise in four overlapping arenas: (1) in the university's external environment (which includes key credentialing and accrediting bodies), (2) at the intellectual core of the professional disciplines, (3) in the involvement of faculty and development of curriculum on campus, and (4) at 'practicum' sites. The chapter explores these challenges, drawing primarily on the recent experiences in one major state university.

The theme of our chapter is this: universities seeking to prepare professionals for interprofessional collaboration must confront the challenges in all four arenas, and must do so not through unilateral action, but in partnership with groups with which the university may not be used to working (clinic or agency staff, licensing bodies, etc.). In brief, we assume that preparation programs for interprofessional, collaborative practice must *themselves* be collaborative and interprofessional, thereby demanding of the university and its faculty the same kinds of skills, attitudes, and knowledge that are expected of human service professionals in the field.

We base the discussion on experiences we have had over the past two years in developing and piloting an interprofessional training project at the University of Washington (UW). UW's Training for Interprofessional Collaboration (TIC) project represents only one of many ways these issues can be addressed, but it is an especially comprehensive example and hence useful for examining the challenges that many universities face. The four responses following this chapter will reconsider the UW experience from the perspective of other campuses engaged in interprofessional preparation.

The TIC project is now two years old. The UW project represents the joint attempt by five professional schools – Social Work, Nursing, Education, Public Affairs, and Public

0268–0939/93 $10·00

Health & Community Medicine – to create a preservice training program that will prepare students in each school for collaborative practice. Now in its first full year of implementation, the project works with a small number of graduate-level students who are simultaneously completing training programs in their respective schools. At present, the TIC project complements and adds to existing training experiences, rather than replacing them. Over the long term, project activities are meant to become more fully integrated into the curriculum of the five schools.

Challenges in the external environment of the university

The university's environment contains powerful groups with an interest in the form and outcome of professional preparation – in particular, credentialing and licensing bodies (typically at the state level), accrediting associations, government agencies involved in the human services professions, and (for public universities) the state legislatures which allocate funds for higher education. These groups are in a position to guide or constrain curriculum, entrance, and exit, and, consequently, the university is challenged to find ways to work within, and, where appropriate or possible, change the requirements imposed on it by its environment.

Of particular importance are the definitions of the trained professional in each discipline, which are enshrined in credentialing requirements and associated measures (e.g., admission-to-practice exams). In most states, these definitions do not reflect the competencies we know to be associated with interprofessional collaborative practice. In some instances, efforts by coalitions that sometimes include the university have begun to set more appropriate standards to guide collaborative practice.

In the case of the TIC project, the pattern of external constraints differs considerably across the five professional disciplines. Licensing and certification requirements are a case in point. For example, the standards which define what beginning social workers need to know (e.g., as set forth by Washington State Administrative Codes related to professional certification of school social workers) are fairly specific about collaborative skills; in contrast, Administrative Codes related to the certification of teachers (defined by the state Office of the Superintendent of Public Instruction) make little or no reference to interprofessional matters, with the exception of individuals preparing for 'special education' roles. Unlike both of these professional roles, service agency administrators and policy analysts are allowed to practice without a credential. Thus, depending on the professional specialty, the requirements of the professional and governmental bodies that control entry into each profession place differing apparent values on interprofessional collaboration.

For reasons that are obvious, professional schools at UW attend to what is required of them, and, not surprisingly, the professional preparation programs have been shaped accordingly. Where interprofessional skills are not a requirement of entry into the profession, the university has tended not to construct programs that feature collaborative elements. So far, neither the TIC project team nor others at UW are actively attempting to change the state's credentialing or licensing requirements *per se*, but over the long term we intend to, once we can demonstrate more clearly the value of doing so and the form that such requirements might take.

Challenges at the intellectual core of the professional disciplines

A second set of challenges derive from the university's role in generating ideas and principles that guide practice in each of the professional disciplines. Universities serve as a central source of intellectual leadership to disciplines involved in interprofessional preparation – social work, teaching, public health work, nursing, human service administration, and so forth. Within universities, units such as professional schools and departments are developed, each concerned with a particular profession; within them, further specialization takes place into divisions or 'pathways'. University-based educators are rewarded and encouraged for both knowing and doing in depth. Within disciplines, a body of knowledge develops that gives a unique perspective on the phenomena central to the discipline. Faculty develop courses to transmit this disciplinary knowledge and define academic program requirements of scope and depth. Most programs espouse the need for electives in other disciplines or units within the discipline; however, the required courses of study typically leave little room for additional foci.

Because there is no natural force within faculties propelling them outside their defined perspectives, the comfort of the known encourages a curriculum that does not incorporate the perspectives, frameworks, theories, or knowledge base of other disciplines. The system of faculty appointment, promotion, and tenure review reinforces this specialization of knowledge. In such a milieu, academic scholars rarely distinguish themselves by interdisciplinary work; the determination of rank and privilege are made by the scholars within that discipline.

Given that disciplines exist, in part, to distinguish areas of special expertise from one another, it is natural that there should arise separate – and often competing – service philosophies, diagnoses of need and pathology, and models of the way the world works. On the other hand, in the world where professionals do their work as teachers, nurses, social workers, therapists, or administrators, they are confronted by challenges that are non-specific, that are related to whole individuals, complex families, and communities. At a minimum, these challenges invite and often require cooperation or coordination among educational, health, and social services. For example, the problem of a child's inattention in the classroom may be related to many matters such as a child-rearing history with a depressed parent, a cognitive deficit, gang fights with which the child is dealing, or poor classroom management. It is not possible for the classroom teacher, or any single professional for that matter, to know both the scope and depth of all matters relevant to the child's apparent learning problem. The teacher needs access to various perspectives on the problem, a range of solutions, and possibly extra help in implementing these solutions.

Universities (including UW) have increasingly paid attention to the whole child (or family or community), and in so doing have set in motion the possibility of integrating heretofore disparate specializations. There have been attempts to provide a structure and strategy within universities for interdisciplinary training, as in University-Affiliated Training and Research Centers set up in the early 1970s for the professions working in mental retardation. More recently, efforts to develop interprofessional curricula (Jacobs 1987) have gone beyond the multidisciplinary philosophy of the past training centers to one that is better described as 'cross-disciplinary'. The goal is an integrative process in which professionals and trainees from different professional preparation programs work together in defining the problem, defining knowledge needs, and developing an integrative framework for action.

This integrative process requires that the university reconceptualize the knowledge base of each profession. In principle, professionals training within each discipline need to know more about the principles and frameworks guiding other disciplines. Social workers, for example, need to know something about the learning process, if they are to work effectively with the families of children experiencing difficulty in school; teachers, on the other hand, need to know more about the social and family dynamics of the children they teach, and so forth. In addition, knowledge of the process of collaboration itself becomes part of the core knowledge new professionals must acquire. Redefining the knowledge base of each profession in this way does not remove the need for specialized professional expertise. No one professional can know enough to meet or anticipate all the needs of the children or families he/she faces.

As will be described in subsequent sections, the TIC project team has been involved in a process of defining interprofessional collaboration and reconsidering the knowledge base of the five collaborating professional disciplines. Underlying all of TIC's efforts has been the attempt to articulate an overall vision of 'interprofessional collaboration,' to which all professional disciplines can agree. In searching for such a vision, we have entertained various alternatives, among them that such collaboration involves: a network of agencies and practitioners, bound together by interagency agreements and professionals in 'case management' roles; a unified team of professionals and community members dealing jointly with a given individual or family; a group of newly trained professionals who share sufficient core knowledge to solve a wide range of problems and who resort less frequently to the help of specialists. From the process of our deliberation, the following generic working definition has emerged:

> Interprofessional collaboration in human service delivery is an interactive process through which individuals and organizations with diverse expertise, experience, and resources join forces to plan, generate, and execute solutions to mutually identified problems related to the welfare of families and children.

This definition, of course, does not resolve more specific definitional matters. We have begun to explore these matters, as we confront the challenges on campus and at practicum sites, as discussed below.

Challenges on campus: faculty involvement, curriculum development and instruction

As the intellectual frameworks for collaborative practice and preparation for it are developed within professional disciplines, universities are in a position to confront the third set of challenges. Specifically, the university must (1) mobilize a critical mass of faculty representing different specializations who care about interprofessional work and who will orient their teaching and research to it; (2) identify a common interprofessional domain as a basis for long-term faculty collaboration and curriculum development; and (3) develop and deliver a curriculum to students who are preparing for collaborative practice. We discuss each of these challenges below.

Various barriers stand in the way of faculty collaboration, collaborative instruction, and the development of a curriculum that transcends disciplinary boundaries. Some derive from the tendency toward specialization discussed above. Others reflect the structural fragmentation of the campus; still others can be traced to the nature of funding for faculty scholarship. Most of the barriers, however, appear to be passive, involving a lack of specific incentives to collaborate, rather than active opposition. Our experience with the TIC project so far suggests that these barriers can be surmounted; however, there remain many questions about the nature and mix of incentives that will sustain collaboration at UW, or would encourage it elsewhere.

Involving faculty

The dynamics of faculty involvement and the conditions supporting it appear to differ somewhat over time as a collaborative effort proceeds through three distinct phases: initiation, nurturing, and institutionalization.

Initiating collaboration entails finding a critical mass of faculty within several schools willing to engage in the effort. They must be sufficiently senior to be knowledgeable and respected in their departments, but must be able to commit sufficient time to meet regularly and draft proposals. Furthermore, the project's content must be shaped to complement their ongoing research activities, or it is bound to lose out in the competition for their time and attention. At least conditional ['OK, let's try it'] support must be gained from the Deans and University Provost, both to provide a safe atmosphere and convince funders of the potential for significant change. Finally, at least one faculty member must be sufficiently committed to assume the role of leader or coordinator, and be rewarded for successfully facilitating the collaborative effort.

At UW, a half dozen faculty from four professional schools (Education, Social Work, Public Affairs, and Public Health & Community Medicine) came together to form the initial project development group, and were subsequently joined by several others as the project gained momentum. Each came with a deep commitment to the idea of collaborative practice, though with different notions of what this might entail. All faculty discovered they had a lot of learning to do in the process, and it took a full year before the basic shape of a project emerged, with which all felt comfortable.

The initial steps towards faculty collaboration at UW were greatly facilitated by special funding. A grant from a well-known private foundation both gave the enterprise legitimacy and indicated the likely reward of engaging in risky behavior. The foundation funding also created a neutral home base for the faculty's work – UW's Human Services Policy Center, which was devoted to projects dealing with service integration in all its many forms. As one of the Center's activities, the TIC project received funds to support the faculty leader as well as partial stipends for the other faculty who contributed time. The foundation grant also subsidized research assistance, which allowed faculty to focus on the most exciting part of the effort, that of engaging their colleagues in discussions of issues they cared passionately about, and learning each others' languages and concepts.

Nurturing collaboration through the initial operational phase of the project brings a new set of issues. It requires resources from the university or external funder for faculty to spend a substantial portion of their time developing, delivering, and refining a pilot curriculum or set of learning experiences, and funding students to serve as research assistants (and, in some cases, as practicum interns). Actually operating a complex project puts additional pressures on the collaborative relationships, since conceptual planning allows many potential conflicts to be blurred or deferred. The immediate needs of students, site practitioners and clients must also be met, even if they exceed the bounds of time bought by the project, and the complexity of operating simultaneously at sites and on campus can feel overwhelming. Finally, the number of tasks multiplies as courses need to be taught, students supervised, field sites developed, and so forth.

Once again, the TIC project relied on foundation funding to support core faculty time (each of the steering group was compensated for 0·20 FTE of their load); most put in more than this, but certain kinds of project needs could not be met adequately by part-time faculty. We found it particularly helpful to hire professional staff whose sole commitment was to the project and who were independent of any professional school. Project staffing has been further augmented by engaging outside consultants for specific tasks – such as a facilitator (yes, a family therapist!) for periodic retreats to work through personal and turf issues with the core faculty group.

Since the period of initial project operations is likely to span several years, the project must be sufficiently flexible to accommodate the changing needs and interests of participating faculty and at the same time cover the expanding needs of the project. The TIC core group recruited additional faculty to implement the required teaching and analytic activities. This entailed a two-way socialization: the new faculty had to be brought up to speed in the work already conducted, but at the same time the core group had to be willing to modify its plans and relationships to accommodate the contributions of the additional participants. While necessary and productive, the socialization of new members has been time-consuming: inevitably, some time and effort was spent rediscovering lessons already learned by the original group members.

Institutionalizing collaboration presents the university with the biggest challenge of all. Ideally institutionalization begins early in the life cycle of the project. During the initial implementation phase, it is necessary to assume ultimate success of the pilot project, and start planning for institutionalization. There is considerable debate about the most appropriate institutional form for interprofessional preparation, as noted in the report of a recent conference dealing with this topic which was developed jointly by the Human Services Policy Center (UW) and the Center for Collaboration for Children (CSUF):

> There is a central tension between (1) establishing preparation as a distinct training program – by embedding it in a separate institute, for example – and (2) incorporating interprofessional elements into the preparation programs of each professional school. A separate institute devoted to interdisciplinary efforts has several advantages: it will always have interprofessional preparation as its central concern, it can respond to changing conditions in both the university and its external environment, and it can provide a home or safe haven for like-minded faculty. At the same time, these advantages carry the cost of marginality: interprofessional preparation can be seen as a 'fringe' activity for a few enlightened or crazed faculty, it can be treated as a dispensable add-on to the 'core' of disciplinary training in each field, and faculty of the institute can be treated as second-class citizens by disciplinary faculty. (Center for Collaboration for Children and Human Services Policy Center 1993: 8)

Conversely, an attempt to subsume collaborative training fully into the core curriculum of each professional school runs the risk of having it disappear as budgetary pressures or fashions in each field shift faculty energy to other concerns before collaboration fully infects the content of each school's curriculum. Each approach has significant costs as well as advantages, thus raising the possibility that mixed models can improve the cost–benefit equation.

Issues surrounding institutionalization have yet to be resolved in the UW case. At the current time, early in the initial operation phase, the TIC project is operating as an independent entity outside the regular preparation programs of the university. Students from each school take TIC coursework in addition to those required by their programs; their fieldwork assignments, which feature collaborative experiences, also involve the full range of practicum learning they might have done outside TIC. The project team is busily exploring ways to embed what it does into the preparation programs of the participating schools.

So far, the project has enjoyed strong support from the five professional school deans, including not only rhetorical encouragement for TIC efforts, but also financial contributions to the project. While this is commendable – and unusual on university campuses – it does not reflect policy-level resolution of the hardest issues confronting collaboration between university units. In its current form as an independent research and development project, TIC has yet to pose to the deans or their respective faculties the tough questions about managing overlap among graduate degree programs, synchronizing schedules, calculating course loads when faculty teach cross-listed courses, or establishing common curricula and compatible expectations for practicum training, to mention only a few of the thorniest matters confronting institutionalization.

The project team is currently taking steps to address these deeper, long-term issues. Over the coming year, the project team plans to (a) analyze the interprofessional content of each school's current core curriculum, and (b) identify a 'common core' of substantive knowledge to be shared by all five professions. We anticipate that this analysis will point the way toward a mixed institutional model, combining elements of a separate institute with substantial absorption of collaborative materials into the 'regular' curriculum of each school.

Defining a common interprofessional domain

To sustain faculty participation and generate the base for curriculum development, some consensus must develop around the common professional domain which is the focus of interprofessional work. This can be done conceptually, in terms of practical applications, or both. The former is relatively easy for faculty to do; the latter is more difficult and may involve a series of steps to develop a shared view of the kinds of knowledge, skills, and beliefs that professionals call on when engaged in interprofessional work.

The TIC project approached this need by systematically assessing the competencies required for collaboration by a variety of practitioners in the field. The assessment involved two interrelated activities: a review of literature addressing interprofessional collaboration and a series of focus-group consultations with practitioners currently engaged in interprofessional collaboration. We learned most from the latter, and consequently we discuss it at somewhat greater length below.

As we embarked on this activity, it became clear that working definitions for key terms and concepts were required, in particular, for 'competence,' 'collaboration' and 'practitioner.' We based our conception of 'competence' on one by Fenichel and Eggbeer (1990), which treats this concept as 'the ability to do the right thing, at the right time, for the right reasons.' Competence thus involves the capacity to analyze a situation, consider alternative approaches, select and skillfully apply the best observation or intervention techniques, evaluate the outcome, and articulate the rationale for each step of the process. Competence generally requires a combination of knowledge, skills, and experience. Competence for work with children and families cannot be inferred from the completion of academic coursework alone; it must be demonstrated.

Before we could identify practitioners who were considered excellent collaborators, we needed to agree on a definition of interprofessional collaboration. We settled on the definition cited in the previous section of the chapter. The more we worked with this definition, the clearer it became to us that we were dealing with more than the activities of professionals providing direct services to clients. Rather, three levels of 'practitioner' were involved:

- *Service delivery level:* practitioners such as school teachers, nurse practitioners, and social workers, who are involved interprofessionally and collaboratively in providing direct services to individual children and their families.
- *Supervisory level:* practitioners such as school principals, health program managers, and managers of family counseling programs, who are involved in supervising and administering collaborative programs for specific populations of children and families.

- *Policy-making level:* practitioners such as local school board members, legislative staff assigned to committees addressing human services, and members of boards overseeing community-based organizations delivering human services, who make policies that initiate, sustain, alter, or otherwise govern collaborative programs for specific populations of children and families.

With these definitions in mind, the TIC project team identified individuals from health, social service, and education organizations who fitted the descriptions for the three levels of practitioners and who were widely viewed as expert collaborators. These individuals participated in a series of focused consultations guided by a variation of the DACUM (Design a Curriculum) process (Myers *et al.* 1989). The group process yielded a large number of competence statements (over 700 in all), which were analyzed and synthesized into a smaller number of themes, organized conceptually into five major domains (intra-personal, interpersonal, group, organizational, sociocultural).

The results of the assessment process provided a conceptual map for major project activities and defined the 'common ground' on which we all stood. Project team members from different disciplines could find in the competency statements attributes of the kinds of professionals we all hoped to prepare.

Developing and delivering curriculum that is interprofessional

Given agreement on a common interprofessional domain, faculty face the challenge of creating and offering a curriculum that transcends the boundaries of particular professional disciplines. Though logistics alone (i.e., scheduling) are nontrivial aspects of this task, the most central concerns are, first, to decide what to teach; second, to resolve how much is generic – that is, common to all professional disciplines – and how much should remain the province of each collaborating professional school; and, third, to find a sufficiently interactive, collaborative format for delivering curriculum. Universities addressing these concerns rapidly encounter the limits of each discipline's professional vocabulary and guiding conceptual frameworks, as well as limits on professors' knowledge of the worlds of practicing professionals.

Deciding what collaborators need to know and what to teach the beginner: Identifying the knowledge of most worth and then further narrowing that knowledge to a core that is teachable to a beginner has been the complex task of the TIC project team. Initially, the team worked with the results of the competency assessment, described above, to see if discrete skills or bodies of information would emerge. In general, however, we found that what collaborating practitioners needed to know and know how to do could not be disaggregated neatly, but rather combined knowledge, skills, and attitudes within the five domains noted above. Aside from presenting the curriculum team with complexity, this result raised questions of teachability and depth. If, as our assessment suggested, collaborative competence was in part a matter of personal flexibility and openness to ideas, could this be taught? While learning activities could be arranged that would highlight the importance of being flexible, encourage students to approach a problem flexibly, and even model flexible behavior, there was no guarantee that the message would get through to individuals with certain kinds of personalities. What knowledge, skills, and attitudes must a practitioner have as a minimum to begin practice? Practically speaking, how much *can* the novice master? The TIC curriculum design has, so far, struck a middle ground between concentrating on particular domains of collaborative competence (e.g., interpersonal skills) and attempting to 'cover' the full range of knowledge and skills that pertain to interprofessional practice.

Universities confront a second set of issues in building and delivering an interprofessional curriculum: how to balance preparation for what exists versus preparation for things as they ought to be. Does one prepare students for collaboration in situations where it is not being practiced regularly or for situations in which collaborative practice is the norm? In the TIC project we have based our thinking and initial curriculum design on information drawn from practitioners who are working under conditions which are frequently not supportive of their interprofessional collaboration. Similarly, the literature we have reviewed expresses the nature of collaborations as it must occur now in often unsupportive environments.

Deciding where the knowledge should be taught and who should teach it: As they decide which competencies to teach, the university faculty must also explore questions about where the knowledge can best be taught and learned (on campus? In the field?) and who should teach it (faculty? practicum site staff? community members? other supervisory staff?). While these questions may seem to be routine matters confronting any professional preparation program, they are especially complex in interprofessional preparation. The balance of campus-based and field-based learning, for example, is complicated by the fact that much of the content to be learned crosses departmental boundaries, as well as boundaries separating professional work in the field. In a similar vein, because no one person 'knows it all,' instructors must be found – or developed – who are conversant with collaborative principles and willing to work collaboratively in teaching teams, which is not the usual mode of instruction for university faculty.

The TIC project has so far resolved the balance of campus-based and field-based learning by creating courses to be taught on campus, primarily by faculty, and by placing students in supervised practicum experiences in communities where they are likely to have opportunities to work together, or at least, with professionals from different disciplines. In these settings (which will be described more fully later in the chapter), agency-based supervisors share in the 'teaching' role, though the extent and nature of that role has yet to be clarified.

Having resolved that some collaborative teaching and learning should take place on campus, university curriculum planners need to figure out what belongs *within* and *across* existing professional preparation programs. Some of what we have to teach is knowledge that all students need to learn regardless of professional specialty, and some is more profession-specific and can therefore be incorporated into the separate professional programs. Further, given the logistics of integrating different professional programs, some things may simply be impossible to teach in joint courses because no feasible way of bringing students together can be found.

To date, TIC curriculum planners have concentrated on developing a joint course, which students from the five participating professional schools must take. In piloting this new curriculum, we expect to identify knowledge that will be better taught in separate programs, rather than in the jointly offered, heterogeneous class. We do not see this kind of parceling out of instructional responsibility as ideal – it may invite the very fragmentation that has characterized professional training heretofore – rather, we view it as a fall-back option, should more integrated experiences prove logistically difficult. But we also recognize that the curriculum content may be safer once embedded in an already established preparation program. Again, as noted earlier, any course developed by a project, especially an interdepartmental project, is vulnerable when resources become tight in any or all departments.

Our early thinking about requiring cross-disciplinary experiences for all brought us up against discrepancies across the five professional schools in program duration and student numbers. Briefly, the preparation programs in the five schools ranged from as short as a year (teaching certificate) to as long as three years (Masters in Nursing). The five schools' student numbers range from less than 25 per year (e.g., students receiving a Masters in Public Health) to over 200 (newly credentialed teachers), numbers which are roughly proportional to the distribution of professions among human services agencies.

The TIC project is currently attempting to cultivate university-based faculty who can teach collaborative competencies. We have discovered that this is not a simple matter, nor does it offer a full solution to the question of who should teach. None of us has sufficient depth of knowledge to arrange learning experiences in the intrapersonal, interpersonal, group process, organizational system, and sociocultural domains. Nor does any single faculty member have the breadth of knowledge of the various agencies and institutions to plan realistic activities related to them. Our initial approach to the challenges of depth and breadth is to use a teaching team of three, drawn from two of the professional schools on campus and a practitioner from a third professional domain. In addition, we are planning to draw on the expertise of guest instructors from the several fields. Even with this arrangement, we face the ultimate dilemma that no one person knows it all and that, to model collaboration, we must teach in varying combinations of faculty and individuals from outside the university.

Challenges at practicum sites

The university has traditionally been a 'cooperative' partner in the experiential component of professional preparation, a partnership which has typically involved the placement of students in one or another kind of supervised 'practicum' experience external to the university setting. The goal of preparation for interprofessional collaboration requires a different kind of practicum, which poses for the university (and for the practicum site) a new set of challenges.

Three challenges arise in the choice of practicum sites and the design of the practicum experience. First of all, the university must arrange opportunities for students to test and extend their learning about collaborative competencies as well as what is learned about a chosen professional field. Second, the field site must model collaborative practice in some degree, and the university has a role in bringing this about, either by facilitating the development of collaborative networks where there are none or by enhancing existing networks. Third, within these collaborative networks, learning experiences must be developed for students so that they actually experience working with professionals from different disciplines.

The act of creating these practicum learning experiences encourages the university to collaborate with field-site staff, community members, and service-providing agencies, more perhaps than has been typical in traditional preparation programs. As part of this collaborative relationship, a two-way learning process develops. On the one hand the university stands to learn a great deal about collaborative practice, which it can use to refine and further develop its interprofessional curriculum. On the other hand, the university has the opportunity – and sometimes the need – to contribute to the ongoing professional development of agency staff at the practicum site.

The TIC project has met these challenges in several ways, and the learning process has only just begun. We review the issues and our experiences to date below, in terms of the three practicum design challenges and the two-way learning process resulting from the university's relationship with the practicum site.

Rethinking the opportunities for students to test campus-based learning in the real world

The traditional way of viewing the practicum experience in professional education – as a chance to test out what one has learned about a particular professional role in a short-term, supervised 'apprentice' situation – needs to be rethought when more than one profession, and the relationship among them, is involved. At a minimum, preparation for inter-professional work raises questions about the content, the value, and the logistics of the practicum.

As far as content is concerned, traditional practicum experiences tend to focus on the attributes of practice that make each professional special and different from others. Inter-professional preparation introduces a new and somewhat contrary emphasis – on the 'common ground' that different professionals share, on the knowledge and skill which directly support collaboration, and on the contribution each profession can make to other professions. How and from whom, at the practicum site, is the student to acquire this kind of knowledge? There are various sources, but orchestrating the students' access to them is no small accomplishment, and every new kind of experience added to the practicum diet means dropping another from an already full learning menu.

Rethinking the content of the practicum leads quickly to questions about the value of practicum learning. As noted earlier in the chapter, the practicum policies of the five participating professional schools differ radically, reflecting sharply different values placed on this kind of learning. At one end of the spectrum, one UW professional school requires continual practicum participation across the two years of the Master's degree program; at the other end, another school does not require a practicum, though students may elect to do this. Some schools insist on compensation for students in practicum roles, thus approximating the conditions of 'real' professional work; others do not. The differing values placed on the practicum pose a fundamental problem to the university in trying to enable students from different professional disciplines to learn with and from each other, and to see their interaction with one another as valued and central to their mutual professional growth.

The differences in practicum policies also generate a major logistical obstacle. Not only are practicums across the five professional schools of different lengths, they also occur at different times in the students' respective degree programs. The university's efforts to arrange suitable collaborative practicums may even contribute to fragmented practices, when students from the five disciplines show up at a practicum site at different times and stay differing lengths of time. (Even the task of arranging practicum activities on the same days of the week is a challenge!)

To date, the TIC project has resolved these matters through a combination of arm-twisting, luck, and expedience. Students' assignments overlap sufficiently to make a variety of collaborative activities possible, at least in principle. But the project has yet to confront the more difficult long-term questions regarding ways to make each participating school's practicum policies more compatible with one another.

Supporting the development of collaborative practice at practicum sites

For students to learn about interprofessional collaboration at training sites, they need to be placed in settings where such collaboration is happening. Typically, this redefines the boundaries of the 'site' and places an additional constraint on site selection. In conventional professional training, the 'site' includes a school, clinic, agency, or other institution in which a given professional specialty is practiced; students need not venture beyond the boundaries of this organization to experience teaching, counseling, or other specialty in a 'real-world' setting. But for students to experience interprofessional practice, the 'site' must expand to include a network or 'community' of collaborating agencies, or some other configuration of different services that makes interaction possible. Though an intern will most likely be homebased in one agency within the network, he or she will need to meet individuals from other agencies, visit different agencies, or otherwise have access to services and staff that are not located at the homebase. For reasons that are obvious, these possibilities will only occur in settings in which services for children and families are approached collaboratively.

The university has the option of selecting practicum sites which already exemplify collaborative practice, or helping other sites to become collaborative. Because full collaboration among health, social services, and education is rare, the university is most likely to be in the position of developing the site's capacity for collaborative practice.

The TIC project team approached this problem by developing criteria for site selection that indicated the extent and nature of collaborative practice among local health, mental health, social welfare, and educational services. Two sites were selected for the first implementation year, one where collaborative practice was well established and one which lacked the necessary preconditions. Each presents a different kind of challenge.

The challenges are easier to address in sites with a well-established collaborative network of human services agencies, as in one TIC site, located in a working-class, industrial community adjacent to Seattle. There, a 30-agency network had grown out of the collaborative interaction of the school district, the city government, and the Cities-in-Schools program. This community needed little help from UW in establishing or maintaining its network, but they welcomed the prospect of students as extra hands to help with the innumerable demands on network participants. In this site we have had to overcome the perception of the university as an organization that pursues its own interests without necessarily giving much in return. It was critical that our approach to this site respect local efforts, build on what site professionals know about collaboration, and attend to their wishes and needs. The subtle tension between satisfying the university's needs (including those of its students) and those of the local agencies continues, however, as available interns express preferences for placements that do not necessarily match the needs as defined by local agencies.

The other practicum site, where a tradition of collaborative practice did not exist, presented a more formidable challenge. Centering on an ethnically mixed inner city school and associated service agencies in the heart of Seattle, many of which had taken UW practicum students before, the site was characterized by a complex and uncoordinated mix of services for children and families, both within the school and external to it. The site was selected, in part, because it typified many urban settings in which collaborative services are most needed.

We have expended considerable energy in stimulating or assisting in the collaborative development of this site. To do so, the TIC project team has (1) facilitated the development of a network of external agencies linked to the school that have served, or might serve, its students; and (2) assisted the school in its efforts to develop a more coordinated internal system for addressing students with specialized needs. In so doing, TIC faculty with prior programmatic connections to the school have had to reassess and redefine their links to the school and to each other.

With the assistance of TIC project staff, a collection of local health, mental health, social service, ethnic, and educational services (several of which have long histories of working with the school) joined forces with the school and identified themselves as a collaborative network. The university played a strong initial role in developing this network but the school has become increasingly active as it works with the agencies to resolve issues related to confidentiality, parental permission, agency waiting lists, and on-site services. The network is still in the process of formation; important issues about the nature of the relationships among the players need to be resolved, and resources need to be found to assure that network activities will be adequately coordinated.

Simultaneously, TIC project staff have attempted to streamline the internal school referral and case management process, which has been seriously bottlenecked with large numbers of referred students waiting for attention from the school's Student Assistance Team. With the assistance of the university, the school is taking steps to create a stronger case-management function.

A key issue for the university faculty was to understand that the school was the focus of the collaborative network; the responsible party. The school was barraged by helpful programs and persons (including several with which TIC faculty had been involved prior to the project's inception), without effective communication or coordination among them. In this context, TIC was experienced as one more program to manage, a small but growing part of the problem. To help the school find a solution, project team members have worked with the principal to develop an operational model to guide the integration of both internal and external services, and to find external funding to implement the model.

In seeking to help this school integrate its services, TIC project faculty have encountered another and unanticipated challenge. Three of us had central roles in different programs operating independently in, or with, the school priot to the inception of TIC. It took us a while to learn that 'collaborative practice' in the school setting meant something more than the sum of the individual projects with which we were associated. To collaborate successfully, one must be willing to blur the boundaries between previously distinct programs.

Developing collaborative learning experiences for students at the practicum site

The existence of collaborative networks or their equivalent at a practicum site is no guarantee that students will undertake, or even observe, collaborative activities during their time on site. To accomplish this goal, the university faces the challenge of arranging ways for students from different disciplines to engage in collaborative problem solving with each other, relevant professional staff, and community members. In addition, supervisors or mentors need to be in place to exploit the learning opportunities as they arise. The responsibility for developing these opportunities is not solely the university's – practicum supervisors, other agency staff, and the students themselves are likely to have good ideas about ways to add a collaborative dimension to their activities on site. As with many aspects of collaborative practice, the responsibility for developing appropriate learning activities is shared but, for obvious reasons, the university must make sure that such activities occur. As a consequence, university staff must invest substantial time arranging site placements, working with various field-based supervisors to make sure an appropriate range of possibilities is considered, and listening carefully to ideas from students and agency staff or community people.

The learning activities can be of many kinds, but often they go beyond the direct provision of services to children or families. In addition to joint problem solving in relationship to particular needy children, families, or classrooms, projects might include the development of common intake instruments which address the commonalties in agency information systems, thereby reducing the length and redundancy of intake interviews; developing legislative advocacy efforts to secure funding for jointly identified needs; or, the collaborative development of new service forms between participating agencies. In undertaking these tasks, students will often need to assume various professional roles such as program developer, policy analyst, and team planner, in addition to traditional direct service roles such as nurse, teacher, or social worker.

In the TIC project, the development of appropriate learning experiences at practicum sites is an evolving activity. Understandably, we underestimated the time it would take to arrange these activities, and, in some cases, students' experiences have been less collaborative than they could or should be. There has been no shortage of ideas, but the biggest challenge has been to focus the student's and supervisor's attention on collaborative possibilities early in the practicum period, at a time when students are still unsure of their primary professional skills as a nurse, teacher, or whatever.

We have also discovered that the university, not to mention participating agencies, must be prepared to adapt curriculum, procedures, and policies if they wish to take advantage of many of the practicum ideas that arise. For example, one nursing student in the TIC project extended her practicum, originally required for only one quarter, so that she could work with social work students to provide services to a particular family. Two agencies changed their referral practices to enable TIC interns to work with families from the school which was at the center of the network in the first project site.

Opportunities for two-way learning in the university's relationship with the practicum site

The adaptations in procedures and policies just mentioned represent one of many ways in which the participating institutions in a collaborative preparation program are affected by their interaction with each other. Substantial opportunities exist for the university and its partners to learn from each other, assuming they approach the relationship with an openness to such learning. It is also probably true that, until they are ready to learn from each other, the partnership may not be sufficiently collaborative to support a viable program.

On the one hand, professionals and community members in the field have much to teach university-based faculty and staff – about conditions in the field, the process of mentoring students in apprentice roles, the practical problems that stand in the way of collaborative practice, and ways to overcome these problems. What these individuals have to say to faculty can suggest changes in those things in which the faculty consider themselves expert, such as the curriculum of the preparation program, the locus of training, and the arrangement of learning activities at the practicum site. On the other hand, university faculty are one source of a vision of collaborative practice that can expand the horizons of those agency staff who have not incorporated collaborative work into their daily routines. By offering staff development or other forms of technical assistance to service providers and policy makers in partner agencies, the university can help to expand their repertoires and thereby make the practicum site a more collaborative learning environment.

The relationship between TIC project staff and people at the two practicum sites is evolving, and a good deal of learning has taken place already by parties on both sides. But the challenge still remains for each partner to acknowledge fully the other's expertise. When we reach that point, the foundation for collaborative interprofessional training will have been laid.

The future of university-based preparation for interprofessional practice

The chapter concludes on a note of cautious optimism. Despite the number and magnitude of these challenges, there is evidence from the UW case that they can be met, and that what now takes the form of a pilot experiment can generate more lasting forms of professional preparation that will ultimately support collaborative practice.

We suspect that the conditions that have made this experiment possible – deep dissatisfaction with fragmentation of services coupled with a diminished pool of resources for new services; energized faculty in an institution with supportive university administrators; the strong desire by practitioners to integrate services more effectively – pertain in many places across the USA. In addition, the considerable attention being paid to curricular renewal in professional schools, aided in some instances by some discretionary seed funding, adds impetus to the attempts by higher education institutions such as UW to build a collaborative dimension into professional preparation.

There are more ways than one to approach interprofessional preparation, some of them alluded to in the responses which follow this chapter. But all must, in some fashion, address the challenges we have outlined. Given the institutional climate at UW and elsewhere, and the ever clearer evidence of need from the field, some or many of these experiments with interprofessional preparation may flourish. Though it means doing business differently, universities may well be up to the challenge.

References

CENTER FOR COLLABORATION FOR CHILDREN (CSUF) & HUMAN SERVICE POLICY CENTER (UNIVERSITY OF WASHINGTON) (1993) *Summary of Discussion: Seattle Conference on Interprofessional Training* (Fullerton, CA: Center for Collaboration for Children, California State University/Fullerton).

MYERS, M., COX, R. and MUELLER, G. (1989) *A Reference Manual for DATA Workshop Facilitators, Recorders, and Coordinators* (Spokane, WA: Spokane Community College).

FENICHEL, E. S. and EGGBEER, L. (1990) *Preparing Practitioners to Work with Infants, Toddlers, and their Families: Issues and Recommendations for the Professions* (Arlington, VA: National Center for Clinical Infant Programs).

JACOBS, L. A. (1987) 'Interprofessional clinical education and practice', *Theory into Practice*, 26(2), pp. 116–123.

POLITICS OF EDUCATION ASSOCIATION YEARBOOK, 1993, 153–155

Defining, supporting, and maintaining interprofessional education

R. Michael Casto

The Interprofessional Commission of Ohio is housed at the Ohio State University (OSU). It is a partnership between eight state professional associations, six professional schools and colleges at OSU and three theological schools. The Commission has two decades of experience coordinating and facilitating collaborative education between six university academic units and three theological schools in central Ohio. The Commission developed its academic program by asking: What is it that we all teach that could be taught more effectively and/or efficiently if we taught it together?

The answer to this question initially generated three areas of common interest: ethical issues common to the helping professions, changing societal values and the professions, and training in the skills needed to engage in collaborative practice in the human services. Based on these three foci, eight courses have been developed, refined and taught by faculty teams from seven disciplines. Over 60 interprofessional continuing professional education and campus conferences have provided hundreds of practitioners, faculty and students with the opportunity to explore the most complex challenges of our society in an interprofessional context.

Definition

The definition of interprofessional collaboration in human service delivery offered in the chapter describing the values, ethos, and programmatic elements of the University of Washington (UW) Training for Interprofessional Collaboration program refers to an 'interactive process' without suggesting specifics about the nature of that process. The experience of hundreds of students in Commission courses suggests that clarity about understanding the process of interprofessional collaboration is an essential component in interprofessional education and practice. Interprofessional team members develop and adopt, over time, a shared set of values with respect both to professional practice and desired outcomes. There is mutuality of respect in an interprofessional context which suggests an equality among and between team members. Team members respect and value the contributions of each other and the client on an equal basis and give full consideration to those contributions as they develop treatment modalities. Clients share fully in the development of a collaborative plan for their care.

We have found that conflict resolution becomes an important dimension in the life of interprofessional teams, since value conflicts over treatment decisions are inevitable. The mark of an interprofessional team is equity and fairness in resolving these conflicts. No single profession has more credibility on an interprofessional team than any other. An interprofessional team will engage in discussion and negotiation until conflicts are resolved and equitable decisions are developed that can be embraced by all team members.

0268–0939/93 $10·00

Funding for interprofessional education

Just as at UW, the Commission was the beneficiary at an early point in its history of significant external funding. That funding was extremely important in allowing the program to develop. However, it was not adequate to provide sustained support. Nor does it seem practical to renew suport from external funding sources indefinitely. Each funding source wants to invest in developing unique programs. It is also difficult for collaborative education programs continually to develop new sources of funding for new projects. Continuing basic work will still need to be sustained with institutional support.

It is not the mission of interprofessional education programs to become ongoing sources of new external revenues for institutions or their participating departments. Rather, the goal of such programs is to provide a new shape and form to both professional education and practice. Therefore, the curricula they develop must become a part of the academic core in professional schools. They are really an attempt to subvert the traditional vertical structures of the universities, their disciplines, and departments. They are an attempt to redefine professional education and to reinvent professional practice. When higher education discovers the radical transformations required to sustain and institutionalize interprofessional education for collaborative practice involving large numbers of students, apparently 'passive' barriers may become 'active' opposition.

At some point institutions of higher education will either integrate education for collaborative practice into the core curricula of their professional education programs, or they will eliminate collaborative features of interprofessional programes. This point is likely to come when institutional resources are limited or when external funding diminishes along with the prospect for major new outside resources. The combination of these two circumstances may be disastrous for interprofessional education programs.

This has been the recent experiences of the Commission housed at OSU. Major foundation support has been lacking for several years. State support for higher education has been significantly reduced. The institution has gone into a significant period of retrenchment. The academic core is being protected by the existing vertical institutional structures, and creative and innovative interdisciplinary programs are being abandoned.

The Commission has responded to these challenges by exploring interinstitutional relationships, generating consultation opportunities based on the expertise of our years of experience, and developing new programs. We remain very optimistic about the prospect of interprofessional collaboration as an important tool for addressing the complex problems of persons in our society. We are considerably less optimistic about the ability of institutions of higher education individually to respond to these challenges.

Faculty participation

The role of faculty in instituting interprofessional education is a key difference between the UW program and that of the Commission. The UW program appears to be faculty initiated and faculty driven. The Commission program was initiated through the collaboration of practitioners, state professional association leaders, and the deans of participating academic units. This difference may signal an important strength of the UW program, at least in the initial stages of development.

Faculty would appear to have more direct access to the core professional curriculum in each school. They may have more freedom to develop new courses and curricula as well as to adjust requirements. They also have direct access to students and may have well-developed relationships to field sites. On the other hand, faculty interest in special projects and new trends is, like that of administrators and institutions, frequently driven by the availability of resources. When resources are limited, fewer faculty will be available and they will have less interest. Again, this has been our experience. Interprofessional collaboration will need to achieve the status of a 'discipline' if it is to overcome the inherent limitations of faculty and the departments in which they are imbedded. It may be that the UW program can achieve this goal.

The Commission at OSU, the TIC program at UW and other endeavours to establish interprofessional education and transform professional practice may be the best hope we have for responding to the overwhelming problems of our society. The challenge for our university-based preparation programs for collaborative interprofessional practice will be to find ways to support and sustain our work. We will need to do this while institutions of higher education undergo the transformations necessary to respond to the critical needs interprofessional collaboration must address.

POLITICS OF EDUCATION ASSOCIATION YEARBOOK, 1993, 157–159

Issues of vision, innovation, mission, outcomes and competent practice

Hal A. Lawson and Katharine Hooper-Briar

We applaud our colleagues at the University of Washington (UW) for their work on the conception, implementation and evaluation of interprofessional education. Their work reflects a fact we all must confront – substantial numbers of children, adults and families have not been effectively served by existing service delivery systems and segregated policy frameworks. In this light, reformist work is the equivalent of tinkering with existing systems and does not promise more effective and efficient services for persons underserved and even harmed by our service systems.

Working to get our existing systems 'right' is of little consequence if our initial framing of human needs, wants, problems was incomplete or wrong. In substitution for existing categorical imperatives, an emergent, relational perspective takes into account ecological and sociocultural contexts. Systemic, relational and socioecological analysis suggests patterns of interconnectedness and interdependence, which demand that we proceed beyond categorical, single-cause, single-profession and single-solution strategies. Moreover, we must search for root causes (e.g., poverty and unemployment) for which other problems (e.g., substance abuse, school failure, child abuse) are the equivalent of symptoms.

A critique

Despite the major work under way at UW, we are unable to derive from our colleagues' chapter an understanding of their guiding vision. What is their vision for the good and just society? How are human services to organize to achieve this vision? Will all of today's professions be needed tomorrow? What roles are assigned to citizens from diverse walks of life? What are our colleagues assuming about citizens' capabilities, potentials, and needs, not only for building themselves, but also in the so-called professional–client relationship? What are the parameters and purposes of collaboration and interprofessional education? Are new service and multidisciplinary initiatives to be guided by consumer-driven approaches, or will traditional hierarchical relationships of expert versus person-in-need prevail? Furthermore, what are the 'theories of change' and 'principles of practice' that drive their work?

At Washington it appears that most, if not all, of the existing professional schools and colleges have been invited to join in planning for interprofessional education and human service collaboration. There are reasons to commend such a generous invitation. On the other hand, if faculty in the respective human services professions are inherently interested in protecting their vested interests, there is little reason to believe that the range and kinds of human service professions will change. In other words, if change is driven through an understanding of the principles that undergird one another's professions, will this be sufficient? The UW 'model' appears to be a reformist strategy for change, not a transformative one. Will this allow us to transcend categorical problem solving, building upon relational or socioecological understandings? We have doubts.

Similarly, in the absence of understandings of a clear guiding vision, a set of desired outcomes, and accompanying theories of change, how can we define or assess competence? Writing competency statements does not guarantee competence. Competency-based education and its close relation – the idea of a singular, scientized and generalizable knowledge base for practice – are legacies of our categorical thinking. We know now the limitations associated with this kind of technical rationality, its reductionism, and its positivist connections.

We must transcend these categorical structures, beginning first with consumers joining with faculty. It continues with the transformation not only of professional schools and colleges, but of entire universities. This transformation includes foundational work with undergraduate students. (Our colleagues do not mention undergraduate education.) There are also crucial questions here about what we claim as knowledge, who generates it, and its communication, transportation and utilization. There are, in addition, questions about multiculturalism and diversity, empowerment and liberation strategies, and the ethical and moral imperatives associated with the human services professions.

Consumer-guided university initiatives

At Miami University, considerable time has been spent in vision setting. The accompanying reformulation and inventions may eventually involve a new human service profession. What began as an education reform agenda has now been revisited as a cross-systems, cross-services, community development agenda which recognizes the importance of being guided by consumers. The university facilitates a collaborative that is the aggregate of 12 schools and representatives of health and social service agencies.

Consumer-driven feedback has been the guiding source for vision, mission, and demonstration projects at the Florida International University Institute on Children and Families at Risk. Guidance by consumers has helped to reformulate the nature of the service delivery and service systems change process. Moreover, the Institute, along with community providers in a number of collaboratives, is forging ways to empower and develop careers for consumers as they move out of a client role.

As we stretch to reformulate the framework for action we find that we require a comprehensive approach, which is multicultural, multigenerational and multidisciplinary. Both universities' endeavors are founded in relational perspectives that are child-centered, family-focused and community-based. Both involve synchronized systems change. This work grows from the belief that there will never be enough social workers, teachers, nurses, police or other human service personnel to address rising needs and their root causes. Based on the African proverb that it takes a village to raise a child, this consumer-guided, problem-solving, and service-delivery vision has proven to be a very effective core for collaboratives and community change strategies.

Problem-setting and the cost of failure

At the heart of our work is a concern with the moral, human and fiscal costs of categorical, top-down and often symptom-based service delivery systems. When 14 or more professionals, who are all working with the same family or its members, do not coordinate, and are not empowered by families themselves as to what they need and want, both consumers and providers may fail. An overhaul of the service delivery approach, involving power sharing, is required. Curricular changes are also required. New core courses may involve: empowerment strategies; child-centered, family-focused and community-based strategies; culturally competent practice; consumer-guided service approaches; collaborative service delivery and problem solving; root-cause versus symptom-based interventions; and new theories of change. These kinds of courses are not likely to develop from competency-based analysis of current practices and delivery systems. In fact, many issues that we now describe as competencies need to be reframed as major civil and human rights issues.

Finally, universities are often barriers to change. Their orientation is often top-down, not bottom-sideways, and expert- rather than consumer-guided. Interprofessional education may provide a breakthrough for universities if it is vision-driven and consumer-guided. Competence, in this perspective, is a target for persons using human service delivery systems, not just a standard for professional providers. This suggests a mission involving the democratization of knowledge and services. Such a priority assigned to democratic processes both in the universities and in service delivery systems connects collaborative projects to a large movement aimed at restoring the democratic political tradition.

POLITICS OF EDUCATION ASSOCIATION YEARBOOK, 1993, 161–163

The integrated services specialist: an interdisciplinary preservice training model

William Wilson, Patricia Karasoff and Barbara Nolan

In the preceding chapter, Knapp and his colleagues at the University of Washington present an excellent illustration of the challenges inherent in the development of an interprofessional training program at the university level. Based on our experience to date developing and implementing an interdisciplinary program at San Francisco State University (SFSU) we will respond to the challenges outlined by our colleagues in Washington and describe our approach to interdisciplinary training.

In 1992, SFSU's Department of Special Education was awarded a five-year Partnership Training Grant from the US Department of Education. This funding has provided California with an opportunity to establish an initial partnership training project for preparing professionals for work in collaboratives which provide school-based or school-linked interagency services for children (Wilson 1992). Unlike UW's Training for Interprofessional Collaboration Project, the training effort at SF State is responding to an immediate need in California for personnel trained with an enhanced set of collaborative and interdisciplinary skills. Therefore our energies have focused on those professionals (masters, post masters, or doctoral level) who have already completed their discipline-specific professional preparation. These individuals are experienced practitioners within their own disciplines who desire additional competencies in the area of integrated service delivery.

While we applaud UW's efforts and agree that there is a need to undertake large-scale systems change in the area of university-based professional preparation programs, we have chosen a different strategy for change. We believe that to respond to the immediate need for a cadre of human service professionals skilled in the arena of collaboration, the university must act swiftly to provide a comprehensive training program within the boundaries of the existing internal and external organizational structure. By creating change within the existing system we can enhance the skills of current professionals while at the same time demonstrate and replicate a preservice training program that is interdisciplinary in nature. In this way we do not wait for total systems change to occur before offering training to those who need it now. However, the long-term plan, not unlike UW's, will then be to incorporate these competencies within discipline-specific programs so that over time there will be no need for an additional training program.

The authors agree with Knapp *et al.* that the university itself must model collaboration and interprofessional practice if they are to deliver a meaningful program to their students. We believe that a truly interdisciplinary program must require that both coursework and fieldwork be taught and supervised by faculty from varying disciplines. By designing a program for those already possessing their discipline-specific license or credential, we have been successful in achieving cross-training and supervision at the course and field placement level without resistance. Furthermore, as Knapp *et al.* have described in detail, accreditation requirements may serve to prevent alternative ways of meeting professional standards. This barrier can be overcome by collaborative teaching, cross-departmental credit, cross-listing a class, or restructuring the discipline-specific curriculum in order to eliminate unnecessary duplication.

SFSU's graduate-level program in the area of collaborative human services began in the fall of 1992. It prepares human service professionals and university students from a variety of backgrounds (e.g., general and special education, nursing, psychology, social work, and administration) at the masters or post-masters level. The program revolves around a 19-unit, three-semester sequence of courses and field experience in which students are provided with the opportunity to apply course content on integrated and collaborative services to school-based or school-linked collaboratives. Coursework and fieldwork are devoted to acquiring competencies in integrated and collaborative services, public policy and legal rights, services within the home, school and community in a multicultual environment, and facilitating change and collaborative practice in education and human services. Like UW, these program competencies were identified through a review of the literature followed by field-based validation, which in our case was done via survey. Credit for several of these courses may also be applied toward the student's masters or doctoral program.

Coursework devoted to service integration is provided concurrently with the practicum experience. As Knapp *et al.* have stated, we believe that it is critically important that the program model collaboration. Therefore our newly developed course on integrated and collaborative services for children is truly an example of cross-training. Using a seminar format, students are exposed to the interdisciplinary nature of service coordination through guest lectures by visiting scholars from within and outside SFSU and practitioners from various disciplines.

The field placement component of the program is vitally important to the success of the program and involves a practicum experience (120 hours) which requires that the students immerse themselves within an existing school-based or school-linked collaborative for 15 weeks. Students are linked with a field supervisor at the site, who is trained in a discipline other than that of the students. There is also a university practicum supervisor. This technique illustrates our emphasis on cross-training by, for example, having social workers supervising educators and educators supervising nurses. As Knapp and his colleagues assert, the critical importance of the practicum site and supervisor cannot be overstated. Therefore our criteria for practicum site selection, which is quite different from UW's, include only those sites where the operation of or formal plans to implement an interagency school-based or school-linked collaborative exist. We realize in this regard we are fortunate in having a number of working examples in California to use as a laboratory. This is in stark contrast to our colleagues in Washington who are faced with the need to create field placements for their students. Practicum students are enrolled concurrently in a student support seminar in which they discuss issues relevant to their practicum experience and present findings from their agency interviews.

The last requirement of the program is the culminating field experience which entails a 120-hour internship within a school-based integrated service system. The internship, as opposed to the practicum, involves the assignment of specific responsibilities which utilize the student's skills in planning, coordinating and delivering comprehensive school-based or school-linked services. The job roles for interns will vary depending on the configuration of the collaborative and the preference for an administrative or service delivery focus and strengths of individual interns.

Finally, as Knapp *et al.* state, the field supervisors from the school-based and school-linked collaborative are seen as critical partners in the training program. These practitioners must be offered an opportunity and incentives to participate as field supervisors and to bring their invaluable field experience to the university via guest lectures, forums, and appointments as adjunct faculty.

References

WILSON, W. (1992) Unpublished survey results of resource specialists and educational administrators, in *Integrated Service Specialist Program: A California Personnel Development Partnership*, US Department of Education Grant No. H029C20053 (San Francisco: Department of Special Education, San Francisco State University).

WILSON, W. and SAILOR, W. (1992) 'Service integration in public schools', *School of Education Review*, 4(Spring), San Francisco State University.

POLITICS OF EDUCATION ASSOCIATION YEARBOOK, 1993, 165–167

Critical teacher education and multicultural issues

Kip Tellez and Jo-Anne Schick

As we see it, the University of Washington (UW) program serves as a vanguard for interprofessional collaboration, but there are two features of professional practice not addressed in the UW program that we would like to explore. First, because we are teacher educators, we view interprofessional practice through a lens that focuses on teacher preparation. Consequently, we find ourselves unsure about how interprofessional training can be implemented in universities where teacher education is limited (often by state lawmakers) in both length and scope, and very often takes place far from or with little concern for urban areas where interprofessional collaboration is needed (Scribner 1985).

Second, multicultural considerations must take center stage when considering interprofessional preparation. We hear few calls for integrated social services in upper class, white neighborhoods. This point is crucial when considering the development of broadly trained professionals.

Teacher education

When considering the interprofessional training of teachers, a number of issues arise: (a) nearly 40% of all teachers receive their certification from a nondoctoral granting institution where teacher certification may be the only profession program on campus (American Association of Colleges for Teacher Education 1991), (b) teacher certification is most often an undergraduate degree program with limited credit hours (American Association of Colleges for Teacher Education 1991), (c) newly certified teachers show a strong preference for suburban teaching (American Association of Colleges for Teacher Education 1987), and (d) there is a growing belief that school district-sponsored alternative certification programs are more effective than university training (Haberman 1992). We question how widely interprofessional programs can be implemented (at least in the UW fashion) when the host institution has no social work, nursing, or public health program, when beginning teachers prefer to work in suburban schools, or when teachers are not even certified through a university. Even a university where professional programs are weak or understaffed may have trouble with a collaborative program.

While the University of Houston (UH) does have a full range of professional programs, we have recently implemented a program that may serve to educate teachers in disciplines beyond education without necessarily involving other disciplines (Tellez and Hlebowitsh in press). As part of a culture study requirement, preservice teacher education students volunteer in social service agencies across the city. Several of our students, for instance, work a minimum of 20 hours in a battered women's shelter, tutoring the children of the women who live there. In their work, they are exposed not only to the social conditions which precipitate violence against women but they also work closely

0268–0939/93 $10·00

with the social workers assigned to the facility. Several other students volunteer in hospital programs, helping to tutor young patients who are confined to critical care facilities.

At the completion of their volunteer assignment, we ask students to write a paper, addressing questions such as, 'What did you learn in your volunteer assignment that will make you a better teacher?' and 'Would schools be different if all teachers could have seen what you did?'. Their responses never fail to overwhelm us. Classroom discussions with our prospective teachers reveal deep and indelible insights into the socioeducational world of urban students. The volunteer assignment has at least one more advantage. Because the Texas state legislature has restricted professional teacher education courses to 18 credit hours, we cannot offer additional courses. The volunteer assignment fits within the space of our constricted program.

The success of our experiences with the volunteer assignment leads us to believe that other teacher education programs, especially those that cannot create an interdisciplinary program, may benefit from a volunteer program. However, universities located far from the urban world, where preservice teachers may not be able to work in a broad range of programs, may not be able to provide such an experience. In general, we argue that teacher preparation must be a priority at comprehensive, rigorous urban universities.

Multicultural issues

The UW group report suggests that they faced considerable difficulties in establishing their program at an ethnically mixed inner city school where a confusing patchwork of social services operated largely independently. This is the type of environment where interprofessional practice is needed most. A recent interprofessional project in Houston convinced us that multicultural issues are central when considering interprofessional collaboration in such settings.

At the University of Houston, we have recently faced the problems of providing interprofessional services. In the spring of 1992, several faculty members and their students from the University of Houston joined with faculty and students from three other institutions of higher learning in the Houston area to collaborate on the problems evident in a near-urban section of the city. There were already several community-based groups active in this area, and it had been chosen as a focus of study due to its dense population, high crime rate, and insufficient health and social service facilities. The population of the area is predominantly immigrant and of low income.

The effort was coordinated by a faculty member with a dual appointment at the University of Houston (UH) and at Rice University. The success of the collaboration was largely due to the tireless efforts of this coordinator who kept in constant contact with all faculty and community representatives, as well as directing his urban design team and finally ensuring the publication of all relevant reports. The study focused on the following areas: social conditions, education, health care, transportation, community organization, and urban design.

The stated mission for the project was the improvement of the quality of life in that community. Unlike the UW program, faculty members and students focused initially on problems within their particular area of expertise. For example, students within the Principles of Curriculum Design in Second Language Education worked in groups to develop effective programs to meet the needs of learners of English as a second language (ESL) enrolled in elementary, secondary, and continuing education (adult) programs in the area. Students and faculty members from all disciplines met a total of four times throughout the semester on Saturday mornings in order to give progress reports to other project members. It was during these meetings that students and faculty from different disciplines gave important feedback to participants in other fields of study. For example, at one meeting it was suggested that the project had insufficient representation from the community, in particular from minority residents. As a result, students from the College of Social Work organized a cultural awareness workshop at which speakers from the Latino, African-American, and Vietnamese communities expressed their concerns. During these meetings, we noticed that the first true collaboration occurred among the various participants and disciplines. The result of the conversations with the community was the realization by all participants that the culture of those being 'served' must be of paramount importance. Perhaps students participating in interprofessional collaboration might benefit from early examinations of the race and class issues.

Conclusion

We hope that teacher educators and other professional program faculty will consider deeply the implementation and consequences of interprofessional collaboration. Too often in teacher preparation we are inclined to alter our existing programs with little evidence to suggest that the old way is not working or that the new way works better. We are not suggesting an overly instrumentalist view of programmatic changes, but evidence that teachers and other professionals are able to do their jobs better as a result of a collaborative training program is necessary for any change. It appears to us that the UW program will be providing the professional training community with that information, and we await the results.

References

AMERICAN ASSOCIATION OF COLLEGES FOR TEACHER EDUCATION (1987) *Teaching Teachers: Facts and Figures* (*RATE I*). (Washington, DC: Author).

AMERICAN ASSOCIATION OF COLLEGES FOR TEACHER EDUCATION (1991) *Teaching Teachers: Facts and Figures* (*RATE IV*). (Washington, DC: Author).

HABERMAN, M. (1992) 'Alternative certification: can the problems of urban education be resolved by traditional teacher education', *Teacher Education and Practice*, 8(1), pp. 13–28.

SCRIBNER, J. D. (1985) 'Colleges of education in urban universities', in C. W. Case and W. A. Matthes (eds) *Colleges of Education: Perspectives on Their Future* (Berkeley, CA: McCutchan), pp. 51–70.

TELLEZ, K. and HLEBOWITSH, P. S. (in press). 'Being there: social service and teacher preparation at the University of Houston', *Innovative Higher Education*.

PART 4
Lessons from the field

POLITICS OF EDUCATION ASSOCIATION YEARBOOK, 1993, 171–178

California's state partnership for school-linked services

William A. White

California's Governor and Superintendent of Public Instruction often find themselves on opposite sides of the fence when debating public policy. Yet both Pete Wilson and former Superintendent Bill Honig have been unwavering in their support of Healthy Start. In a unique collaborative effort, the Governor, the Superintendent, the Legislature, and a consortium of private foundations mustered their forces in support of major systems reforms in children's services.

Senate Bill 620, 'Healthy Start', (Chapter 759, Statutes of 1991, authored by Senator Robert Presley) was sponsored by Governor Wilson as the centerpiece of his prevention-focused initiative for children. Healthy Start involves schools in community partnerships to restructure services to children and their families. The first projects were funded in 1991–92 with an appropriation of $20 million.

Legislative history

This cross-cutting initiative began with no organized constituency and the potential of strong opposition from entrenched categorical programs. But with strong support from the Governor and key legislators, SB 620 met relatively little opposition in the Legislature. Although some members of the education lobby expressed concern that the initiative was funded out of the budget allocation for education rather than health, none publicly opposed the bill. The only public opposition came from conservative groups who feared students might gain access to family planning services.

During the legislative process SB 620 gained support from a consortium of private foundations active in children's services. Following the passage of SB 620, the foundations joined with the Governor, the Superintendent of Public Instruction, the Department of Health Services, and other state agencies to support implementation. At the same time, plans were developed to broaden and expand on the options offered by SB 620. The overall California effort – called Comprehensive Integrated School-linked Services (CISLS) – has three major objectives. First is developing models through Healthy Start. Second is building new financing mechanisms to sustain and expand the models. Finally, the partnership works for ongoing systems change.

What motivates these program partners to take the risks and pay the price of collaboration? Perhaps one reason is the growing need for services to low-income families. Currently, over 1.5 million California children receive Aid to Families With Dependent Children. The percentage of California children who have no health insurance, either private or public, continues to grow. Children Now reports that, in 1989, 26% of California's children fell into this category (Children Now 1992), comprising working poor families and large numbers of undocumented immigrants. California is in the midst of a public policy and fiscal crisis of epic proportions. As the recession continues, program caseloads grow. Expenditures of formula-driven programs continue to expand. Tax revenues have not kept pace.

Program cuts intended to deal with a projected $14.3 billion deficit in 1991–92 were not enough. Legislators agonized for weeks beyond their statutory deadline before agreeing to budget compromises intended to deal with a $10.7 billion shortfall in 1992–93. Welfare grants were cut; the sales tax increased; the budget for schools, through creative accounting, was funded by regarding part of the previous year's budget as counting toward 1992–93; higher education fees increased; and most major programs suffered cutbacks. But that was enough either. With all of the easy cuts, and many very hard ones, already taken, the Legislature must deal with a 1993–94 deficit first projected at $8.6 billion, but now appearing to be $2 billion higher.

With many other programs, Healthy Start rode the budget roller coaster in 1992. The Governor proposed $40 million in funding, double the first year's level. The Legislature cut until they hit zero. The State Partnership and Healthy Start supporters in the Legislature were finally able to restore $15.6 million. For 1993–94, the Governor's proposal of $38 million was cut in half by the Legislature.

As the fiscal crisis has worsened in California, so has the outlook for programs serving children and families. What could state government do? The treasury had run dry. A sagging economy meant brisk demand for services. Boosting funding or lopping off customers was clearly impractical. In the short term the only viable answer was a more efficient service network. In this one way, crisis meant opportunity. To a bureaucracy, stable funding often equates to resistance to change. In contrast, fiscal pressure may make organizations willing to explore new ways to do business.

Prior to Healthy Start, efforts to coordinate children's services had little success. Many well-intentioned plans fell victim to turf battles among vested interests. During a December 1988 hearing of California's Senate Select Committee on Children and Youth, Jack Hailey of the Senate Office of Research described this undistinguished history:

> Since 1970, numerous reports and proposals have addressed the need for a comprehensive children's service system. ... These proposals bring about ... three significant patterns. First, the principals were usually new to the issue ... Second, most of the opposition ... came from within the children's services arena connected to fear of losing categorical funding or ... influence and identity. And third, for 18 years, none of these proposals was seized by a governor or by the leadership of either party of either house. (California Legislature 1988: 14–15)

Little progress was made in building collaborative services systems until the late 1980s. At that time, a cluster of significant initiatives laid the groundwork for Healthy Start and other parts of the Comprehensive School-Linked Services effort:

- Presley–Brown Interagency Children's Service Act of 1989 (SB 997): authorizes county-wide interagency children and youth service councils who may apply for waivers of state regulations.
- School-Based Early Mental Health Intervention and Prevention Services for Children Act of 1991 (AB 1650): provides grants to schools offering mental health services to low-income children in grades K–3.
- Child Mental Disease (AB 377): Four-county demonstration providing integrated services to prevent out-of-home placement.
- Demonstration of Restructuring in Public Education Act (Senate Bill 1274): offers grants to schools to improve student outcomes by changing operations and policies.
- Healthy Kids, Healthy California: launched in 1989 by the California Department of Education, promotes school/community collaboration to design comprehensive health programs.

- Medi-Cal Managed Care Initiative (AB 336): initiates an expanded system of managed care for Medi-Cal recipients.

Each of these initiatives, along with Healthy Start, offers the potential for better coordination of services and collaboration in service delivery. However, for this potential to be realized, state agencies must assume an atypical role.

> For state agencies, this initiative requires them to think and act as 'change agents', with the goal of empowering other constituents and actors in this process, rather than trying to control or provide the new service system directly. Given the size of the State, and the distance between state government and the actual point of community service delivery, a direct role by state-level agencies in community change is clearly impossible. What state actors must do is to constantly watch that the incentives for change are in the right direction, that the tools for change are in the most appropriate hands, and that the state-level commitment to channel refinanced dollars . . . to local communities, is maintained. This requires . . . great sophistication in managing change, as well as . . . commitment to a new vision of services. (Farrow 1993: 41–42)

A related initiative, Superintendent of Public Instruction Honig's Healthy Kids, Healthy California initiative was designed to 'bring together the skills of all educators and support staff in a school and to develop partnerships with partners and the community . . . to influence the overall health and well-being of students' (CDE 1988: page titled 'A Message from the Superintendent').

Honig was well aware of the problems with children's services: 'California has approximately 160 children and youth-serving programs, overseen by 37 different state entities, located in seven different state departments. These state programs are implemented through 20 different types of programs at the county level, with . . . over 25 different and often conflicting eligibility criteria . . .' (California Legislature 1988: 107). In the Superintendent's view, what was needed was 'a strategy for collaborative planning, funding, and delivery among the state departments providing services to families and their children. Families needing assistance from multiple agencies should have to deal with only one person . . .' (California Legislature 1988: 111–112).

The Foundation Consortium

A major partner in this initiative is the Foundation Consortium for School-Linked Services. The Foundation Consortium represents 13 grant-making foundations based in California. The Consortium was born out of members' perceptions that local grants do not lead to large-scale change, and often cannot be sustained past the grant period. Systems barriers have proven an obstacle to local success. Influencing the mainstream of state-level policy offers the potential for greater impact on more people than isolated projects.

'The advantages from the foundations' perspective are that, one, we can leverage a great many more funds', says Howard Kahn (Southern California Association for Philanthropy 1992: 10), president of the California Wellness Foundation and chair of the Consortium.

> Foundations generally are important funders, and they're creative funders but by and large are not large funders compared to the resources that go to schools and to county health systems, which the state provides. By being partners in the decision-making process, we are able to leverage those funds in directions we think are creative, and that we think are most meaningful. (p. 10)

The systems changes of most interest to the foundation partners are those which offer:

- better ways to identify children and families needing service;
- unified planning and record-keeping;

- noncategorical budgeting;
- flexible, integrated funding at the local level.

The Consortium has committed $1.75 million annually in support of the initiative. This pays for the statewide evaluation of Healthy Start and for staff to help design systems changes. Funding state staff is very unusual for foundations. But the Consortium members had, individually, been funding local collaboration, and had a deep understanding of the time and effort needed. Foundation funding gives the flexibility to attack major problems quickly, without the usual bureaucratic restrictions. Foundations are used to thinking on the cutting edge, testing the latest concepts. State agencies on the other hand tend to move more slowly, often because staff are fully occupied maintaining existing programs. The staffing relief provided by the foundations allows the state agency partners to accelerate their change agenda. On the other hand, each of the partners relinquishes some autonomy. Trust becomes increasingly important as foundations agree to less control over how their funds are spent and state government accedes to negotiating significant policy issues.

The State Partnership

The Governor, the Superintendent, and the foundations first came together in the halls of the Legislature during the debate on SB 620 – and discovered they shared compatible visions of the future for children's services. Further, all realized that the existing service structure was failing many families. The dialogue from these encounters grew into an agreement on how to construct a new paradigm. This Agreement in Principle, signed by Governor Wilson, Superintendent of Public Instruction Honig, and the Foundation Consortium, forged a public/private partnership focusing on school-linked services (Executive Department, State of California 1992).

To turn the Agreement's philosophy into reality, a state-level collaborative evolved. The State Partnership is governed by what has become known as the Principals Group. Senate Bill 620, setting up the Healthy Start program, designated a governing council: the Superintendent of Public Instruction, the Secretary of the Health and Welfare Agency, the Secretary of Child Development and Education, and the directors of the departments of Health Services, Social Services, Alcohol and Drug Programs, and Mental Health. This group plus the foundation representatives form the core of the Principals Group.

In monthly meetings of the principals and their key staff, a plan for a statewide school-linked services system is unfolding. Based on agreements reached in these meetings, the members set state policy on family and children's services. To guide their efforts, the principals have developed vision statements – their view of the future possible for children, families, communities, and systems. Strategic decisions of the principals are transformed into action by the principals' senior staff, who meet weekly. Also attending these meetings are members of individual work groups which also meet weekly and focus on evaluation, technical assistance, Medi-Cal, and financing. In these small groups the compromises needed to transform philosophy into action are hammered out.

The Agreement in Principle guides the work of the state collaborative. The work plan comprises three interlocking objectives which are the first major steps toward developing a new service model.

Healthy Start

One objective of the Agreement in Principle is to develop program models based on the experiences gained at Healthy Start sites. SB 620, administered by the California Department of Education, encourages development of comprehensive, integrated, school-linked services models. The initiative requires strong community collaborative links among public and private agencies serving families. In this way Healthy Start is a catalyst for broader change – valuable in its own right, and even more important for the patterns it establishes for broader system reform. The program, fiscal, and political arrangements encouraged by Healthy Start are basic building blocks of the larger system.

Healthy Start is California's first statewide effort to place comprehensive support services at or near schools. Funding for this initiative is not primarily aimed at buying services. Instead, Healthy Start covers the costs of building local partnerships. Thus, Healthy Start money is glue money, cementing together the carefully shaped pieces of the new systems. Careful fitting makes the strongest bond and uses the least glue. Healthy Start sites are fitting together a wide array of services for families at or near local schools. But this initiative goes well beyond co-location. The confusing mix of eligibility standards, application processes, and service categories is being melded into a system which is accessible, friendly, and responsive to family needs.

Several key concepts are central to Healthy Start site plans:

- *Collaborative* partnerships bring together key people and agencies in health and human services, county government, county offices of education, school districts, and others to create new child-centered service systems.
- *Schools act as sites for service integration* where the problems of children are likely to be identified and where they can most easily be served.
- *Integrated services* at Healthy Start sites must provide a minimum of four services. The statute lists some possibilities – immunizations, dental, health, counseling, parenting education, family preservation, nutrition, academic support – and allows for any other services based on needs. Healthy Start promotes reconfiguring systems to better fit the needs of clients. A key feature of many projects is a service center, providing one-stop shopping.
- *Family and community participation* is assured when parents, teachers, students, the school, district and county leadership, and the community and agency service providers all help govern, build, and carry out Healthy Start programs.
- *Individualized case management* is based on a personalized plan for students and family members. The plan is developed with the help of a case manager who makes referrals and follows progress.
- *Targeting low-income and at-risk youth* is a priority; although Healthy Start aims to make services available for all families. Priority is given to low-income and limited English-proficient students and families.
- *Measurable outcomes* are critical. Healthy Start projects are expected to improve such outcomes as school attendance and performance, physical and social health, and family functioning. To gauge program effects, local initiatives evaluate services delivery and collaborative functioning. A statewide evaluation of Healthy Start operational sites, plus similar projects supported by Foundation Consortium members, is also under way. This evaluation focuses on education, health, and social outcomes, and systems change.

Healthy Start offers funding to school districts and county offices of education, and their collaborative partners for planning or operational grants. Planning grants are for a one- or two-year period, for up to $50,000. Operational grants are for three years and are for up to $400,000. At least 90% of the schools that receive grants must qualify by having 50% of more of the students meet specific low-income criteria or have a large population of students with limited English proficiency. For 1991–92, 40 operational proposals were selected to pioneer the program. One hundred and ten planning proposals were funded. The 1992–93 grant cycle added 25 operational grants, 19 of which were former planning grantees, and 72 new planning grants.

Healthy Start projects range from a single school site to a countywide collaborative of multiple school districts and schools. The 65 operational grantees encompass 210 schools; 491 schools are included in the 163 planning sites. Implementation of the 1991–92 grants began in the fall of the 1992 school year. An unexpected delay in start-up resulted from the Legislature and the Governor laboring more than two months past the statutory deadline before adopting the 1992–93 budget. Even though Healthy Start grant monies were from the previous year's budget, many local boards of education would not allow hiring staff and beginning new programs until the district's overall budget was finalized.

The schools' partners in the community had their own budget problems. Faced with cuts in staff and funding, many felt the need to rethink their commitments to provide resources to the collaborative. While most concluded that meeting these commitments was a high priority, the process of reconsideration delayed implementation in some sites.

Confidentiality of client data had been expected to be a major issue in implementation. However, a statutory change in 1991 (Assembly Bill 2184) removed many potential barriers by allowing integrated service programs to share information necessary to a client's service plan. Thus, confidentiality posed few true problems among collaborative partners, but was still often raised as a means of defending turf. An unanticipated problem with confidentiality has arisen in some sites using parents as advocates. These agencies have learned the need to ensure that the advocates follow the same standards as agency staff when dealing with sensitive information about families. This will be a significant training issue at a number of sites – how you ask for information, where you put it, and who has access.

Workshops held for operational site grantees have helped them to home in on program areas needing immediate attention. Prime among these is determining how to encourage greater parent involvement, both in governance and in service delivery. Many sites also expressed a need for assistance in setting up case management systems.

While most sites have made considerable progress, all have areas where they feel the need for expert assistance. Fortunately, for each site with a problem, there are several sites which have successfully addressed that problem. Thus, a major focus in coming months will be to foster mentor relationships among the sites.

The first available operational site service data gathered by the statewide evaluator is for the initial quarter of 1993. Sites sorted their services into 95 categories in ten major groupings. Although incomplete, the data show considerable diversity among sites in the kinds of services offered. Most sites, as expected, offer significant educational services, public assistance advocacy, and health and mental health services, but show wide variance in which services are frequently provided. Some sites have had high demand for basic needs – food, clothing, housing assistance, etc. Many sites have identified an unmet need for services to help families deal with violence – within the family and in the community. Most sites have informally identified dental service as an area of high need, but few sites are offering these services. At this point, it appears that the diversity of services is both a function of the needs of the community and the availability of resources to meet those needs.

Financing mechanisms

A second major objective of the Agreement in Principle is to provide new or better funding streams for children's services. As a first step, the Partnership has developed a Medi-Cal billing option for schools. A Medicaid State Plan Amendment, approved in March 1993, allows schools to enroll as providers. Schools may bill for the services to students and families. The potential scope of services is very broad providing an option for dealing with service gaps that cannot be filled by local collaborative members. Additionally, reimbursement for existing services provides new funds for reinvestment in school-linked support services. The provider agreement each school district must sign requires that Medi-Cal payments be reinvested in expanded services and that local collaboratives help decide how funds will be spent.

The State Partnership committed to putting an education provider category in place quickly. To speed approval, it was agreed to make no changes in eligibility, in qualifications for people delivering services, or in covered services. This move to 'pick the low-hanging fruit' from the fiscal tree was a first step. The longer-range strategy is to explore new ways to finance other services of local collaboratives, as well as additional Medicaid strategies. The financial goal of each school-linked services collaborative should be stable, long-term financing – becoming self-sustaining through a mix of continuing funding and reimbursements.

Sustained systems change

A final objective of the Agreement in Principle is sustained systems change which envisions a statewide service system that: integrates state, county and local resources to minimize conflict, fragmentation, duplication, and inconsistency; expands school-linked services; and eliminates barriers to service delivery. Federal waivers will be sought to test innovative strategies. Medicaid waivers could involve presumptive eligibility or capitated case management and services. Education waivers may be sought to allow flexibility in categorical programs, such as Chapter I and Special Education.

The immediate priorities of the California Partnership are to implement their strategic plan by: (1) designing new cost-effective program models; (2) cultivating new financing mechanisms; (3) expanding experimentation with school-linked service approaches and with school Medi-Cal providers; (4) developing options for overcoming barriers to services; and (4) generating an intergovernmental strategy for implementing and evaluating the statewide school-linked service system. An immediate need as systems change begins is preventing duplication and overlap between Healthy Start and county managed care systems. Similarly, gaps and overlaps in categorical programs must be reexamined.

The state-level effort to build California's Comprehensive School-Linked Services initiative bodes well for children's services. In a recent briefing for state staff by the Partnership, the panel was asked why there is so much confidence in this initiative. 'None of this is new. Each of these concepts has been tried and failed before. What makes you think it will work this time?' The answers summarize the lessons learned by the State Partnership:

- Research has taught us we are most likely to succeed if we target our efforts on comprehensive support of families, rather than categorical services to individuals.

- We are making more effective use of meoney. Funding streams are being redesigned to be flexible and to provide incentives.
- Stakeholders at all levels are involved: public and private; local, county, state, and federal; health, education, social service; and community, school, family. Most earlier efforts bypassed some of these groups.
- There is a much better appreciation of how tough the job is and how important it is.

California has made excellent progress, but has much work remaining. Comprehensive school-linked services are still a long way from reality – perhaps not until the end of the decade – but when completed will revolutionize the way support systems serve our children and families.

References

CALIFORNIA DEPARTMENT OF EDUCATION (1988) *Healthy Kids, Healthy California* (Sacramento, CA: Author).

CALIFORNIA DEPARTMENT OF HEALTH SERVICES (1992) *Delivering the Future – Recommendations from the AB 99 Steering Committee Regarding Health Care for Women, Children, and Adolescents in California* (Sacramento, CA: Author).

CALIFORNIA LEGISLATURE (1988) *Hearing on Coordinating Children's Services in California, Senate Select Committee on Children and Youth* (Sacramento, CA: Joint Publications, State Capitol).

CHILDREN NOW (1992) *California: The State of Our Children, California State 1992 Report Card: Data Supplement* (Santa Monica, CA: Children Now).

CONGRESSIONAL RECORD – US SENATE (1990, 7 February) (Washington, DC), p. S946.

EXECUTIVE DEPARTMENT, STATE OF CALIFORNIA (1992) *Agreement in Principle Between the State of California and the California Wellness Foundation, the Walter S. Johnson Foundation, the Henry J. Kaiser Family Foundation, the Marin Community Foundation, the San Francisco Foundation, the Sierra Foundation, the Stuart Foundations, and the Zellerbach Family Fund* (Sacramento, CA: Author).

FARROW, F. (1993) *Improving Outcomes for California's Children – A Strategy to Build Comprehensive Community Services* (Washington, DC: Center for the Study of Social Policy).

SOUTHERN CALIFORNIA ASSOCIATION FOR PHILANTHROPY (1992, fall) *Southern California Philanthropy* 1(4).

POLITICS OF EDUCATION ASSOCIATION YEARBOOK, 1993, 179–187

On the cutting edge: Family Resource/Youth Service Centers in Kentucky

Charles J. Russo and Jane Clark Lindle

Introduction

Kentucky stagnated in the backwater of public education until a maelstrom of judicial, executive, and legislative forces propelled the state into the vanguard of reform. In 1989, the Kentucky Supreme Court's findings in *Rose* v. *Council for Better Education, Inc.* struck down the existing system of public school funding as violative of a state constitutional mandate that all students be provided with adequate educations. This unprecedented ruling ushered in needed changes in public education. With the General Assembly acting as architect, the Governor signed into law the Kentucky Education Reform Act (KERA), perhaps the most comprehensive structural reform in the last decade (Walker 1990: 1).

In enacting KERA, the General Assembly eschewed a 'quick fix' for meaningful reform. KERA accomplished sweeping changes in finance, governance, and curriculum, but this radical reform went beyond academic matters to address the physical and emotional needs of students. KERA is grounded on the precepts that (1) all children should begin school ready to learn, (2) parental and family involvement is critical for educational success, and (3) the community should provide services to increase the educative capacities of families and schools (Roeder 1992a, Coe *et al.* 1991, Hornbeck 1990, Legislative Research Commission 1990). KERA links schools and social service agencies as integral partners in educating Kentucky's children and youth for the 21st century and provides Family Resource/Youth Services Centers (FRYSCs) in schools throughout the state (Kentucky Revised Statutes 1992: 156.497). Centers are located in or near schools to coordinate social service delivery for preschool to high school students and families.

During the first year of funding (1991–92), 133 Centers serving 232 schools (23% of eligible schools) were in operation (Status Report 1991: 6, Roeder 1992b: 6). More than half of these were Family Resource Centers (FRCs), another 25% were Youth Services Centers (YSCs), and 26 were combined FRYSCs (Status Report 1991: 6). During the 1992–93 academic year 222 Centers, serving 103 of Kentucky's 176 school districts, were operational (Kentucky Department of Education 1993). Initial reports indicate that the Centers have been successful (Roeder 1992b, Cohen 1992, Coe *et al.* 1991).

This article is divided into two parts to explain the emerging relationship between the educational and social service systems in Kentucky. The first half presents a legal history of FRYSCs and KERA. The second half describes the Centers' development. Due to the embryonic stage of FRYSC implementation, the data used in the second half of this article are primarily qualitative. Interviews with employees of state and local agencies, FRYSC and schools were triangulated with media reports and state and local documentation of FRYSC development.

KERA: a legal history

Kentucky's education reformers were influenced by the national reform reports of the 1980s and galvanized by the state's poor records on virtually all global indicators of educational performance (Combs 1991: 367), including the lowest percentage of citizens in the USA completing high school (Bureau of the Census 1984: 135). In 1985, the Council for Better Education incorporated. The Council – a coalition of 66 school districts with low property wealth and thus a weak tax base, joined by seven boards of education and 22 students from the seven districts – sought to challenge the disparity in Kentucky's educational funding. Bert Combs, former Governor and partner in one of the state's leading law firms, was prevailed upon to serve as lead attorney in the Council's lawsuit (Combs 1991).

The Council's challenge to the adequacy of Kentucky's funding of public education was part of a national trend. Including the Tennessee Supreme Court's March 1993 decision, 12 of 25 challenges to the adequacy of state funding systems in recent years have been successful (Schmidt 1993, Dayton 1992). And since 1989 six states have been ordered by their highest courts to find an equitable way to fund their public schools (Diegmueller 1993). The Kentucky challenge was ruled on about the same time as a similar finding was made in Texas. The immediate consequence of the Texas and Kentucky cases was a contrast in political responsiveness (Harp 1991a, 1991b). Unlike Texas, Kentucky's response galvanized immediate systemic change in the state's structure for public schooling.

By a five to two ruling in *Rose* v. *Council for Better Education* [hereafter *Rose*] (1989), the Kentucky Supreme Court affirmed a lower court decision which struck down the state's entire public school system for failing to comply with the constitutional mandate to 'provide an efficient system of common schools throughout the state' (Kentucky Constitution, Section 183). The court then 'directed the General Assembly to recreate and redesign a new system that will comply with the standards' (*Rose* 1989: 212). While recognizing the General Assembly's exclusive duty to establish an efficient system, but desiring to assure compliance with its dictates, the court withheld the finality of judgment until 90 days after the adjournment of the regular 1990 legislative session (*Rose* 1989: 216).

Between the court's June 1989 ruling in *Rose* and the General Assembly's regular session, Governor Wallace Wilkinson appointed a Task Force of legislative representatives. The Governor's Task Force on Educational Reform began meeting with a wide range of national consultants on virtually every aspect of education (Legislative Research Commission 1990). The general Assembly convened in January 1990, and quickly set about the task of educational reform. In March 1990, the General Assembly passed House Bill 940, and on 11 April, 1990 the Governor signed into law The Kentucky Education Reform Act.

Among KERA's innovative reforms, the creation of FRYSCs as a link between schools and social service agencies is one of the most comprehensive. Family Resource Centers are patterned on Centers in Connecticut, the Lexington, KY Department of Social Services Family Care Center, and Parent And Child Education which was an existing Kentucky program. Youth Services Centers are modeled on similar facilities in New Jersey (Hornbeck 1990, Levy and Shephardson 1992). FRYSCs also are designed in part after the Kentucky Integrated Delivery System which was piloted in 1988 (Cabinet for Human Resources and the Kentucky Department of Education 1990, Hornbeck 1990).

The legislation authorizing the development (Kentucky Revised Statutes 1992: 156.497) and funding (Kentucky Revised Statutes 1992: 156.4977) of FRYSCs provides a great deal of information about their legal organization. Kentucky Revised Statutes 156.497, 'Interagency Task Force on Family Resource Centers and Youth Services Center – Formulation of Five-Year Plan – Implementation', is the heart of the new law. The Secretary of the Cabinet for Human Resources (CHR) was authorized to assemble a 16 member Task Force to formulate a five-year plan. The Task Force included representatives from such diverse groups as the Kentucky Department of Education (KDE); the Departments of Health Services, Social Services, and Social Insurance in CHR; the Governor's Office; parents; teachers; local school administrators; and local school boards. The Task Force elects its chair who is eligible for annual re-election. The CHR provided staffing for the implementation phase. The Task Force must monitor the development of Centers until it ceases to exist on 31 December 1995.

Due to legislative debate over whether oversight of the FRYSCs should reside in Kentucky Department of Education or the Cabinet for Human Resources, the Task Force reports to the Secretary of the Cabinet for Human Resources, the State Board for Elementary and Secondary Education, the Governor, and the Legislative Research Commission. This pattern of oversight was an important recognition of the necessity for collaboration on the state level as a model for local level collaboration and implementation of FRYSCs. A precedent for such collaboration was established in the 1988 development of the Kentucky Integrated Delivery System (KIDS). KIDS was envisioned by the then Secretary of the Cabinet for Human Resources, Harry J. Cowherd, and the State Superintendent for Education, John Brock (North Central Regional Educational Laboratory 1992, Steffy 1993). Brock approached members of the Cabinet for Human Resources and the Department of Education to participate in dropout prevention training. As members from both agencies came together, the idea of KIDS was formed. Cowherd threw the weight of his office behind the school districts and local agencies piloting the concept. Cowherd and Brock were still in office when the FRYSC strand of KERA was designed. To many in Kentucky, FRYSCs looked like KIDS in concept, a concept with which they had already experienced a measure of success (Steffy 1993: 191).

The Task Force completed its implementation plan by the legislated date of 1 January 1991. Two hundred and forty-five schools responded with proposals by 30 June 1991 (Status Report 1991: 5). Slightly over 200 additional proposals were submitted by May 1992 (Proposal Review Session 1992). Although the legislature had estimated that 500 Kentucky schools would be eligible for FRYSCs, a survey conducted by the FRYSC Branch of the Cabinet for Human Resources in 1990 showed that over 1100 of Kentucky's 1400 schools would qualify (Proposal Review Session 1992, Steffy 1993). Using a consortia model of grouping nearby schools for one Family Resource or Youth Service Center, by 30 June 1992, FRYSCs were established in or near at least one-quarter (222) of eligible schools (Kentucky Department of Education 1993). An additional quarter will be served over each of the next three years.

Initial uncertainty over service eligibility was clarified in a 1992 revision of the law. The clarification was provoked by fundamentalist religious groups who wished to limit services on the basis of socio-economic status (interview with interagency Task Force member 1992). The legislative revision stipulated that services are available to all students to ensure success but, in the event of limited resources, 'students and families who are the most economically disadvantaged shall receive priority status for receiving services' (Kentucky Revised Statutes 1992: 156.497[2]).

Family Resources Centers, for elementary schools, and Youth Services Centers, for schools serving children over 12 years of age, are established in or near schools where 20% or more of students are eligible for free lunches. Family Resources Centers are required to provide 'core' services including preschool and after-school child care, prenatal education for new parents, parent and child education, training for day care providers, and health services (Kentucky Revised Statutes 1992: 156.497[3]). Youth Services Centers are mandated to provide the 'core' service of referrals for health and social services, employment services, summer/part-time job development, drug and alcohol abuse counseling, as well as family crisis and mental health counseling (Kentucky Revised Statutes 1992: 156.497[4]). FRYSCs are prohibited from counseling or referrals for abortion (Kentucky Revised Statutes 1992: 156.497[6]). However, all Centers are encouraged to develop additional service components. The suggested optional components range from recreational activities to crisis intervention, but Cabinet for Human Resources documents emphasize preventive services and community collaboration (Family Resource Coalition 1992, Interagency Task Force 1991).

Kentucky Revised Statutes 156.4977, 'Grants to Local School Districts for Family Resource and Youth Service Centers', lays out eligibility requirements for funding of Centers up to the 1995 fiscal year. Instructions and scoring procedures for grant proposals were developed by Cabinet for Human Resources staff following Task Force recommendations. Kentucky educators, social workers and citizens recommended by Interagency Task Force members reviewed proposals for funding (Steffy 1993). Proposals are required to include information on: governance, needs, services and activities, training plans, job descriptions, Center location and accessibility, contracts and letters of agreement, financial strategy and budget, public relations issues (including a 'de-stigmatizing' plan) and program evaluation.

Kentucky's precepts that all children can learn with critical involvement from parent(s), family and community are embedded in the 'de-stigmatizing' facets of FRYSC implementation. One of the national organizations which promotes a community-based interagency approach to family support, the Family Resource Coalition, was utilized as a resource by the Interagency Task Force early in its planning stages. Its 'Checklist of Family Support Principles' begins with this question:

> Are services provided in the most family-friendly, non-stigmatizing environment, and wherever possible, in the home? (Family Resource Coalition Report 1990: 7)

Kentucky's Interagency Task Force extended the concept of non-stigmatizing environments to promotion of family/community ownership in the Centers (Interagency Task Force 1991: 16). As a result, the 'Solicitation of Proposals' for FRYSCs grants included a required plan for reducing stigma. The purpose of this requirement was to encourage participation by all members of the community in FRYSC development and support (Family Resource and Youth Services Centers Branch 1993). A community-centered philosophy drives the mission of FRYSCs.

The programmatic mission for FRYSCs is to co-ordinate and identify gaps in the existing service delivery system. This single directive is an outgrowth of concern that Kentucky's human and social services prior to KERA were 'piecemeal, limited and/or dependent on soft funds' (Hornbeck 1990, Interagency Task Force 1991: 11). Furthermore, local FRYSC efforts are predicted on a belief that interagency coordination is best negotiated within the community rather than mandated by the state (Interagency Task Force 1991: 13). These beliefs are buttressed by the Interagency Task Force's 'Guiding Principles':

- All children can learn and most at high levels.

- Create an atmosphere that empowers the child, youth and/or family to acquire the competencies necessary to meet the needs and achieve the goals of attaining an education.
- Develop an interagency focus.
- Assure community ownership.
(Cabinet for Human Resources 1992, Interagency Task Force 1991: 15–17)

The empowerment and community ownership principles guarantee local variability in implementation. This design accommodates an assortment of community conditions affecting students, families, education, and service delivery systems. The following section is descriptive of the current level of implementation. Due to the nascent stage of implementation, this report is limited to qualitative data obtained from state and local FRYSCs and school staffs.

A snapshot of FRYSC implementation

To illustrate implementation, data were gathered from interviews, media reports, sociological reports, and state and local documentation of FRYSC development. Comments from interviews were triangulated with other data sources to insure validity. Several themes emerged from the data which may foreshadow the success of Kentucky's FRYSCs. The data included the following issues of implementation:

- providing services versus coordinating services;
- initial enthusiasm and staying-power; and
- macro- and micro-level tensions.

Providing vs. coordinating

FRYSCs have produced dramatic results in increased access to services by children and families (Roeder 1992b: 2). FRYSC directors are accomplished raconteurs and advocates for students and families in need (field notes 1992, Roeder 1992: 3). Several directors noted that interagency collaboration was catalyzed by the plight of children and families referred to their FRYSCa (interviews western Kentucky 1992, central Kentucky 1992). A nurse employed by an FRYSC in western Kentucky made this point:

> The thing that really got us started was we had this family that came to our county from Florida. They had *nothing*. They had this baby. [The FRYSC nurse] talked the grocery into giving them some staples. Then [the FRYSC nurse and secretary] sent them to [volunteers who run the charity for area council of churches]. They helped with housing and getting them on their feet. Everything, everyone, just came together. (interview July 1992)

While the directors of the local FRYSCs are sure that they are coordinating services, the variance in local operational definitions of 'coordination' versus 'provision' of services is great (Roeder 1992b: 13). One former Cabinet for Human Resources staff member speculates that this exists not solely by design, but because of the history of social service delivery in the state. Now a school administrator, this individual expressed the following concerns:

> FRYSCs appear to be addressing the gaps in service at the local level, but not at the state level. This program was supposed to shore up the social service delivery system. That hasn't happened yet. In some ways, FRYSCs are becoming a secondary social service system. I'm not sure anyone is really watching this carefully. (interview November 1992)

Coordination of services was the intent of the legislation (Hornbeck 1990). But, not everyone is wary of FRYSCs becoming a secondary delivery site. In some counties, FRYSCs are seen as a positive addition or alternative to existing delivery sites (field notes 1992).

Local coordinators measure success by the families and students they have helped (Cohen 1992: 17, Roeder 1992b: 15–16). Their enthusiastic client focus is the source of their skills in leveraging local interagency resources.

Enthusiasm and staying power

Early successes of FRYSCs seem to be directly related to the zeal of Center Coordinators. There is no question that many of the original coordinators are passionate advocates of children and clients (Proposal Review Session 1992, Roeder 1992b).

Interviews with coordinators reveal spirited, confident, change agents committed to the principles of family support. The entire state seems to be blessed with these energetic champions of FRYSCs (Cohen 1992, Dunn 1992, Lucke 1992, Roeder 1992). An FRYSC nurse noted that:

> Our coordinator is very persistent with red tape. She just keeps on 'til she gets through. She's learning, too, but she's very smart. (interview July 1992)

A similar point was made by a FRYSC Coordinator:

> No one says 'no' to me! (interview July 1992)

Hiring and supporting coordinators who have a high level of enthusiasm appears to be one directive from the Interagency Task Force which local FRYSC advisory boards followed explicitly. The Cabinet for Human Resources' *Guide for Implementation and Planning* suggests:

> The single most important decision for a new FRYSC program is who the center coordinator will be. This staff person in many cases will BE the program .... The most important qualification for a ... director is a proven capacity for building strong personal relationships .... Other personal qualities ... include a high level of initiative .... (Family Resource Coalition 1992: 16)

Not all of CHR's suggestions are as well accepted for local implementation as this one. The typical tensions of change are found in the macro and micro concerns of implementing FRYSCs (McLaughlin 1990).

Macro and micro pressures

> I worry that the evaluation of FRYSCs will keep them from maintaining their uniqueness by forcing them to do some things the same. I know there have to be similarities, but I don't want us to measure success by how many phone calls we took. (interview with Interagency Task Force member, 1992)

Both Center Coordinators and Cabinet for Human Resources staff have reservations about the current monitoring and reporting system (Cohen 1992, Roeder 1992b). Cabinet for Human Resources staff are counselled to develop a technology-based monitoring and evaluation system (field notes 1992, Roeder 1992b). In turn, the Interagency Task Force advises local FRYSC planning teams to develop 'quantitative' evaluation plans. On the other hand, design and proposal guidelines promote 'unique', community-based flexibility in implementation (Cabinet for Human Resources 1992, Family Resource Coalition 1992). The clash between local implementation variability and the state agency's political needs for an accountability system is felt at both the local and state level (Roeder 1992b). Comments from our interviewees also note these tensions.

> I sometimes think that Frankfort [the capital] is just making it up as we go along. For instance, we coordinators had a big flare up over child abuse information. CHR staff wanted us to send out all this information on the child abuse reporting requirements to parents. Statewide, we banded together against this for several reasons. For one thing, it's an old law on the books long before KERA. For another, we've [coordinators] spent a lot of time trying to lower the stigma that might be attached to seeking help from FRYSCs. Just when we've begun to establish trust with families that really need this, the state wants to scare them with the legal stuff. In the end, we talked them out of doing this (interview with FRYSC Coordinator 1992)

> I worry that sometimes these coordinators can't see the forest for the trees. They know they are successful with this family or that kid, but in each case, they probably uncovered something about the existing service delivery system that should be changed. But we won't know about it at the state level. (interview with school administrator 1992)

In a lesser way, local accountability is also an issue. Although most school officials have been supportive of the FRYSC coordinators and services, they have some misgivings about the relationship between FRYSC personnel and schools (Roeder 1992b). For example, principals worry about liability in the supervision of building personnel. Even though many FRYSC Coordinators do not report to school administrators, the principals of schools where Centers are housed hire or evaluate staff who work for the coordinator (field notes 1992). These kinds of efforts require close working relationships (Roeder 1992b) and local variability in implementation.

The macro- and micro-level concerns are tied to the tension between flexible, decentralized design and rigid, centralized notions of accountability. Rather than viewing the incomparability of FRYSCs as a sign of systemic health in the integration of policy, state agency and legislative personnel may fall into the trap of demanding uniformity and, ultimately, mediocrity (McLaughlin 1990).

Conclusion

With the adoption of KERA, Kentucky catapulted from a back-bench seat among the states' education systems to a prominent leadership role in educational reform. The significance of Kentucky's reform is that it is a systemic revolution, not only in education but also in the infrastructure of local social service delivery. The early reports suggest that divergent political and economic forces can spur equally competitive judicial, executive, and legislative powers to design a robust revolution in collaboration, education, and social service delivery. Yet, the most stringent test of success – time – has yet to be faced by Kentucky's grand educational experiment.

Some critical deadlines loom in the future of Kentucky's FRYSCs. As noted earlier, KERA's centralized funding reforms provide a serious counterpoint to the singular decentralized designs of the local FRYSCs. By 1995, the legislative authorization for the Interagency Task Force expires. Several unanswered questions loom toward that date. Under what state agency's aegis will the future for FRYSCs be found? By 1995, will all funds for FRYSCs be allocated to those already operating? What about eligible schools/communities which never developed acceptable FRYSC proposals although definitive needs exist? And finally, how will the accountability and evaluation issues be addressed while preserving the local adaptability of FRYSC programs? Whether Kentucky represents a new trend in public education or is viewed as an outlier remains to be seen and will depend in large part on how successful its reforms are in the long run.

References

ALEXANDER, K. (1990) 'The courts and the governor show the way in Kentucky', *Politics of Education Bulletin*, 16, pp. 1–3.

BUREAU OF THE CENSUS (1984) *United States Department of Commerce, Statistical Abstracts of the United States 1985* (105th edn.) (Washington, DC: US Government Printing Office).

CABINET FOR HUMAN RESOURCES (1992) *Solicitation of Proposals* (Frankfort: Cabinet for Human Resources).

CABINET FOR HUMAN RESOURCES AND THE KENTUCKY DEPARTMENT OF EDUCATION (1990) *Delivering Human Services to K.I.D.S. and Their Families* (Frankfort, KY: Division of Community Education, Kentucky Department of Education).

COE, P., KANNAPEL, and LUTZ, P. (1991) *Initial Reactions to the Kentucky Education Reform Act in Six Rural Districts* (State policy program, Charleston, WV: Appalachia Educational Laboratory).

COHEN, D. L. (1992, 23 September) Kentucky family support centers a success, study finds', *Educational Week*, 12(3), pp. 17, 19.

COMBS, B. T. (1991) 'Creative constitutional reform in Kentucky', *Harvard Journal of Legislation*, 28, pp. 367–378.

DAYTON, J. (1992) 'An anatomy of school funding litigation', *Education Law Reporter*, 77, pp. 627–648.

DIEGMULLER, K. (1993, 23 June) 'Mass. court rules finance system is unconstitutional', *Education Week*, pp. 1,30.

DUNN, R. (1992) 'Focus: Education reform's foundation: Family Resource/Youth Services Centers', *Perspectives*, 3, pp. 4–5.

FAMILY RESOURCE COALITION (rev. 1992) *Kentucky Family Resource and Youth Services Centers: Guide for Planning and Implementation* (Chicago: Family Resource Coalition).

FAMILY RESOURCE CALITION REPORT (1990) *Building Communities*, 9, pp. 1–19 (Chicago: Family Resource Coalition).

FAMILY RESOURCES AND YOUTH SERVICES CENTERS BRANCH (1993) *Solicitation of Proposals* (Frankfort, KY: Cabinet for Human Resources).

HARP, L. (1991a, 10 April) 'Texas judge gives another chance to equity order: Vows drastic steps if no accord is reached', *Education Week*, pp. 1, 19.

HARP, L. (1991b, 5 June) 'Texas legislature approves Richard's reform bill', *Education Week*, p. 22.

HORNBECK, D. W. (1990) *Recommendations related to Curriculum* (Frankfort, KY: Legislative Research Commission).

INTERAGENCY TASK FORCE ON FAMILY RESOURCE AND YOUTH SERVICES CENTERS (1991) *State Implementation Plan* (Frankfort, KY: Cabinet for Human Resources).

KENTUCKY DEPARTMENT OF EDUCATION (1993) 'Kentucky Education Reform Act progress report', *Kentucky Teacher*, pp. 4–5.

KENTUCKY REVISED STATUTES (1992) Sections 156.497, 156.4977, Kentucky Education Reform Act.

LEGISLATIVE RESEARCH COMMISSION (1990) *A Guide to the Kentucky Education Reform Act of 1990* (Frankfort, KY: Legislative Research Commission).

LEVY, J. F. and KANNAPEL, P. (1991) 'Family Resource/Youth Service Centers', *Notes from the Field: Education Reform in Rural Kentucky*, 1, pp. 1–2.

LEVY, J. F. and SHEPARDSON, W. (1992) 'A look at current school-linked service efforts', *The Future of Children*, 2, pp. 44–55.

LUCKE, J. (1992, 3 February) 'Sandgap school puts reforms into action', *Lexington Herald – Leader*, pp. B1–B2.

MCLAUGHLIN, M. W. (1990) 'The Rand Change Agent Study revisited: macro perspectives and micro realities', *Educational Researcher*, 19, pp. 11–16.

NORTH CENTRAL REGIONAL EDUCATIONAL LABORATORY (1992) 'Guidebook 8: Integrating community services', *Schools That Work: The Research Advantage* (Oak Brook, IL: North Central Regional Educational Laboratory).

PROPOSAL REVIEW SESSION (1992) Jabez, KY: Family Resources and Youth Services Center Branch.

ROEDER, P. W. (1992a) *Family Centers in Kentucky Schools: Politics and Policy in Education and Welfare Delivery* (Lexington, KY: Prichard Committee).

ROEDER, P. W. (1992b) *Assessment of Family Resource and Youth Service Centers* (Lexington, KY: Prichard Committee).

Rose v. Council for Better Education, Inc. 790 S.W.2d 186 (Ky. 1989).

SCHMIDT, P. (1993, 31 March) 'School finance system in Tennessee is struck down', *Education Week*, 12(27), pp. 1, 22.

STATUS REPORT (1991) *Family Resources and Youth Services Centers Status Report for 1991* (Frankfort, KY: Cabinet for Human Resources).

STEFFY, B. E. (1993) *The Kentucky Education Reform: Lessons for America* (Lancaster, PA: Technomic).

WALKER, R. (1990, 4 April) 'Lawmakers in Ky. approve landmark school-reform bill', *Education Week*, 9(28), pp. 34–35.

POLITICS OF EDUCATION ASSOCIATION YEARBOOK, 1993, 189–199

Afterword

Sid Gardner

This review will focus on the two major themes carried through several of the chapters: (1) the value of school-linked services as a form of services integration and (2) the prospects that preservice and in-service university education may be able to produce a new generation of professionals who can work effectively in these new, better-integrated systems.

School-linked services: inescapable logic vs projectitis

Common themes in these selections include the political difficulty and the programmatic imperatives of linking the services which students need with the schools they attend. These chapters show both how hard it will be to transform current practices, and how essential the task has become. Mitchell and Scott diagnose the problem bluntly: 'solving agency problems becomes the driving force . . .' – not solving the problems of students and families. They underscore how we substitute specialization for professionalism (p. 4).

The word collaboration is used in this volume to mean at least four distinct kinds of linkages – collaborations among: (1) schools and universities, (2) schools and other children-serving agencies, (3) schools and parents, and (4) schools and the community at large. It is important to make clear which of these we mean when we use so 'loaded' a term, since one person's collaboration may well be another's insularity. For a university's education school to work with local school districts is far less innovative, after all, than for an education school to work with a law school or a school of medicine. We patrol the boundaries of our disciplines with much greater care, typically, than we use in negotiating university–community contacts within familiar networks of agencies in the same discipline or profession.

In their excellent work in Philadelphia, cited in Stefkovich and Guba's article, the Philadelphia Children's Network under Ralph Smith has adopted the slogan 'help the children; fix the system.' It is a powerful reminder of the need for balance – balance between our client-level concerns for students and their families and our system-level concerns for the ways that organizations attempt to work with each other in the best interests of children.

There is profound logical failure in the linked notions that (1) schools cannot do it all and (2) schools are in this all alone. Yet most of the time schools act as if both were true. Most of the time schools act as if they could effectively address the problems of students who are physically in school during only 9% of their lives from birth to adulthood. We sometimes call that '9% thinking' – the solipsistic myth that schools, or any agency, can by itself solve the problems of children. But that is the prevailing assumption in the daily practice of most professionals who work with children.

To confront that myth and to reach out beyond the walls of the school, the norms of teacher education and the status quo of the profession are politically feasible – but will require leaders who want help, and who recognize they should neither be held accountable for doing it all nor should they try to do their part of the job alone. These chapters have shown examples of uncommon leadership in providing new models of extraordinary practice.

Stefkovich and Guba suggest (p. 11) the importance of going beyond the school assessment mode to a wider concern for assessments of nonschool factors. Some schools are using family assessment tools, while others are trying to adapt the risk assessment approaches of child protective services, with a new influx of child welfare workers who are 'reinventing' their profession while based at schools.

The lessons of most of these state and local policy initiatives are still too new to summarize with confidence. The three discussions of California's Healthy Start program (in White, Koppich, and in Mitchell and Scott) are remarkably different in their views of the same reality, in large part because they focus on a program which is not yet fully two years old. White, as part of the management team now directing the program, emphasizes its potential; Koppich stresses the political issues that surround the initiation of the program; while Mitchell and Scott make clear the scale of the problems faced by Healthy Start, describing schools in which one-quarter of all students are referred for special education. Mitchell and Scott underscore the realities of collaboration: 'interdisciplinary cooperation, no matter how expert it might be, cannot solve systemic breakdown' (p.84).

But for all the newness of this round of reforms, there are powerful lessons that can be extracted from earlier cycles of reform. One of the most important of these is the critical role of teachers and parents, and several of the articles deal well with these issues. Another is the likelihood that systems reform will revert to mere projects.

The power of the project mentality

The issue of 'projects' arises in at least two ways in these articles. First, there is the segmentation of reform into separate, parallel reform projects which rarely combine for maximum effect, and often compete for attention and resources. Second, there is the lack of strategic impact of projects which never seem to change the system, but merely exist apart from it. Let us look at each of these in greater depth.

Education reform is operating almost entirely separate from these school-linked services efforts which build new links to external agencies. Adding new services projects onto the already confused categorical landscape of most high-needs schools is at best an incremental strategy. It is one which can easily coexist with an equally incremental education reform strategy which adds a few pedagogical innovations to the repertoire of the school, but leaves basic governance and the categorical system intact. This add-on approach is the norm, and, as we shall see below, it also characterizes much higher education reform as well.

The implicit message of this kind of fragmented reform is clear: education reform is what we do inside the classroom and the school; collaboration is what we do outside with other agencies. As long as that artificial separation is maintained, the two trains will proceed on separate, diverging tracks, both carrying inadequate resources to get the job done.

The point is critical. For the students most likely to fail to reap the benefits of education restructuring, it is the additional support from external sources (including parents as active members of a student services team) that is the only basis for optimism.

While Mitchell and Scott raise some important points about the scale at which case management efforts can operate successfully, what education reform efforts have typically overlooked are the substantial resources represented by the staff of external agencies *who are working with the same students*.

That overlap is the best answer to educators who argue that the idea of partnerships with outside agencies will founder on their inadequate funding and huge caseloads. This lesson has been clear in those few schools which have been willing to do their homework and document how many other agencies are working with their at-risk students. Consistently, data matches of at-risk students and agency caseloads have documented that the most educationally at-risk students are simultaneously in the caseloads of three or four other agencies. So the caseload problem is not the worker who has 100 students in his/her caseload; it is the student who has five agencies or isolated projects trying to help him/her, and three others working with other members of the same family – all unknown to each other.

A few years ago in an Eastern city, a local foundation was asked to replicate funding for a successful youth development program. The project had used a youth mentor to work with a caseload of students in five local schools, and the project had more than met its goals. The local funder was asked to support seven more schools, with a new mentor coordinator to be based at each school. The funder then asked a powerful question: 'How many youth workers are there in this city who could do this work?'. At first, no one knew. Finally, the answer came back: there were more than 300 identifiable 'youth workers' in that community. The funder then asked the second powerful question: 'What are our chances of convincing some of them that this program works and getting some of them to do this work, instead of seven new workers?' Ultimately, that was what was done.

That reallocation mentality is very different from the grant/project mentality. The tipoff is how many of these chapters describe grant-driven innovation versus reallocation of resources already in the system. Too many of these success stories are based on new grant funding, rather than any serious discussion of reallocation of the base of funding already in the schools and in the surrounding neighborhoods. It is not that these funds are sufficient – it is that they are overlapping. As a result, it is unlikely that we will get substantial funding increases until we can better inventory all of the funds now used to serve children and describe the outcomes of the resources we already use.

For many of these projects, the solution was getting a grant. This add-on instinct is deep in our attitudes, because it is how we do new things in a world of categorical grant funding. But what the 'get-a-grant' mentality ignores is two things: (1) the $300 billion we are spending annually to help children and families and (2) the critical need to *do better* before we can make the case to *receive more*. The grant mentality feeds into the kind of 'projectitis' that has dotted the educational landscape with pilot projects serving 15 students here and 30 families there. These projects are mounted as facades, behind which lies an unchanged system, like latter-day Potemkin villages. Such projects can distract us from the basic tasks of reform on the front lines of innovation in education and other children-serving agencies.

Pilot projects are, of course, one way of changing the system. But far too many are begun without a clue as to how the replication strategy should proceed. Projects become tactical in their style, trying to run an isolated operation, without any strategic content that is explicit. The strategic ingredients of future funding, evaluation targets, or personnel retraining are acknowledged – but soon, the pilot project staff find that operations always drive out policy, and that their need for a long-term strategy gets swamped in the day-to-day demands of running a project.

Experience has repeatedly proven that it is impossible to use categorical funding to provide lasting incentives for collaboration. Programmatic funding can only fund separatist efforts to organize collaboration around a single discipline, as in some mental health or employment-driven models – or in the most educentric of the models described in this compilation. These represent attempts to build an empire around a single service, not a partnership of true equals.

For example, in one recent discussion of a school-linked services model, the idea was floated for a new position, vice-principal for student and family services, which would be filled *by a professional from an external agency working within the school*. This model of power-sharing was presented; there were a few puzzled looks, and the discussion moved on. The episode seemed to suggest that the idea was simply too foreign to the outlooks of professionals who had, after all, spent their lives in categorical systems that separated professionals into their own agencies and disciplines and simply could not accommodate their thinking to the concept of shared accountability across agency and professional lines.

In another site, during a recent policy debate about a budget for an education reform project that would have emphasized health and social services, a teacher's union representative said 'I thought all the new money was supposed to go into the classroom' when told about a proposal for new health and family services coordination staff in a model school.

There are some sites that are experimenting with such approaches, to be sure. But they are far too few, and receive far less concrete support from educational hierarchies than laudatory rhetoric.

Learning new norms takes time. It takes uncommon leadership that will reach out from the schools. And it takes willing partners on the other side of the table, in the agencies which serve students while schools are trying to teach them. These are extraordinary resources, and they are not always available.

The final power of the project mentality comes in subverting reform itself. In some communities, the fragmentation of reform itself has become a growing barrier to reform. This is due to the proliferation of categorical collaboration initiatives, in a pattern in which federal or foundation funders each require a collaborative council, which further fragments the system. In the past 20 years, we have had programs that fund schools and other agencies for dropout prevention, delinquency prevention, substance abuse prevention, child abuse prevention, teen pregnancy prevention, gang prevention, and now, finally, we have violence prevention programs. In some schools, these separately funded staffs literally line up in little offices along the halls or out in the portables, working largely in isolation from each other, and making almost no effort to determine *how often they are really working with the same students under different labels*.

School-linked services then revert to becoming just one more project because so many other reform projects compete for attention. Some sites, in fact, have been compelled to develop an inventory of reforms as a way of addressing this problem, using a matrix of collaboratives to enable information exchange across collaboratives.

Line workers as the source of systems change

At the same time we must recognize that we are often asking the front-line workers to pay most of the costs of change. A social services worker relocated to a school is often coming to a less safe environment, doing an unfamiliar job, with fewer rules and routines, and on an unfamiliar team. This is a worker who needs more than the usual level of support and rewards. He/she needs compensation for paying the costs of change, and for taking the risks of innovation. Far too often, though, we reward such people only as long as the grant holds out – and then we send them 'back home,' ignoring the lessons they have learned and the skills they have acquired by working across traditional boundaries.

In fact, the people who have done it – who have collaborated in new settings – are our greatest human resources. We have treasures in their humor, ability to work across cultures and disciplines, ability to explore new ways of doing things rather than clinging to 'the comforts of the known,' as Knapp puts it. It is to them that I want to dedicate this summary: Lucinda, Glorious, Elaine, Pat, Debbie, Karen, Christine, Pam, Lynette, Bonnie, Yolande, Jeanne, Jane, Rachel, Emily, and Connie.

The gender of these names is relevant – there are gender skills in these worlds of collaboration, and Louise Adler is right to highlight Carol Gilligan and those who write about gender. It has been noted that interpersonal ingredients make up at least half of the success factors connected with collaboration across agencies and disciplines, and the interpersonal attributes in any team are critical to its effectiveness.

Some of these issues are ethical

These are political issues because agency and disciplinary protectionism is part of the problem. But these are also ethical issues, because we must ask if we have done enough to work across systems to help the clients, and if we are involved in agency-centered practice or client-centered practice. That is where we find ourselves facing the *moral imperatives of collaboration*. For if we believe that in helping a child who needs help from two or more disciplines – from a nurse as well as a teacher – good service means getting *both* services, then 'the system' *and the two professionals within it* share a burden of providing the needed services effectively. And 'effectively' means in an integrated manner which gives assurance that the child is going to be connected with the services required.

The healthy agency, then, collaborates with other agencies and professionals because it is a client-centered agency, and it recognizes that the needs of its clients cannot be met by a single agency. The healthy agency sees the trends in services and needs, and understands that the children and families who need the most help increasingly are found in the caseloads of more than one agency at the same time. And those organizations know and accept that it is rare that they can solve that family's problems working in isolation. They know it takes more than one profession, more than one agency, and more than one discipline to help the families that need the most help.

Another, blunter way to frame this issue is to bring in the well-established professional concept of *malpractice*. While this is a highly uncomfortable term for professionals to discuss, it helps greatly to clarify basic responsibilities. If surgeons, for example, were educated without any familiarity with the role of the anesthesiologist, training them and sending them forth to do surgery would constitute malpractice. But if we believe some of the most at-risk children and families need the simultaneous services of health, education, and social services professionals, is it not also a form of malpractice to teach and train these professionals without equipping them to work as closely as surgeons and anesthesiologists do?

This ethics of effectiveness helps us to measure the competency of existing services systems against the needs they attempt to meet. It also helps us judge the governance of those systems against a new standard: can we get the job done for children and families through the current structures of interagency collaboration and the existing 'system' of subnational government, with its framework of fragmented roles among thousands of states, counties, cities, school districts, and nonprofit providers of services? Or do we need new forms of governance that are accountable across their boundaries for child outcomes, in the same way that we had to create new forms of governance to handle air pollution across boundaries of local government which had failed to respond to that new need?

The need for greater emphasis on outcomes

We must accept also the strong critique, quoted by Mawhinney from Townsend and others, of the 'technocratic and centralist bias' inherent in some approaches to school-linked services and the larger services integration movement. One of the most important correctives to that bias is an emphasis on the outcomes of collaboration, rather than becoming overly romantic about the benefits of its processes. Collaboration for its own sake is a diversion of energies from what matters much more: improving outcomes for the children who are most at risk of failing to achieve their full potential.

Schorr (1993) argues that the label 'services integration' is less descriptive than 'effective services,' since it is the *outcomes* of the services rather than the process by which they are linked which must be central. Others have pointed out that good services integration is community-building, and I agree. There is a false dichotomy between the 'top-down' and 'bottom-up' approaches to reforming services for children and families, and we must take care not to be drawn into such polarities.

The outcomes emphasis is understated in most of these articles, and in some it is almost totally missing. There is a passing reference to the intended result of the collaborations under discussion, but the critical need to evaluate those processes by the outcomes they yield needs further emphasis.

The California Healthy Start planning guide included a slogan which planning teams were urged to take seriously as they did their work. The slogan was 'Start with the kids.' It was intended to signal the importance of moving from the needs of the children and families to developing shared goals and a vision, drawing on those in turn for program design and the measures of success that would indicate whether the programs were successful *in meeting the needs of the children*. Unhappily, some programs failed to achieve that flow from needs to programs to measures of success. These unsuccessful sites tended to start with the schools, or the planning team, or the budget, or some other artifact that was not fundamentally about the needs of the students.

The power of a greater emphasis on outcomes is that it returns professionals' attention to the importance, underscored in many of these articles, of the issue of community. Outcomes which measure client impact are fundamentally about a community's values and its goals. Outcome measures without community consensus on goals are just numbers. Used effectively, outcomes are a signal that a community has begun the process of setting goals. Outcomes are a starting point for the kind of community-wide collaboration that is much more than just meetings. Collaboration with a mission is about goals, not meetings, and the mission can only be expressed in terms of outcomes which the community cares about enough to count in a public, regular, and accountable way.

So collaboration across agencies and across the whole community is essential for outcomes to have meaning. Outcomes are meaningless without being closely related to *the goals which they measure*. The goals, in turn, are meaningless unless they reflect a community's consensus developed by collaboration across agencies and neighborhoods.

This emphasis on outcomes returns accountability to where it belongs – at the level of the community leaders and the agencies they support. The means of achieving the goals then become less important than the goals – which reverses the current emphasis on agency-centered systems instead of client-centered systems. If we hold the outcomes constant, but agree to vary the activities we use to achieve those outcomes, we have finally developed a learning organization, in Peter Senge's terms: an organization that keeps trying to achieve its goals in different ways that are not measured by the means but by the goals.

Context matters

The policy context of school-linked service matters, and budget cuts have been the context in many sites during the current fiscal period of national and regional recession. As a result, some of the goals of school-linked services have become politically harder, while others have become politically easier.

Professional concerns are at a peak due to layoffs of support service personnel in some states and districts. When a new school-linked services program becomes available, such as California's Healthy Start program, professional groups which have just seen nurses and psychologists in the school system laid off are understandably suspicious of new, external personnel who may be providing health and counseling assistance similar to that provided by the recently eliminated staff. The budget cuts also obviously make it harder for county and other agencies to support schools with their personnel and other resources.

Yet the budget stringency also works for innovation in some settings. One principal who was planning a Healthy Start project said to a planning team meeting 'We have nothing to lose at this point by doing things differently, because we've run out of resources to do it the same way we've been doing it in the past.'

Assumptions about systems change: can we get there from here?

A basic question which is, for the most part, unanswered by this collection is whether the categorical funding system of the past 30 years can be reformed sufficiently to enable success for school-linked services or any other strategy of support for students and families. Some have begun to argue that 'you can't get there from here.' In a categorically funded system, the emphasis on clients will always be on their categorically defined deficits, rather than their strengths, and on students who are separately 'treated,' rather than families supported across agencies. This argument goes on to assert that it will be impossible to empower communities to set their own priorities in a system which funds local projects based on funding allocations set in state capitals and in Washington, rather than those set at the local level through collaborative processes.

In one school-based services planning session recently, a planning team had repeatedly said they lacked resources to work with at-risk students. The team finally was helped to inventory their categorical funding for at-risk students. They had 17 separate programs totalling approximately $300,000 a year, which was funding portions of the time of 12 staff members. Once the inventory had been compiled, the group was asked how they would use the funds differently if they could design their own system for at-risk students without any categorical restrictions. The brief, inconclusive discussion that followed felt to some of the outsiders in the meeting as though someone had asked the fish to describe the water. The group simply could not imagine a system which they would design themselves, without responding to outside mandates. The categorical funding environment was so omnipresent, so accepted and so given, that it was impossible to see or understand its overwhelming impact, much less determine how to reshape it.

None of the chapters addressed this issue head on, and, by omission, all seemed to accept the categorical system as given. But the prescription for community-based, family-focused, multidisciplinary work within a system that can only approach such issues in categorical, deficit driven ways becomes a much harder one to realize. Without proposals to move toward community-determined priorities, in an outcomes-driven funding system, the burden of proof faced by proponents of school-linked services may become far more difficult.

The university context: teaching it wrong, getting it right

During the time that this volume was written:

- a professor in the California State system launched a written diatribe against uncredentialed school-based counselors from community agencies who were not, in her view, as competent as her fully credentialed peers;
- a field visit from leaders of a national accrediting organization to a major school of social work questioned the collaborative content in the curriculum as being at odds with 'good social work practice';
- numerous department heads and representatives of national groups of disciplinary associations made clear their strong beliefs that 'we're already doing it' when discussing the need for greater interdisciplinary work – and then proceeded to describe models in which their discipline was clearly at the center of a coalition which they controlled, rather than participating as co-equal partners in a network of services accountable for outcomes in terms of clients, and not professional norms.

It is not enough that excellent work is being done by the University of Washington, and nearly 30 other public and private universities involved in this volume and other work around the nation and in Canada. We must measure these beginnings against the immensely greater amount of professional education which remains content with a narrow disciplinary focus on getting one kind of credential to serve one categorically defined target group of youth.

The preceding chapters suggest a framework for discussing the role of universities in working with children- and family-serving professionals and organizations:

1. *Curriculum review and revision*, in which courses are both revised and added to enrich the multidisciplinary content of preservice education at both graduate and undergraduate levels.
2. *Changes in field placement, internships and supervision of field-based education*, in which teams of students from different professional areas are assigned to work and learn together at common sites such as schools, family resource centers, health clinics, or community-based services centers.
3. *In-service training and extended education*, which recognizes that far more of the professionals who will staff education and human services education agencies in the next 20 years are already in professional careers than will be added to these fields. Thus retraining and in-service education are important ingredients in

multidisciplinary education. This area is especially important because spending on staff development and in-service training in federal and state budgets, despite recent cutbacks, remains a significant item. Like the private sector, the public sector has moved to increase its staff development and professional education budgets, in recognition that the skills which a professional needs to do his/her job are likely to change several times during his/her career.

4. *Technical assistance for collaborative state and local efforts*, including joint projects undertaken with state and local agencies and community-based organizations, in which the university role is to provide facilitation, disciplinary expertise, a neutral forum, or some other form of supportive consultation.
5. *Evaluation of collaborative state and local efforts*, which uses program evaluation methods as well as a newer set of evaluation tools needed to evaluate collaborative service delivery.
6. *Policy research across disciplines*, in support of state or local policy development, including development of proposed children and family policy initiatives, outcomes measures, indicators or 'scorecards' on conditions of children and families.

As Knapp, Wilson, and others note, we cannot preach what we cannot do. Telling school districts to work more closely with health providers, in a university where the dean of education and the dean of health sciences have not worked together for years, is hardly credible advice.

We *are* still teaching it wrong. The best of these articles remind us how rarely we use cases like these to teach students how to work across the boundaries, instead of within the lines that protect the status quo of professionalism from any external challenge. For all the progress represented in these chapters, the vast majority of subject-matter we put before students reinforces insularity of disciplines, rather than broadening horizons.

We also need to remember the scale at which we are now working, and compare it with the scale at which we could be working. The California State University graduates around 10,000 professionals each year who go to work with children and families – as teachers, social workers, counselors, home economists, nurses, and recreation leaders. To change the way those 10,000 professionals work with each other, across the boundaries of programs and agencies, is a far greater potential impact on systems change than the finest model program could ever hope to have. Moving large institutions, as Max Weber said of politics, is 'a strong and slow boring of hard boards. It takes both passion and perspective' (128). But the potential payoffs are very large.

And so audacity is needed, not playing safe. For universities, there is no more than a 50–50 chance that we will be able to meet the growing demands for these new professionals who are able to work across the boundaries of their professions, and able to work with families as equal partners, in a setting that values cultural competence. A good deal of the training expertise and innovation in the field of collaborative services and policy is in the hands of some excellent nonprofit institutions such as the Institute for Educational Leadership, the Georgia Academy, the Council of Governor's Policy Advisors, and other consortia of funders and training providers. These institutions do not take two years to change a course, or five years to develop a new program; they can innovate as needs for in-service education present themselves, and they can ignore issues of turf protectionism in producing a product with cross-disciplinary competencies.

Change is going to happen, and these articles show its clear direction: toward boundary-spanning competencies, not border patrol operations that protect the worst of past insularity. Universities will need to develop more of these boundary-spanning competencies – or risk being left watching their nonprofit colleagues become even more of a factor in the world of in-service education and leadership development. Relying on credential-granting powers may relegate universities to a negative gate-keeping role, rather than elevating them to a position of leadership in providing the new professionals our communities and agencies need so much. The 'reorientation of professional norms' which Mitchell and Scott call for will demand the same kind of uncommon leadership within universities which school-linked services require at the community level.

So what are the bases for optimism? The students are the reality. Thank God, they are also a big part of the future, and they want to get there working in new ways. They want to be trained to work in teams. Every time I ask a class 'would you rather work separately or in a team with other professions,' they look at me as if the answer is overwhelmingly obvious. 'It's the team, stupid' that can get the job done, in their minds. They are right. As a far wiser man once said:

> It is not enough to teach a [person] a specialty. Through it he may become a kind of useful machine, but not a harmoniously developed personality. It is essential that the student acquire an understanding of and a lively feel for values. He must acquire a vivid sense of the beautiful and of the morally good. Otherwise, he – with his specialized knowledge – more closely resembles a trained dog than a harmoniously developed person. He must learn to understand the motives of human beings, their illusions, and their sufferings in order to acquire a proper relationship to individual fellowmen and the community. (Albert Einstein, *Ideas and Opinions*, 1955, quoted in Goodlad 1990: 227)

The other basis for optimism comes in the quiet growth of these initiatives, and the ways in which innovators in higher education settings have begun what seems to be a 'two-track' strategy: confronting the institution when it must, but using the flexibility (or the absent-mindedness) in institutional practices to make progress. For example, in setting up the collaborative services seminar which we operate here at Fullerton, the critical event was the scheduling changes required to enable five classes in five departments to meet at the same time in the same place. In the early discussions of these changes, one colleague spoke with satisfaction of the changes just negotiated: 'The academic schedule – now that is where the real institutional power lies.' She was right, and the willingness which she and her colleagues showed to move through the arcane levels of that system produced a remarkable educational experience for 120 students. By using existing courses as part of a five-course consortium experience, it was unnecessary to navigate the university's clearance processes for more elaborate course changes and development of new courses.

The parallels between the school-based services agenda and the university reform agenda are many. In the excellent dialogue between Knapp and his colleagues and the respondents to their chapter, a strong emphasis is given to the add-on, separate project mentality which was described earlier as characteristic of many school-based services projects. Knapp also points out that it was external grant funding that began their efforts at interprofessional education, in the same way that grant funding has been at the base of many of the school-linked services efforts. Casto's commentary stresses the need to penetrate the core funding sources of the university, in the same way that school-linked service advocates need to seek reallocation of existing grant resources, rather than depending on new external funding. And the issue of institutionalization which Knapp honestly frames as unresolved is the same issue encountered in the governance debates between collaborative forms which are co-equal versus educentric models of school-linked services.

Knapp also underscores how important it is for student field placements to reinforce curriculum emphases on collaborative practice. We have found at Fullerton that a strong preference emerges from some of the best of the students who have taken our collaborative seminars. These students want to work in settings that *are* collaborative. The problem is obvious: many field settings *are not*, which creates a need to identify sites where field work and practica can be focused on the best of collaborative practice. If the ethos at the field placement undermines the message of the classroom, neither will be credible for long.

Conclusion

This work is not just about good practice. It has become urgent, possibly because it represents our last chance to show better results from the system as it is configured today and led by those who lead it today. If we fail, by only tinkering with a few pilot projects, the system will be changed – but from outside. Proposals for vouchers, 'cashing out the system' at the neighborhood level, radical privatization of children's services, and other 'reforms' are as politically appealing as they are simplistic and wrong. The movement toward outcomes as a way of increasing accountability will be diverted into outcomes as fiscal controls, and the punitive use of such accountability measures will overwhelm efforts to use them to assist and reward good performance.

I must acknowledge a colleague, Marianne Pennekamp, who first cited the following quote from Alice Walker (1984: 5) as a way of reminding us all of the great importance of our work in better integrating what we try to do for children and families:

> What is always needed in the appreciation of art, or in life, is the larger perspective. Connections made, or at least attempted, where none existed before, the straining to encompass in one's glance at the varied world the common thread, the unifying theme through immense diversity, a fearlessness of growth, of search, of looking, that enlarges the private and the public world. And yet, in our particular society, it is the narrowed and narrowing view of life that often wins.

It need not be that narrowing view that wins – if we can sustain the kinds of connections made across disciplines and in communities which are described in this volume.

References

GOODLAD (1990) *Teachers for Our Nation's Schools* (San Francisco: Jossey-Bass Publishers).

SCHORR, LISBETH B. (1992) 'Daring to learn from our successes: services, supports, and systems that improve outcomes for children,' discussion paper prepared for the Aspen Institute Domestic Strategy Group, 1992.

WALKER, ALICE (1984) *In Search of Our Mothers' Gardens* (New York: Harcourt Brace Jovanovich Publishers).

WEBER, MAX (1948) 'Politics as a vocation,' in H. N. Gerth & C. Wright Mills (eds.) *From Max Weber* (London: Routledge & Kegan Paul).

Index